Scriptures at Your Fingertips

Over 200 Topics and 2000 Verses

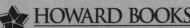

Compiled by
Merry Graham
and Rachel Bye

HOWARD BOOKS
A DIVISION OF SIMON & SCHUSTER
New York   London   Toronto   Sydney

Our purpose at Howard Books is to:
- *Increase faith* in the hearts of growing Christians
- *Inspire holiness* in the lives of believers
- *Instill hope* in the hearts of struggling people everywhere
Because He's coming again!

Published by Howard Books, a division of Simon and Schuster, Inc.
1230 Avenue of the Americas, New York, NY 10020
www.howardpublishing.com

Scriptures at Your Fingertips © 2006 by Merry Graham and Rachel Bye.

Library of Congress Cataloging-in-Publication Data
Bible. English. New King James. Selections. 2006.
  Scriptures at your fingertips / compiled by Merry Graham.
    p. cm.
  ISBN 13: 978-1-58229-613-5
  ISBN 10: 1-58229-613-8
  1. Bible—Indexes. 2. Bible—Quotations. I. Graham, Merry. II. Bye, Rachel. III. Title.
  BS432.B45   2006
  220.5'208—dc22   2006049532

06 07 08 09 10 11 12 13 RRD 10 9 8 7 6 5 4 3 2 1

Manufactured in the United States of America

For information regarding special discounts for bulk purchases, please contact: Simon & Schuster Special Sales at 1-800-456-6798 or business@simonandschuster.com.

Cover design by John Mark Luke Designs
Interior design by Inside Out Design & Typesetting

All Scripture
is given by inspiration of God,
and is profitable for doctrine,
for reproof,
for correction,
for instruction in righteousness,
that the man of God may be complete,
thoroughly equipped
for every good work.

2 TIMOTHY 3:16–17 NKJV

CONTENTS

CONTENTS

CONTENTS

CONTENTS

Exodus 4:10-12 NRSV But Moses said to the Lord, "O my Lord, I have never been eloquent, neither in the past nor even now that you have spoken to your servant; but I am slow of speech and slow of tongue." Then the Lord said to him, "Who gives speech to mortals? Who makes them mute or deaf, seeing or blind? Is it not I, the Lord? Now go, and I will be with your mouth and teach you what you are to speak."

1 Chronicles 4:10 NASB Now Jabez called on the God of Israel, saying, "Oh that You would bless me indeed and enlarge my border, and that Your hand might be with me, and that You would keep me from harm that it may not pain me!" And God granted him what he requested.

John 14:26 WNT But the Advocate, the Holy Spirit whom the Father will send at my request, will teach you everything, and will bring to your memories all that I have said to you.

Romans 12:6-8 NKJV Having then gifts differing according to the grace that is given to us, let us use them: if prophecy, let us prophesy in proportion to our faith; or ministry, let us use it in our ministering; he who teaches, in teaching; he who exhorts, in exhortation; he who gives, with liberality; he who leads, with diligence; he who shows mercy, with cheerfulness.

Philippians 4:13 NASB I can do all things through Him who strengthens me.

1 Timothy 1:12 NKJV And I thank Christ Jesus our Lord who has enabled me, because He counted me faithful, putting me into the ministry.

1 Peter 4:10-11 NIV Each one should use whatever gift he has received to serve others, faithfully administering God's grace in its various forms. If anyone speaks, he should do it as one speaking the very words of God. If anyone serves, he should do it with the strength God provides, so that in all things God may be praised through Jesus Christ.

Matthew 18:4–5 WEB Whoever therefore humbles himself as this little child, the same is the greatest in the Kingdom of Heaven. Whoever will receive one such little child in my name receives me.

John 1:12–13 WEB But as many as received him, to them he gave the right to become God's children, to those who believe in his name: who were born not of blood, nor of the will of the flesh, nor of the will of man, but of God.

John 14:18 NKJV I will not leave you orphans; I will come to you.

Romans 8:14–17 NCV The true children of God are those who let God's Spirit lead them. The Spirit we received does not make us slaves again to fear; it makes us children of God. With that Spirit we cry out, "Father." And the Spirit himself joins with our spirits to say we are God's children. If we are God's children, we will receive blessings from God together with Christ. But we must suffer as Christ suffered so that we will have glory as Christ has glory.

2 Corinthians 6:18 NCV "I will be your father, and you will be my sons and daughters, says the Lord Almighty."

Ephesians 1:3–6 WNT Blessed be the God and Father of our Lord Jesus Christ, who has crowned us with every spiritual blessing in the heavenly realms in Christ; even as, in His love, He chose us as His own in Christ before the creation of the world, that we might be holy and without blemish in His presence. For He pre-destined us to be adopted by Himself as sons through Jesus Christ—such being His gracious will and pleasure—to the praise of the splendor of His grace with which He has enriched us in the beloved One.

James 1:27 NKJV Pure and undefiled religion before God and the Father is this: to visit orphans and widows in their trouble, and to keep oneself unspotted from the world.

Jeremiah 29:11 NLT "For I know the plans I have for you," says the LORD. "They are plans for good and not for disaster, to give you a future and a hope."

Jeremiah 32:40-41 NLT And I will make an everlasting covenant with them, promising not to stop doing good for them. I will put a desire in their hearts to worship me, and they will never leave me. I will rejoice in doing good to them and will faithfully and wholeheartedly replant them in this land.

2 Corinthians 5:17 TMB Therefore if any man be in Christ, he is a new creature: old things are passed away; behold, all things have become new.

Galatians 2:20 TMB I am crucified with Christ, nevertheless I live; yet not I, but Christ liveth in me. And the life which I now live in the flesh, I live by the faith of the Son of God, who loved me and gave Himself for me.

Ephesians 3:16-20 NCV I ask the Father in his great glory to give you the power to be strong inwardly through his Spirit. I pray that Christ will live in your hearts by faith and that your life will be strong in love and be built on love. And I pray that you and all God's holy people will have the power to understand the greatness of Christ's love—how wide and how long and how high and how deep that love is. Christ's love is greater than anyone can ever know, but I pray that you will be able to know that love. Then you can be filled with the fullness of God. With God's power working in us, God can do much, much more than anything we can ask or imagine.

Colossians 2:9-10 NKJV For in Him dwells all the fullness of the Godhead bodily; and you are complete in Him, who is the head of all principality and power.

1 John 1:7 NCV If we live in the light, as God is in the light, we can share fellowship with each other. Then the blood of Jesus, God's Son, cleanses us from every sin.

Genesis 15:1 NCV After these things happened, the LORD spoke his word to Abram in a vision: "Abram, don't be afraid. I will defend you, and I will give you a great reward."

Psalm 28:6-7 NASB Blessed be the LORD, because He has heard the voice of my supplication. The LORD is my strength and my shield; my heart trusts in Him, and I am helped; therefore my heart exults, and with my song I shall thank Him.

Psalm 56:3-4 NKJV Whenever I am afraid, I will trust in You. In God (I will praise His word), in God I have put my trust; I will not fear. What can flesh do to me?

PSALM 91:9-12 WEB Because you have made Yahweh your refuge, and the Most High your dwelling place, no evil shall happen to you, neither shall any plague come near your dwelling. For he will put his angels in charge of you, to guard you in all your ways. They will bear you up in their hands.

Proverbs 3:24-26 WEB When you lie down, you will not be afraid. Yes, you will lie down, and your sleep will be sweet. Don't be afraid of sudden fear, neither of the desolation of the wicked, when it comes: for Yahweh will be your confidence, and will keep your foot from being taken.

2 Timothy 1:7-9 NIV For God did not give us a spirit of timidity, but a spirit of power, of love and of self-discipline. So do not be ashamed to testify about our Lord, or ashamed of me his prisoner. But join with me in suffering for the gospel, by the power of God, who has saved us and called us to a holy life.

Hebrews 13:5-6 WNT Your lives should be untainted by love for money. Be content with what you have; for God Himself has said, "I will never, never let go your hand: I will never forsake you." So that we fearlessly say, "The Lord is my helper; I will not be afraid: what can man do to me?"

Proverbs 20:1 NIV Wine is a mocker and beer a brawler; whoever is led astray by them is not wise.

Proverbs 23:19-21 NASB Listen, my son, and be wise, and direct your heart in the way. Do not be with heavy drinkers of wine, with gluttonous eaters of meat; for the heavy drinker and the glutton will come to poverty, and drowsiness will clothe one with rags.

Proverbs 23:29-33 NASB Who has woe? Who has sorrow? Who has contentions? Who has complaining? Who has wounds without cause? Who has redness of eyes? Those who linger long over wine, those who go to taste mixed wine. Do not look on the wine when it is red, when it sparkles in the cup, when it goes down smoothly; at the last it bites like a serpent and stings like a viper. Your eyes will see strange things and your mind will utter perverse things.

Hosea 4:11 NKJV Harlotry, wine, and new wine enslave the heart.

Romans 13:13-14 NIV Let us behave decently, as in the daytime, not in orgies and drunkenness, not in sexual immorality and debauchery, not in dissension and jealousy. Rather, clothe yourselves with the Lord Jesus Christ, and do not think about how to gratify the desires of the sinful nature.

Romans 14:21 NIV It is better not to eat meat or drink wine or to do anything else that will cause your brother to fall.

1 Corinthians 6:9-10 NKJV Do not be deceived. Neither fornicators, nor idolaters, nor adulterers, nor homosexuals, nor sodomites, nor thieves, nor covetous, nor drunkards, nor revilers, nor extortioners will inherit the kingdom of God.

Ephesians 5:18 NIV Do not get drunk on wine. . . . Instead, be filled with the Spirit.

Psalm 27:4 NLT The one thing I ask of the LORD—the thing I seek most—is to live in the house of the LORD all the days of my life, delighting in the LORD's perfections and meditating in his Temple.

Proverbs 23:4-5 NKJV Do not overwork to be rich; because of your own understanding, cease! Will you set your eyes on that which is not? For riches certainly make themselves wings; they fly away like an eagle toward heaven.

Jeremiah 45:5 NKJV "And do you seek great things for yourself? Do not seek them; for behold, I will bring adversity on all flesh," says the LORD. "But I will give your life to you as a prize in all places, wherever you go."

Micah 6:8 NCV The LORD has told you, human, what is good; he has told you what he wants from you: to do what is right to other people, love being kind to others, and live humbly, obeying your God.

Luke 13:23-24 NKJV Then one said to Him, "Lord, are there few who are saved?" And He said to them, "Strive to enter through the narrow gate, for many, I say to you, will seek to enter and will not be able."

1 Corinthians 14:12 NCV Since you want spiritual gifts very much, seek most of all to have the gifts that help the church grow stronger.

1 Thessalonians 4:10-12 WNT And indeed you do love all the brethren throughout Macedonia. And we exhort you to do so more and more, and to vie with one another in eagerness for peace, every one minding his own business and working with his hands, as we ordered you to do: so as to live worthy lives in relation to outsiders, and not be a burden to any one.

Exodus 23:20 NIV See, I am sending an angel ahead of you to guard you along the way and to bring you to the place I have prepared.

Psalm 34:7 NKJV The angel of the LORD encamps all around those who fear Him, and delivers them.

Psalm 91:11-12 NASB For He will give His angels charge concerning you, to guard you in all your ways. They will bear you up in their hands, that you do not strike your foot against a stone.

Psalm 103:20 NIV Praise the LORD, you his angels, you mighty ones who do his bidding, who obey his word.

Matthew 18:10 TMB Take heed that ye despise not one of these little ones; for I say unto you that in Heaven their angels do always behold the face of My Father who is in Heaven.

Acts 5:19-20 NCV But during the night, an angel of the Lord opened the doors of the jail and led the apostles outside. The angel said, "Go stand in the Temple and tell the people everything about this new life."

Colossians 2:18 NKJV Let no one cheat you of your reward, taking delight in false humility and worship of angels, intruding into those things which he has not seen, vainly puffed up by his fleshly mind.

Hebrews 1:14 NASB Are they not all ministering spirits, sent out to render service for the sake of those who will inherit salvation?

Hebrews 13:1-2 NIV Keep on loving each other as brothers. Do not forget to entertain strangers, for by so doing some people have entertained angels without knowing it.

Psalm 103:8 NCV The LORD shows mercy and is kind. He does not become angry quickly, and he has great love.

Proverbs 15:1 NASB A gentle answer turns away wrath, but a harsh word stirs up anger.

Proverbs 19:11 WEB The discretion of a man makes him slow to anger. It is his glory to overlook an offense.

Proverbs 22:24-25 WEB Don't befriend a hot-tempered man, and don't associate with one who harbors anger: lest you learn his ways, and ensnare your soul.

Ecclesiastes 7:9 NLT Don't be quick-tempered, for anger is the friend of fools.

Jeremiah 30:24 NKJV The fierce anger of the LORD will not return until He has done it, and until He has performed the intents of His heart. In the latter days you will consider it.

Ephesians 4:26-27 NKJV Be angry and do not sin: do not let the sun go down on your wrath, nor give place to the devil.

Ephesians 6:4 NCV Fathers, do not make your children angry, but raise them with the training and teaching of the Lord.

Colossians 3:8 NIV But now you must rid yourselves of all such things as these: anger, rage, malice, slander, and filthy language from your lips.

James 1:19-21 NIV Everyone should be quick to listen, slow to speak and slow to become angry, for man's anger does not bring about the righteous life that God desires. Therefore, get rid of all moral filth and the evil that is so prevalent and humbly accept the word planted in you, which can save you.

Psalm 37:5-7 NLT Commit everything you do to the LORD. Trust him, and he will help you. He will make your innocence as clear as the dawn, and the justice of your cause will shine like the noonday sun. Be still in the presence of the LORD, and wait patiently for him to act. Don't worry about evil people who prosper or fret about their wicked schemes.

Psalm 62:5-6 NKJV My soul, wait silently for God alone, for my expectation is from Him. He only is my rock and my salvation; He is my defense; I shall not be moved.

Psalm 94:17-19 NIV Unless the LORD had given me help, I would soon have dwelt in the silence of death. When I said, "My foot is slipping," your love, O LORD, supported me. When anxiety was great within me, your consolation brought joy to my soul.

Psalm 127:2 NKJV It is vain for you to rise up early, to sit up late, to eat the bread of sorrows; for so He gives His beloved sleep.

Proverbs 12:25 NKJV Anxiety in the heart of man causes depression, but a good word makes it glad.

Proverbs 16:3 NASB Commit your works to the LORD and your plans will be established.

Isaiah 41:13 TMB "For I, the LORD thy God, will hold thy right hand, saying unto thee, 'Fear not; I will help thee.' "

Luke 12:29-31 WEB Don't seek what you will eat or what you will drink; neither be anxious. For the nations of the world seek after all of these things, but your Father knows that you need these things. But seek God's Kingdom, and all these things will be added to you.

John 14:1 NCV Jesus said, "Don't let your hearts be troubled. Trust in God, and trust in me."

John 14:27 NKJV "Peace I leave with you, My peace I give to you; not as the world gives do I give to you. Let not your heart be troubled, neither let it be afraid."

Ephesians 1:3-6 WNT Blessed be the God and Father of our Lord Jesus Christ, who has crowned us with every spiritual blessing in the heavenly realms in Christ; even as, in His love, He chose us as His own in Christ before the creation of the world, that we might be holy and without blemish in His presence. For He pre-destined us to be adopted by Himself as sons through Jesus Christ—such being His gracious will and pleasure—to the praise of the splendor of His grace with which He has enriched us in the beloved One.

Philippians 4:6-7 NKJV Be anxious for nothing, but in everything by prayer and supplication, with thanksgiving, let your requests be made known to God; and the peace of God, which surpasses all understanding, will guard your hearts and minds through Christ Jesus.

Hebrews 4:15-16 NKJV For we do not have a High Priest who cannot sympathize with our weaknesses, but was in all points tempted as we are, yet without sin. Let us therefore come boldly to the throne of grace, that we may obtain mercy and find grace to help in time of need.

Hebrews 6:19-20 NCV We have this hope as an anchor for the soul, sure and strong. It enters behind the curtain in the Most Holy Place in heaven, where Jesus has gone ahead of us and for us.

1 Peter 5:6-7 NIV Humble yourselves, therefore, under God's mighty hand, that he may lift you up in due time. Cast all your anxiety on him because he cares for you.

John 6:37-39 NCV The Father gives me my people. Every one of them will come to me, and I will always accept them. I came down from heaven to do what God wants me to do, not what I want to do. Here is what the One who sent me wants me to do: I must not lose even one whom God gave me, but I must raise them all on the last day.

John 10:27-29 NRSV My sheep hear my voice. I know them, and they follow me. I give them eternal life, and they will never perish. No one will snatch them out of my hand. What my Father has given me is greater than all else, and no one can snatch it out of the Father's hand.

Romans 8:38-39 NKJV For I am persuaded that neither death nor life, nor angels nor principalities nor powers, nor things present nor things to come, nor height nor depth, nor any other created thing, shall be able to separate us from the love of God which is in Christ Jesus our Lord.

Romans 11:29 WEB For the gifts and the calling of God are irrevocable.

Philippians 1:6 WEB Being confident of this very thing, that he who began a good work in you will complete it until the day of Jesus Christ.

Colossians 2:2-3 NIV My purpose is that they may be encouraged in heart and united in love, so that they may have the full riches of complete understanding, in order that they may know the mystery of God, namely, Christ, in whom are hidden all the treasures of wisdom and knowledge.

Hebrews 10:22-23 NIV Let us draw near to God with a sincere heart in full assurance of faith, having our hearts sprinkled to cleanse us from a guilty conscience and having our bodies washed with pure water. Let us hold unswervingly to the hope we profess, for he who promised is faithful.

Leviticus 17:11 NIV For the life of a creature is in the blood, and I have given it to you to make atonement for yourselves on the altar; it is the blood that makes atonement for one's life.

Matthew 26:27-28 NKJV Then He took the cup, and gave thanks, and gave it to them, saying, "Drink from it, all of you. For this is My blood of the new covenant, which is shed for many for the remission of sins."

Mark 10:45 NCV In the same way, the Son of Man did not come to be served. He came to serve others and to give his life as a ransom for many people.

Romans 5:8-11 NASB While we were yet sinners, Christ died for us. Much more then, having now been justified by His blood, we shall be saved from the wrath of God through Him. For if while we were enemies we were reconciled to God through the death of His Son, much more, having been reconciled, we shall be saved by His life. And not only this, but we also exult in God through our Lord Jesus Christ, through whom we have now received the reconciliation.

Colossians 1:13-14 NIV For he has rescued us from the dominion of darkness and brought us into the kingdom of the Son he loves, in whom we have redemption, the forgiveness of sins.

Hebrews 10:12-14 NKJV But this Man, after He had offered one sacrifice for sins forever, sat down at the right hand of God, from that time waiting till His enemies are made His footstool. For by one offering He has perfected forever those who are being sanctified.

1 John 2:1-2 NKJV And if anyone sins, we have an Advocate with the Father, Jesus Christ the righteous. And He Himself is the propitiation for our sins.

Proverbs 29:2 NKJV When the righteous are in authority, the people rejoice; but when a wicked man rules, the people groan.

Matthew 10:1 TMB He gave them power against unclean spirits to cast them out, and to heal all manner of sickness and all manner of disease.

Matthew 28:18-20 WEB Jesus came to them and spoke to them, saying, "All authority has been given to me in heaven and on earth. Go, and make disciples of all nations, baptizing them in the name of the Father and of the Son and of the Holy Spirit, teaching them to observe all things which I commanded you."

John 17:1-2 WEB Jesus said these things, and lifting up his eyes to heaven, he said, "Father, the time has come. Glorify your Son, that your Son may also glorify you; even as you gave him authority over all flesh, that to all whom you have given him, he will give eternal life."

Acts 1:8 NKJV But you shall receive power when the Holy Spirit has come upon you.

Romans 13:1-2 NIV Everyone must submit himself to the governing authorities, for there is no authority except that which God has established. The authorities that exist have been established by God. Consequently, he who rebels against the authority is rebelling against what God has instituted, and those who do so will bring judgment on themselves.

Colossians 2:9-10 WEB For in him all the fullness of the Godhead dwells bodily, and in him you are made full, who is the head of all principality and power.

Titus 2:15 NKJV Speak these things, exhort, and rebuke with all authority. Let no one despise you.

Matthew 3:11-15 WEB I indeed baptize you in water for repentance, but he who comes after me is mightier than I, whose shoes I am not worthy to carry. He shall baptize you in the Holy Spirit . . . Then Jesus came from Galilee to the Jordan to John, to be baptized by him. But John would have hindered him, saying, "I need to be baptized by you." . . . Jesus said, "Allow it . . . this is the fitting way for us to fulfill all righteousness."

Matthew 3:16-17 NKJV When He had been baptized, Jesus came up immediately from the water; and behold, the heavens were opened to Him, and He saw the Spirit of God descending like a dove and alighting upon Him. And suddenly a voice came from heaven, saying, "This is My beloved Son, in whom I am well pleased."

Matthew 28:18-20 NIV Then Jesus came to them and said, "All authority in heaven and on earth has been given to me. Therefore go and make disciples of all nations, baptizing them in the name of the Father and of the Son and of the Holy Spirit, and teaching them to obey everything I have commanded you. And surely I am with you always, to the very end of the age."

Mark 16:15-18 WNT Then He said to them, "Go the whole world over, and proclaim the Good News to all mankind. He who believes and is baptized shall be saved, but he who disbelieves will be condemned. And signs shall attend those who believe, even such as these. By making use of my name they shall expel demons. They shall speak new languages. They shall take up venomous snakes, and if they drink any deadly poison it shall do them no harm whatever. They shall lay their hands on the sick, and the sick shall recover."

Luke 3:3 WEB He came into all the region around the Jordan, preaching the baptism of repentance for remission of sins.

John 3:5 TMB Jesus answered, "Verily, verily I say unto thee, unless a man be born of water and of the Spirit, he cannot enter into the Kingdom of God."

Acts 2:38-39 NIV Peter replied, "Repent and be baptized, every one of you, in the name of Jesus Christ for the forgiveness of your sins. And you will receive the gift of the Holy Spirit. The promise is for you and your children and for all who are far off—for all whom the Lord our God will call."

Acts 22:14-16 NCV He said, "The God of our ancestors chose you long ago to know his plan, to see the Righteous One, and to hear words from him. You will be his witness to all people, telling them about what you have seen and heard. Now, why wait any longer? Get up, be baptized, and wash your sins away, trusting in him to save you."

Romans 6:2-4 NCV No! We died to our old sinful lives, so how can we continue living with sin? Did you forget that all of us became part of Christ when we were baptized? We shared his death in our baptism. When we were baptized, we were buried with Christ and shared his death. So, just as Christ was raised from the dead by the wonderful power of the Father, we also can live a new life.

Galatians 3:25-27 WEB But now that faith is come, we are no longer under a tutor. For you are all children of God, through faith in Christ Jesus. For as many of you as were baptized into Christ have put on Christ.

Ephesians 4:4-6 NKJV There is one body and one Spirit, just as you were called in one hope of your calling; one Lord, one faith, one baptism; one God and Father of all, who is above all, and through all, and in you all.

Colossians 2:11-13 NKJV In Him you were also circumcised with the circumcision made without hands, by putting off the body of the sins of the flesh, by the circumcision of Christ, buried with Him in baptism, in which you were also raised with Him through faith in the working of God, who raised Him from the dead. And you, being dead in your trespasses and the uncircumcision of your flesh, He has made alive together with Him.

1 Samuel 1:5 NKJV But to Hannah he would give a double portion, for he loved Hannah, although the LORD had closed her womb.

1 Samuel 1:20 NKJV So it came to pass in the process of time that Hannah conceived and bore a son, and called his name Samuel, saying, "Because I have asked for him from the LORD."

Psalm 113:9 TMB He maketh the barren woman to keep house, and to be a joyful mother of children. Praise ye the LORD!

Psalm 138:8 TMB The LORD will perfect that which concerneth me; Thy mercy, O LORD, endureth for ever; forsake not the works of Thine own hands.

Isaiah 43:18-19 NASB Do not call to mind the former things, or ponder things of the past. Behold, I will do something new, now it will spring forth; will you not be aware of it?

Isaiah 54:1 NASB "Shout for joy, O barren one, you who have borne no child; break forth into joyful shouting and cry aloud, you who have not travailed; for the sons of the desolate one will be more numerous than the sons of the married woman," says the LORD.

Luke 1:13-15 WNT But the angel said to him, "Do not be afraid, Zechariah, for your petition has been heard: and your wife Elizabeth will bear you a son, and you are to call his name John. Gladness and exultant joy shall be yours, and many will rejoice over his birth. For he will be great in the sight of the Lord; no wine or fermented drink shall he ever drink; but he will be filled with the Holy Spirit from the very hour of his birth."

John 10:10 NKJV "I have come that they may have life, and that they may have it more abundantly."

1 Samuel 16:7 NKJV But the LORD said to Samuel, "Do not look at his appearance or at his physical stature, because I have refused him. For the LORD does not see as man sees; for man looks at the outward appearance, but the LORD looks at the heart."

Psalm 27:4 WEB One thing have I asked of Yahweh, that will I seek after, that I may dwell in the house of Yahweh all the days of my life, to see Yahweh's beauty, and to inquire in his temple.

Psalm 145:4-6 NKJV One generation shall praise Your works to another, and shall declare Your mighty acts. I will meditate on the glorious splendor of Your majesty, and on Your wondrous works. Men shall speak of the might of Your awesome acts, and I will declare Your greatness.

Proverbs 31:30 NLT Charm is deceptive, and beauty does not last; but a woman who fears the LORD will be greatly praised.

Ecclesiastes 3:11 NLT God has made everything beautiful for its own time.

Romans 10:15 WEB As it is written: "How beautiful are the feet of those who preach the Good News of peace, who bring glad tidings of good things!"

1 Timothy 2:9-10 WNT And I would have the women dress becomingly, with modesty and self-control, not with plaited hair or gold or pearls or costly clothes, but—as befits women making a claim to godliness—with the ornament of good works.

1 Peter 3:3-4 NKJV Do not let your adornment be merely outward—arranging the hair, wearing gold, or putting on fine apparel—rather let it be the hidden person of the heart, with the incorruptible beauty of a gentle and quiet spirit, which is very precious in the sight of God.

Mark 9:23 NLT "What do you mean, 'If I can'?" Jesus asked. "Anything is possible if a person believes."

Luke 17:5-6 WNT And the Apostles said to the Lord, "Give us faith." "If your faith," replied the Lord, "is like a mustard seed, you might command this black-mulberry-tree, 'Tear up your roots and plant yourself in the sea,' and instantly it would obey you."

John 3:35-36 NKJV The Father loves the Son, and has given all things into His hand. He who believes in the Son has everlasting life; and he who does not believe the Son shall not see life, but the wrath of God abides on him.

John 7:37-38 NIV On the last and greatest day of the Feast, Jesus stood and said in a loud voice, "If anyone is thirsty, let him come to me and drink. Whoever believes in me, as the Scripture has said, streams of living water will flow from within him."

John 8:31-32 WNT Jesus therefore said to those of the Jews who had now believed in Him, "As for you, if you hold fast to my teaching, then you are truly my disciples; and you shall know the Truth, and the Truth will make you free."

John 11:25-27 WNT "I am the Resurrection and the Life," said Jesus; "he who believes in me, even if he has died, he shall live; and every one who is living and is a believer in me shall never, never die. Do you believe this?" "Yes, Master," she replied; "I thoroughly believe that you are the Christ, the Son of God, who was to come into the world."

John 11:40-42 NKJV Jesus said to her, "Did I not say to you that if you would believe you would see the glory of God?" Then they took away the stone from the place where the dead man was lying. And Jesus lifted up His eyes and said, "Father, I thank You that You have heard Me. And I know that You always hear Me, but because of the people who are standing by I said this, that they may believe that You sent Me."

John 12:44-46 NIV Then Jesus cried out, "When a man believes in me, he does not believe in me only, but in the one who sent me. When he looks at me, he sees the one who sent me. I have come into the world as a light, so that no one who believes in me should stay in darkness."

John 14:11-13 NIV Believe me when I say that I am in the Father and the Father is in me; or at least believe on the evidence of the miracles themselves. I tell you the truth, anyone who has faith in me will do what I have been doing. He will do even greater things than these, because I am going to the Father. And I will do whatever you ask in my name, so that the Son may bring glory to the Father.

John 17:25-26 NASB O righteous Father, although the world has not known You, yet I have known You; and these have known that You sent Me; and I have made Your name known to them, and will make it known, so that the love with which You loved Me may be in them, and I in them.

Romans 10:10-11 WNT For with the heart men believe and obtain righteousness, and with the mouth they make confession and obtain salvation. The Scripture says, "No one who believes in Him shall have reason to feel ashamed."

1 Timothy 4:12-15 NCV Do not let anyone treat you as if you are unimportant because you are young. Instead, be an example to the believers with your words, your actions, your love, your faith, and your pure life. Until I come, continue to read the Scriptures to the people, strengthen them, and teach them. Use the gift you have, which was given to you through prophecy when the group of elders laid their hands on you. Continue to do those things; give your life to doing them so your progress may be seen by everyone.

Hebrews 11:6 NKJV But without faith it is impossible to please Him, for he who comes to God must believe that He is, and that He is a rewarder of those who diligently seek Him.

Exodus 20:14-16 NLT Do not commit adultery. Do not steal. Do not testify falsely against your neighbor.

Psalm 55:22 NKJV Cast your burden on the LORD, and He shall sustain you; He shall never permit the righteous to be moved.

Proverbs 10:12 NCV Hatred stirs up trouble, but love forgives all wrongs.

Mark 13:12-13 NKJV Now brother will betray brother to death, and a father his child; and children will rise up against parents and cause them to be put to death. And you will be hated by all for My name's sake. But he who endures to the end shall be saved.

Luke 6:27-28 WEB But I tell you who hear: love your enemies, do good to those who hate you, bless those who curse you, and pray for those who mistreat you.

Romans 12:20-21 WEB "If your enemy is hungry, feed him; if he is thirsty, give him a drink; for in doing so, you will heap coals of fire on his head." Don't be overcome by evil, but overcome evil with good.

1 Corinthians 13:4-7 NKJV Love suffers long and is kind; love does not envy; love does not parade itself, is not puffed up; does not behave rudely, does not seek its own, is not provoked, thinks no evil; does not rejoice in iniquity, but rejoices in truth; bears all things, believes all things, hopes all things, endures all things.

1 Thessalonians 4:3-6 NKJV For this is the will of God, your sanctification: that you should abstain from sexual immorality; that each of you should know how to possess his own vessel in sanctification and honor, not in passion of lust, like the Gentiles who do not know God; that no one should take advantage of and defraud his brother in this matter, because the Lord is the avenger of all such.

Numbers 6:22-26 NASB Then the LORD spoke to Moses, saying, "Speak to Aaron and to his sons, saying, 'Thus you shall bless the sons of Israel. You shall say to them: "The LORD bless you, and keep you; The LORD make His face shine on you, and be gracious to you; the LORD lift up His countenance on you, and give you peace." ' "

Psalm 71:6 NLT Yes, you have been with me from birth; from my mother's womb you have cared for me. No wonder I am always praising you!

Psalm 127:3-5 NKJV Behold, children are a heritage from the LORD, the fruit of the womb is a reward. Like arrows in the hand of a warrior, so are the children of one's youth. Happy is the man who has his quiver full of them.

Isaiah 54:13 WEB All your children shall be taught of Yahweh, and great shall be the peace of your children.

Jeremiah 1:4-5 NKJV Then the word of the LORD came to me, saying: "Before I formed you in the womb I knew you; before you were born I sanctified you; I ordained you a prophet to the nations."

Matthew 19:14 NIV Jesus said, "Let the little children come to me, and do not hinder them, for the kingdom of heaven belongs to such as these."

Luke 1:42 NKJV Then she spoke out with a loud voice and said, "Blessed are you among women, and blessed is the fruit of your womb!"

Philippians 4:6-7 NKJV Be anxious for nothing, but in everything by prayer and supplication, with thanksgiving, let your requests be made known to God; and the peace of God, which surpasses all understanding, will guard your hearts and minds through Christ Jesus.

Romans 13:12-14 WNT We must therefore lay aside the deeds of darkness, and clothe ourselves with the armour of Light. Living as we do in broad daylight, let us conduct ourselves becomingly, not indulging in revelry and drunkenness, nor in lust and debauchery, nor in quarrelling and jealousy. On the contrary, clothe yourselves with the Lord Jesus Christ, and make no provision for gratifying your earthly cravings.

Ephesians 4:30-32 WEB Don't grieve the Holy Spirit of God, in whom you were sealed for the day of redemption. Let all bitterness, wrath, anger, outcry, and slander be put away from you, with all malice. And be kind to one another, tenderhearted, forgiving each other, just as God in Christ also forgave you.

Colossians 3:12-13 NKJV Therefore, as the elect of God, holy and beloved, put on tender mercies, kindness, humility, meekness, longsuffering; bearing with one another, and forgiving one another, if anyone has a complaint against another; even as Christ forgave you, so you also must do.

Colossians 3:19 WEB Husbands, love your wives, and don't be bitter against them.

James 3:14-18 NKJV But if you have bitter envy and self-seeking in your hearts, do not boast and lie against the truth. This wisdom does not descend from above, but is earthly, sensual, demonic. For where envy and self-seeking exist, confusion and every evil thing are there. But the wisdom that is from above is first pure, then peaceable, gentle, willing to yield, full of mercy and good fruits, without partiality and without hypocrisy. Now the fruit of righteousness is sown in peace by those who make peace.

Hebrews 12:14-15 NKJV Pursue peace with all people, and holiness, without which no one will see the Lord: looking carefully lest anyone fall short of the grace of God; lest any root of bitterness springing up cause trouble.

Numbers 6:24-26 NKJV The LORD bless you and keep you; the LORD make His face shine upon you, and be gracious to you; the LORD lift up His countenance upon you, and give you peace.

Psalm 5:11-12 NIV But let all who take refuge in you be glad; let them ever sing for joy. Spread your protection over them, that those who love your name may rejoice in you. For surely, O LORD, you bless the righteous; you surround them with your favor as with a shield.

Psalm 65:4 NKJV Blessed is the man You choose, and cause to approach You, that he may dwell in Your courts.

Psalm 112:1-2 NKJV Blessed is the man who fears the LORD, who delights greatly in His commandments. His descendants will be mighty on earth; the generation of the upright will be blessed.

Proverbs 10:22 NLT The blessing of the LORD makes a person rich, and he adds no sorrow with it.

John 13:16-17 NLT How true it is that a servant is not greater than the master. Nor are messengers more important than the one who sends them. You know these things – now do them! That is the path of blessing.

Ephesians 1:3 TMB Blessed be the God and Father of our Lord Jesus Christ, who hath blessed us with all spiritual blessings in heavenly places in Christ.

2 Thessalonians 2:16-17 NKJV Now may our Lord Jesus Christ Himself, and our God and Father, who has loved us and given us everlasting consolation and good hope by grace, comfort your hearts and establish you in every good word and work.

1 Corinthians 3:9-10 NKJV For we are God's fellow workers; you are God's field, you are God's building. According to the grace of God which was given to me, as a wise master builder I have laid the foundation, and another builds on it.

1 Corinthians 12:11-12 NCV One Spirit, the same Spirit, does all these things, and the Spirit decides what to give each person. A person's body is only one thing, but it has many parts. Though there are many parts to a body, all those parts make only one body. Christ is like that also.

1 Corinthians 12:17-18 NIV If the whole body were an eye, where would the sense of hearing be? If the whole body were an ear, where would the sense of smell be? But in fact God has arranged the parts in the body, every one of them, just as he wanted them to be.

1 Corinthians 12:24-27 WNT But it was God who built up the body, and bestowed more abundant honor on the part that felt the need, that there might be no disunion in the body, but that all the members might entertain the same anxious care for one another's welfare. And if one part is suffering, every other part suffers with it; or if one part is receiving special honor, every other part shares in the joy. As for you, you are the body of Christ, and individually you are members of it.

1 Corinthians 12:28-31 NKJV And God has appointed these in the church: first apostles, second prophets, third teachers, after that miracles, then gifts of healings, helps, administrations, varieties of tongues. Are all apostles? Are all prophets? Are all teachers? Are all workers of miracles? Do all have gifts of healings? Do all speak with tongues? Do all interpret? But earnestly desire the best gifts.

Ephesians 1:22-23 NKJV And He put all things under His feet, and gave Him to be head over all things to the church, which is His body, the fullness of Him who fills all in all.

Joshua 1:9 NKJV Be strong and of good courage; do not be afraid, nor be dismayed, for the LORD your God is with you wherever you go.

Acts 4:13-14 WEB Now when they saw the boldness of Peter and John, and had perceived that they were unlearned and ignorant men, they marveled. They recognized that they had been with Jesus. Seeing the man who was healed standing with them, they could say nothing against it.

Acts 4:29-31 WEB "Now, Lord, look at their threats, and grant to your servants to speak your word with all boldness, while you stretch out your hand to heal; and that signs and wonders may be done through the name of your holy Servant Jesus." When they had prayed, the place was shaken where they were gathered together. They were all filled with the Holy Spirit, and they spoke the word of God with boldness.

Romans 1:16 TMB For I am not ashamed of the Gospel of Christ, for it is the power of God unto salvation to every one who believeth.

Ephesians 6:19-20 NKJV That I may open my mouth boldly to make known the mystery of the gospel, for which I am an ambassador in chains; that in it I may speak boldly, as I ought to speak.

Hebrews 4:16 NKJV Let us therefore come boldly to the throne of grace, that we may obtain mercy and find grace to help in time of need.

Hebrews 13:6 NKJV So we may boldly say: "The LORD is my helper; I will not fear. What can man do to me?"

1 John 5:14 NLT And we can be confident that he will listen to us whenever we ask him for anything in line with his will.

Psalm 138:8 NLT The LORD will work out his plans for my life—for your faithful love, O LORD, endures forever. Don't abandon me, for you made me.

Romans 11:29 NLT For God's gifts and his call can never be withdrawn.

Romans 12:6-8 NIV We have different gifts, according to the grace given us. If a man's gift is prophesying, let him use it in proportion to his faith. If it is serving, let him serve; if it is teaching, let him teach; if it is encouraging, let him encourage; if it is contributing to the needs of others, let him give generously; if it is leadership, let him govern diligently; if it is showing mercy, let him do it cheerfully.

1 Corinthians 14:1 NKJV Pursue love, and desire spiritual gifts, but especially that you may prophesy.

Ephesians 4:1-4 NKJV Walk worthy of the calling with which you were called, with all lowliness and gentleness, with longsuffering, bearing with one another in love, endeavoring to keep the unity of the Spirit in the bond of peace. There is one body and one Spirit, just as you were called in one hope of your calling.

Ephesians 4:11-16 NRSV The gifts he gave were that some would be apostles, some prophets, some evangelists, some pastors and teachers, to equip the saints for the work of ministry, for building up the body of Christ, until all of us come to the unity of the faith and of the knowledge of the Son of God, to maturity, to the measure of the full stature of Christ. We must no longer be children, tossed to and fro and blown about by every wind of doctrine, by people's trickery, by their craftiness in deceitful scheming. But speaking the truth in love, we must grow up in every way into him who is the head, into Christ, from whom the whole body, joined and knit together by every ligament with which it is equipped, as each part is working properly, promotes the body's growth in building itself up in love.

Philippians 1:6 NKJV Being confident of this very thing, that He who has begun a good work in you will complete it until the day of Jesus Christ.

Colossians 1:9-10 NKJV That you may you be filled with the knowledge of His will in all wisdom and spiritual understanding; that you may walk worthy of the Lord, fully pleasing Him, being fruitful in every good work and increasing in the knowledge of God.

1 Timothy 3:1-7 WNT "If any one is eager to have the oversight of a Church, he desires a noble work." A minister then must be a man of irreproachable character, true to his one wife, temperate, sober-minded, well-behaved, hospitable to strangers, and with a gift for teaching; not a hard drinker nor given to blows; not selfish or quarrelsome or covetous; but ruling his own household wisely and well, with children kept under control with true dignity. (If a man does not know how to rule his own household, how shall he have the Church of God given into his care?) He ought not to be a new convert, for fear he should be blinded with pride and come under the same condemnation as the Devil. It is needful also that he bear a good character with people outside the Church, lest he fall into reproach or a snare of the Devil.

1 Timothy 3:13 NASB For those who have served well as deacons obtain for themselves a high standing and great confidence in the faith that is in Christ Jesus.

2 Timothy 1:8-9 NASB Therefore do not be ashamed of the testimony of our Lord or of me His prisoner, but join with me in suffering for the gospel according to the power of God, who has saved us and called us with a holy calling, not according to our works, but according to His own purpose and grace which was granted us in Christ Jesus.

Psalm 121:1-8 NRSV I lift up my eyes to the hills—from where will my help come? My help comes from the Lord, who made heaven and earth. He will not let your foot be moved; he who keeps you will not slumber. He who keeps Israel will neither slumber nor sleep. The Lord is your keeper; the Lord is your shade at your right hand. The sun shall not strike you by day, nor the moon by night. The Lord will keep you from all evil; he will keep your life. The Lord will keep your going out and your coming in from this time on and forevermore.

Isaiah 58:6-7 NKJV Is this not the fast that I have chosen: To loose the bonds of wickedness, to undo the heavy burdens, to let the oppressed go free, and that you break every yoke? Is it not to share your bread with the hungry, and that you bring to your house the poor who are cast out; when you see the naked, that you cover him, and not hide yourself from your own flesh?

Matthew 25:38-40 NIV "When did we see you a stranger and invite you in, or needing clothes and clothe you? When did we see you sick or in prison and go to visit you?" The King will reply, "I tell you the truth, whatever you did for one of the least of these brothers of mine, you did for me."

Luke 14:13-14 NASB But when you give a reception, invite the poor, the crippled, the lame, the blind, and you will be blessed, since they do not have the means to repay you; for you will be repaid at the resurrection of the righteous.

Romans 12:10-13 WEB In love of the brothers be tenderly affectionate one to another; in honor preferring one another; not lagging in diligence; fervent in spirit; serving the Lord; rejoicing in hope; enduring in troubles; continuing steadfastly in prayer; contributing to the needs of the saints; given to hospitality.

Deuteronomy 8:2-5 NRSV Remember the long way that the LORD your God has led you these forty years in the wilderness, in order to humble you, testing you to know what was in your heart, whether or not you would keep his commandments. He humbled you by letting you hunger, then by feeding you with manna, with which neither you nor your ancestors were acquainted, in order to make you understand that one does not live by bread alone, but by every word that comes from the mouth of the LORD. The clothes on your back did not wear out and your feet did not swell these forty years. Know then in your heart that as a parent disciplines a child so the LORD your God disciplines you.

Psalm 37:23-25 NCV When a person's steps follow the LORD, God is pleased with his ways. If he stumbles, he will not fall, because the LORD holds his hand. I was young, and now I am old, but I have never seen good people left helpless or their children begging for food.

Psalm 37:37-40 NKJV Mark the blameless man, and observe the upright; for the future of that man is peace. But the transgressors shall be destroyed together; the future of the wicked shall be cut off. But the salvation of the righteous is from the LORD; He is their strength in the time of trouble. And the LORD shall help them and deliver them; He shall deliver them from the wicked, and save them, because they trust in Him.

Proverbs 22:1 NLT Choose a good reputation over great riches, for being held in high esteem is better than having silver or gold.

Matthew 5:16 NLT In the same way, let your good deeds shine out for all to see, so that everyone will praise your heavenly Father.

Romans 5:3-5 NKJV We also glory in tribulations, knowing that tribulation produces perseverance; and perseverance, character; and character, hope. Now hope does not disappoint, because the love of God has been poured out in our hearts by the Holy Spirit who was given to us.

1 Corinthians 11:1 NCV Follow my example, as I follow the example of Christ.

1 Corinthians 15:33–34 NCV Do not be fooled: "Bad friends will ruin good habits." Come back to your right way of thinking and stop sinning.

Galatians 5:25 WEB If we live by the Spirit, let us also walk by the Spirit.

Titus 2:6–8 WEB Likewise, exhort the younger men to be sober minded; in all things showing yourself an example of good works; in your teaching showing integrity, seriousness, incorruptibility, and soundness of speech that can't be condemned; that he who opposes you may be ashamed, having no evil thing to say about us.

1 Peter 1:13–16 NKJV Therefore gird up the loins of your mind, be sober, and rest your hope fully upon the grace that is to be brought to you at the revelation of Jesus Christ; as obedient children, not conforming yourselves to the former lusts, as in your ignorance; but as He who called you is holy, you also be holy in all your conduct, because it is written, "Be holy, for I am holy."

2 Peter 1:3–8 WNT His divine power has given us all things that are needful for life and godliness, through our knowledge of Him who has appealed to us by His own glorious perfections. It is by means of these that He has granted us His precious and wondrous promises, in order that through them you may, one and all, become sharers in the very nature of God, having completely escaped the corruption which exists in the world through earthly cravings. But for this very reason—adding, on your part, all earnestness—along with your faith, manifest also a noble character: along with a noble character, knowledge; along with knowledge, self-control; along with self-control, power of endurance; along with power of endurance, godliness; along with godliness, brotherly affection; and along with brotherly affection, love. If these things exist in you, and continually increase, they prevent your being either idle or unfruitful in advancing towards a full knowledge of our Lord Jesus Christ.

Proverbs 1:7 TMB The fear of the LORD is the beginning of knowledge, but fools despise wisdom and instruction.

Proverbs 20:11 TMB Even a child is known by his doings, whether his work be pure and whether it be right.

Proverbs 22:15 NKJV Foolishness is bound up in the heart of a child; the rod of correction will drive it far from him.

Matthew 18:10-11 NKJV Take heed that you not despise one of these little ones, for I say to you that in heaven their angels always see the face of My Father who is in heaven. For the Son of Man has come to save that which was lost.

Matthew 21:16 NCV They asked Jesus, "Do you hear the things these children are saying?" Jesus answered, "Yes. Haven't you read in the Scriptures, 'You have taught children and babies to sing praises'?"

Luke 2:40 TMB And the Child grew and waxed strong in spirit, filled with wisdom, and the grace of God was upon Him.

Ephesians 2:10 NKJV For we are His workmanship, created in Christ Jesus for good works, which God prepared beforehand that we should walk in them.

Ephesians 5:1-2 NKJV Therefore be imitators of God as dear children. And walk in love, as Christ also has loved us and given Himself for us, an offering and a sacrifice to God for a sweet-smelling aroma.

Ephesians 6:1-3 NKJV Children, obey your parents in the Lord, for this is right. "Honor your father and mother," which is the first commandment with promise: "that it may be well with you and you may live long on the earth."

Colossians 3:20 NCV Children, obey your parents in all things, because this pleases the Lord.

2 Timothy 2:10 NKJV Therefore I endure all things for the sake of the elect, that they also may obtain the salvation which is in Christ Jesus with eternal glory.

2 Timothy 3:14-15 NKJV But you must continue in the things which you have learned and been assured of, knowing from whom you have learned them, and that from childhood you have known the Holy Scriptures, which are able to make you wise for salvation through faith which is in Christ Jesus.

2 Peter 3:18 NLT But grow in the special favor and knowledge of our Lord and Savior Jesus Christ.

1 John 2:12 NIV I write to you, dear children, because your sins have been forgiven on account of his name.

1 John 2:28-29 NIV And now, dear children, continue in him, so that when he appears we may be confident and unashamed before him at his coming. If you know that he is righteous, you know that everyone who does what is right has been born of him.

1 John 3:2-3 WEB Beloved, now we are children of God, and it is not yet revealed what we will be. But we know that, when he is revealed, we will be like him; for we will see him just as he is. Everyone who has this hope set on him purifies himself, even as he is pure.

1 John 4:4 NLT But you belong to God, my dear children. You have already won your fight with these false prophets, because the Spirit who lives in you is greater than the spirit who lives in the world.

Deuteronomy 30:19-20 NRSV I call heaven and earth to witness against you today that I have set before you life and death, blessings and curses. Choose life so that you and your descendants may live, loving the LORD your God, obeying him, and holding fast to him; for that means life to you and length of days, so that you may live in the land that the LORD swore to give to your ancestors, to Abraham, to Isaac, and to Jacob.

Psalm 25:12-14 NIV Who, then, is the man that fears the LORD? He will instruct him in the way chosen for him. He will spend his days in prosperity, and his descendants will inherit the land. The LORD confides in those who fear him; he makes his covenant known to them.

Psalm 119:102-105 NRSV I do not turn away from your ordinances, for you have taught me. How sweet are your words to my taste, sweeter than honey to my mouth! Through your precepts I get understanding; therefore I hate every false way. Your word is a lamp to my feet and a light to my path.

Matthew 6:33 WEB But seek first God's Kingdom, and his righteousness; and all these things will be given to you as well.

Romans 13:13-14 WEB Let us walk properly, as in the day; not in reveling and drunkenness, not in sexual promiscuity and lustful acts, and not in strife and jealousy. But put on the Lord Jesus Christ, and make no provision for the flesh, for its lusts.

Colossians 1:9-11 WEB That you may be filled with the knowledge of his will in all spiritual wisdom and understanding, that you may walk worthily of the Lord, to please him in all respects, bearing fruit in every good work, and increasing in the knowledge of God; strengthened with all power, according to the might of his glory, to all endurance and perseverance with joy.

Psalm 17:15 WEB As for me, I shall see your face in righteousness. I shall be satisfied, when I awake, with seeing your form.

Matthew 7:1-2 NCV Don't judge other people, or you will be judged. You will be judged in the same way that you judge others, and the amount you give to others will be given to you.

Romans 12:1-2 NKJV I beseech you therefore, brethren, by the mercies of God, that you present your bodies a living sacrifice, holy, acceptable to God, which is your reasonable service. And do not be conformed to this world, but be transformed by the renewing of your mind, that you may prove what is that good and acceptable and perfect will of God.

2 Corinthians 3:18 NLT And all of us have had that veil removed so that we can be mirrors that brightly reflect the glory of the Lord. And as the Spirit of the Lord works within us, we become more and more like him and reflect his glory even more.

Colossians 3:12-16 WEB Put on therefore, as God's chosen ones, holy and beloved, a heart of compassion, kindness, lowliness, humility, and perseverance; bearing with one another, and forgiving each other, if any man has a complaint against any; even as Christ forgave you, so you also do. Above all these things, walk in love, which is the bond of perfection. And let the peace of Christ rule in your hearts, to which also you were called in one body; and be thankful. Let the word of Christ dwell in you richly; in all wisdom teaching and admonishing one another with psalms, hymns, and spiritual songs, singing with grace in your heart to the Lord.

1 John 3:2 NASB Beloved, now we are children of God, and it has not appeared as yet what we will be. We know that when He appears, we will be like Him, because we will see Him just as He is.

Psalm 118:22-23 NRSV The stone that the builders rejected has become the chief cornerstone. This is the Lord's doing; it is marvelous in our eyes.

Psalm 122:1 TMB I was glad when they said unto me, "Let us go into the house of the LORD."

Matthew 16:16-18 NKJV Simon Peter answered and said, "You are the Christ, the Son of the living God." Jesus answered and said to him, "Blessed are you, Simon Bar-Jonah, for flesh and blood has not revealed this to you, but My Father who is in heaven. And I also say to you . . . on this rock I will build My church, and the gates of Hades shall not prevail against it."

Acts 9:31 NCV The church everywhere in Judea, Galilee, and Samaria had a time of peace and became stronger. Respecting the Lord by the way they lived, and being encouraged by the Holy Spirit, the group of believers continued to grow.

Acts 20:28 NCV Be careful for yourselves and for all the people the Holy Spirit has given to you to care for. You must be like shepherds to the church of God, which he bought with the death of his own son.

Galatians 6:10 TMB As we therefore have opportunity, let us do good unto all men, especially unto those who are of the household of faith.

Ephesians 2:19-22 NKJV You are no longer strangers and foreigners, but fellow citizens with the saints and members of the household of God, having been built on the foundation of the apostles and prophets, Jesus Christ Himself being the chief cornerstone, in whom the whole building, being fitted together, grows into a holy temple in the Lord, in whom you also are being built together for a dwelling place of God in the Spirit.

Deuteronomy 30:5-6 NIV He will bring you to the land that belonged to your fathers, and you will take possession of it. He will make you more prosperous and numerous than your fathers. The LORD your God will circumcise your hearts and the hearts of your descendants, so that you may love him with all your heart and with all your soul, and live.

.

Jeremiah 32:38-40 NIV They will be my people, and I will be their God. I will give them singleness of heart and action, so that they will always fear me for their own good and the good of their children after them. I will make an everlasting covenant with them: I will never stop doing good to them, and I will inspire them to fear me, so that they will never turn away from me.

Ezekiel 11:19-21 NRSV "I will give them one heart, and put a new spirit within them; I will remove the heart of stone from their flesh and give them a heart of flesh, so that they may follow my statutes and keep my ordinances and obey them. Then they shall be my people, and I will be their God. But as for those whose heart goes after their detestable things and their abominations, I will bring their deeds upon their own heads," says the Lord GOD.

Romans 2:28-29 WEB For he is not a Jew who is one outwardly, neither is that circumcision which is outward in the flesh; but he is a Jew who is one inwardly, and circumcision is that of the heart, in the spirit not in the letter; whose praise is not from men, but from God.

Colossians 2:11-13 NKJV In Him you were also circumcised with the circumcision made without hands, by putting off the body of the sins of the flesh, by the circumcision of Christ, buried with Him in baptism, in which you also were raised with Him through faith in the working of God, who raised Him from the dead. And you, being dead in your trespasses and the uncircumcision of your flesh, He has made alive together with Him, having forgiven you all trespasses.

Matthew 26:26–28 NASB While they were eating, Jesus took some bread, and after a blessing, He broke it and gave it to the disciples, and said, "Take, eat; this is My body." And when He had taken a cup and given thanks, He gave it to them, saying, "Drink from it, all of you; for this is My blood of the covenant, which is poured out for many for forgiveness of sins."

Acts 2:42–43 TMB And they continued steadfastly in the apostles' doctrine and fellowship, in the breaking of bread and in prayers. And fear came upon every soul, and many wonders and signs were done by the apostles.

1 Corinthians 10:15–17 NASB I speak as to wise men; you judge what I say. Is not the cup of blessing which we bless a sharing in the blood of Christ? Is not the bread which we break a sharing in the body of Christ? Since there is one bread, we who are many are one body; for we all partake of the one bread.

1 Corinthians 11:23–30 WEB The Lord Jesus on the night in which he was betrayed took bread. When he had given thanks, he broke it, and said, "Take, eat. This is my body, which is broken for you. Do this in memory of me." In the same way he also took the cup, after supper, saying, "This cup is the new covenant in my blood. Do this, as often as you drink, in memory of me." For as often as you eat this bread, and drink this cup, you proclaim the Lord's death until he comes. Therefore whoever eats this bread or drinks the Lord's cup in a way unworthy of the Lord, will be guilty of the body and the blood of the Lord. But let a man examine himself, and so let him eat of the bread, and drink of the cup. For he who eats and drinks in an unworthy manner eats and drinks judgment to himself, if he doesn't discern the Lord's body. For this cause many among you are weak and sickly, and not a few sleep.

2 Corinthians 13:14 TMB The grace of the Lord Jesus Christ, and the love of God, and the communion of the Holy Ghost, be with you all. Amen.

Psalm 65:5 NKJV You will answer us, O God of our salvation, You who are the confidence of all the ends of the earth, and of the far-off seas.

Psalm 118:8-9 TMB It is better to trust in the LORD than to put confidence in man. It is better to trust in the LORD than to put confidence in princes.

Proverbs 14:26 NKJV In the fear of the LORD there is strong confidence, and His children will have a place of refuge.

Isaiah 30:15 NCV This is what the Lord GOD, the Holy One of Israel, says: "If you come back to me and trust me, you will be saved. If you will be calm and trust me, you will be strong." But you don't want to do that.

Philippians 1:6 WEB Being confident of this very thing, that he who began a good work in you will complete it until the day of Jesus Christ.

Philippians 3:3-4 NCV We are the ones who are truly circumcised. We worship God through his Spirit, and our pride is in Christ Jesus. We do not put trust in ourselves or anything we can do, although I might be able to put trust in myself.

Hebrews 3:14 WEB For we have become partakers of Christ, if we hold fast the beginning of our confidence firm to the end.

1 John 2:28 TMB And now, little children, abide in Him, that when He shall appear we may have confidence, and not be ashamed before Him at His coming.

1 John 5:14-15 NKJV Now this is the confidence that we have in Him, that if we ask anything according to His will, He hears us. And if we know that He hears us, whatever we ask, we know that we have the petitions that we have asked of Him.

1 Timothy 3:8-10 NIV Deacons, likewise, are to be men worthy of respect, sincere, not indulging in much wine, and not pursuing dishonest gain. They must keep hold of the deep truths of the faith with a clear conscience. They must first be tested; and then if there is nothing against them, let them serve as deacons.

1 Timothy 4:1-2 NIV The Spirit clearly says that in later times some will abandon the faith and follow deceiving spirits and things taught by demons. Such teachings come through hypocritical liars, whose consciences have been seared as with a hot iron.

Hebrews 9:13-14 NKJV For if the blood of bulls and goats and the ashes of a heifer, sprinkling the unclean, sanctifies for the purifying of the flesh, how much more shall the blood of Christ, who through the eternal Spirit offered Himself without spot to God, cleanse your conscience from dead works to serve the living God?

Hebrews 10:22-23 NCV Let us come near to God with a sincere heart and a sure faith, because we have been made free from a guilty conscience, and our bodies have been washed with pure water. Let us hold firmly to the hope that we have confessed, because we can trust God to do what he promised.

1 Peter 3:8-9 NIV Finally, all of you, live in harmony with one another; be sympathetic, love as brothers, be compassionate and humble. Do not repay evil with evil or insult with insult, but with blessing, because to this you were called so that you may inherit a blessing.

1 John 3:20-22 WEB If our heart condemns us, God is greater than our heart, and knows all things. Beloved, if our hearts don't condemn us, we have boldness toward God; and whatever we ask, we receive from him, because we keep his commandments and do the things that are pleasing in his sight.

Psalm 16:5-6 NLT LORD, you alone are my inheritance, my cup of blessing. You guard all that is mine. The land you have given me is a pleasant land. What a wonderful inheritance!

Matthew 6:27, 34 NKJV Which of you by worrying can add one cubit to his stature? . . . Therefore do not worry about tomorrow, for tomorrow will worry about its own things. Sufficient for the day is its own trouble.

Philippians 4:11-13 NIV I am not saying this because I am in need, for I have learned to be content whatever the circumstances. I know what it is to be in need, and I know what it is to have plenty. I have learned the secret of being content in any and every situation, whether well fed or hungry, whether living in plenty or in want. I can do everything through him who gives me strength.

Colossians 2:9-11 WNT For it is in Christ that the fullness of God's nature dwells embodied, and in Him you are made complete, and He is the Lord of all princes and rulers. In Him also you were circumcised with a circumcision not performed by hand, when you threw off your sinful nature in true Christian circumcision.

1 Timothy 6:6-8 NIV But godliness with contentment is great gain. For we brought nothing into the world, and we can take nothing out of it. But if we have food and clothing, we will be content with that.

2 Timothy 4:8 NLT And now the prize awaits me—the crown of righteousness that the Lord, the righteous Judge, will give me on that great day of his return. And the prize is not just for me but for all who eagerly look forward to his glorious return.

Hebrews 13:5 NIV Keep your lives free from the love of money and be content with what you have, because God has said, "Never will I leave you; never will I forsake you."

Psalm 39:1 NCV I said, "I will be careful how I act and will not sin by what I say. I will be careful what I say around wicked people."

Psalm 141:3 TMB Set a watch, O LORD, over my mouth; keep the door of my lips.

Proverbs 10:19-21 NKJV In the multitude of words sin is not lacking, but he who restrains his lips is wise. The tongue of the righteous is choice silver; the heart of the wicked is worth little. The lips of the righteous feed many, but fools die for lack of wisdom.

Proverbs 11:11-13 NASB By the blessing of the upright a city is exalted, but by the mouth of the wicked it is torn down. He who despises his neighbor lacks sense, but a man of understanding keeps silent. He who goes about as a talebearer reveals secrets, but he who is trustworthy conceals a matter.

Proverbs 13:3 WEB He who guards his mouth guards his soul. One who opens wide his lips comes to ruin.

Proverbs 29:11 NCV Foolish people lose their tempers, but wise people control theirs.

Matthew 12:34-37 WEB You offspring of vipers, how can you, being evil, speak good things? For out of the abundance of the heart, the mouth speaks. The good man out of his good treasure brings out good things, and the evil man out of his evil treasure brings out evil things. I tell you that every idle word that men speak, they will give account of it in the day of judgment. For by your words you will be justified, and by your words you will be condemned.

Romans 12:2 NKJV And do not be conformed to this world, but be transformed by the renewing of your mind, that you may prove what is that good and acceptable and perfect will of God.

Deuteronomy 4:40 NKJV You shall therefore keep His statutes and His commandments which I command you today, that it may go well with you and with your children after you, and that you may prolong your days in the land which the LORD your God is giving you for all time.

Psalm 34:14 TMB Depart from evil and do good; seek peace and pursue it.

Psalm 73:24-26 NASB With Your counsel You will guide me, and afterward receive me to glory. Whom have I in heaven but You? And besides You, I desire nothing on earth. My flesh and my heart may fail, but God is the strength of my heart and my portion forever.

Psalm 101:3-4 NCV I will not look at anything wicked. I hate those who turn against you; they will not be found near me. Let those who want to do wrong stay away from me; I will have nothing to do with evil.

Psalm 112:1-3 NIV Praise the LORD. Blessed is the man who fears the LORD, who finds great delight in his commands! His children will be mighty in the land; the generation of the upright will be blessed. Wealth and riches are in his house; and his righteousness endures forever.

Psalm 119:111-112 NASB I have inherited Your testimonies forever, for they are the joy of my heart. I have inclined my heart to perform Your statutes forever, even to the end.

Proverbs 1:7 TMB The fear of the LORD is the beginning of knowledge, but fools despise wisdom and instruction.

Proverbs 1:33 NCV But those who listen to me will live in safety and be at peace, without fear of injury.

Joshua 1:8-9 NKJV This Book of the Law shall not depart from your mouth, but you shall meditate in it day and night, that you may observe to do according to all that is written in it. For then you will make your way prosperous, and then you will have good success. Have I not commanded you? Be strong and of good courage; do not be . . . dismayed, for the LORD your God is with you wherever you go.

Psalm 27:14 NASB Wait for the LORD; be strong and let your heart take courage; yes, wait for the LORD.

Psalm 29:11 TMB The LORD will give strength unto His people; the LORD will bless His people with peace.

Psalm 31:24 WEB Be strong, and let your heart take courage, all you who hope in Yahweh.

Psalm 107:28-30 WEB Then they cry to Yahweh in their trouble, and brings them out of their distress. He makes the storm a calm, so that its waves are still. Then are they glad because it is calm, so he brings them to their desired haven.

Romans 16:20 NIV The God of peace will soon crush Satan under your feet. The grace of our Lord Jesus be with you.

Philippians 1:19-20 WEB For I know that this will turn out to my salvation, through your supplication and the supply of the Spirit of Jesus Christ, according to my earnest expectation and hope, that I will in no way be disappointed, but with all boldness, as always, now also Christ will be magnified in my body, whether by life, or by death.

1 John 5:14 NLT And we can be confident that he will listen to us whenever we ask him for anything in line with his will.

Deuteronomy 28:1-2 NKJV If you diligently obey the voice of the Lord your God, to observe carefully all His commandments which I command you today, that the Lord your God will set you high above all nations of the earth. And all these blessings shall come upon you and overtake you, because you obey the voice of the Lord your God.

Psalm 25:14 TMB The secret of the Lord is with them that fear Him, and He will show them His covenant.

Isaiah 59:21 NIV "As for me, this is my covenant with them," says the Lord. "My Spirit, who is on you, and my words that I have put in your mouth will not depart from your mouth, or from the mouths of your children, or from the mouths of their descendants from this time on and forever," says the Lord.

Mark 14:24 NLT And he said to them, "This is my blood, poured out for many, sealing the covenant between God and his people."

Hebrews 7:22 NCV This means that Jesus is the guarantee of a better agreement from God to his people.

Hebrews 8:10-12 WEB "For this is the covenant that I will make with the house of Israel. After those days," says the Lord; "I will put my laws into their mind, I will also write them on their heart. I will be their God, and they will be my people. They will not teach every man his fellow citizen, every man his brother, saying, 'Know the Lord,' for all will know me, from the least of them to the greatest of them. For I will be merciful to their unrighteousness. I will remember their sins and lawless deeds no more."

Hebrews 13:20-21 NIV May the God of peace, who through the blood of the eternal covenant brought back from the dead our Lord Jesus, that great Shepherd of the sheep, equip you with everything good for doing his will, and may he work in us what is pleasing to him, through Jesus Christ, to whom be glory for ever and ever. Amen.

Genesis 1:1, 26, 31 NKJV In the beginning God created the heavens and the earth. . . . Then God said, "Let Us make man in Our image, according to Our likeness; let them have dominion over the fish of the sea, over the birds of the air, and over the cattle, over all the earth and over every creeping thing that creeps on the earth." . . . Then God saw everything that He had made, and indeed it was very good.

Psalm 33:6-8 NLT The LORD merely spoke, and the heavens were created. He breathed the word, and all the stars were born. He gave the sea its boundaries and locked the oceans in vast reservoirs. Let everyone in the world fear the LORD, and let everyone stand in awe of him.

Isaiah 45:6-8 NLT So all the world from east to west will know there is no other God. I am the LORD, and there is no other. I am the one who creates the light and makes the darkness. I am the one who sends good times and bad times. I, the LORD, am the one who does these things. Open up, O heavens, and pour out your righteousness. Let the earth open wide so salvation and righteousness can sprout up together. I, the LORD, created them.

Romans 8:19-21 WEB For the creation waits with eager expectation for the children of God to be revealed. For the creation was subjected to vanity, not of its own will, but by reason of him who subjected it, in hope that the creation itself also will be delivered from the bondage of decay into the liberty of the glory of the children of God.

Colossians 1:15-18 WNT Christ is the visible representation of the invisible God, the Firstborn and Lord of all creation. For in Him was created the universe of things in heaven and on earth, things seen and things unseen, thrones, dominions, princedoms, powers—all were created, and exist through and for Him. And HE IS before all things and in and through Him the universe is a harmonious whole. Moreover He is the Head of His Body, the Church. He is the Beginning.

Psalm 19:14 WEB Let the words of my mouth and the meditation of my heart be acceptable in your sight, Yahweh, my rock and my redeemer.

Psalm 34:11-13 WEB Come, you children, listen to me. I will teach you the fear of Yahweh. Who is someone who desires life, and loves many days, that he may see good? Keep your tongue from evil, and your lips from speaking lies.

Proverbs 15:4 TMB A wholesome tongue is a tree of life, but perverseness therein is a breach in the spirit.

Proverbs 21:23 NCV Those who are careful about what they say keep themselves out of trouble.

Matthew 7:3-5 WEB Why do you see the speck that is in your brother's eye, but don't consider the beam that is in your own eye? Or how will you tell your brother, 'Let me remove the speck from your eye;' and behold, the beam is in your own eye? You hypocrite! First remove the beam out of your own eye, and then you can see clearly to remove the speck out of your brother's eye.

Ephesians 5:1-2 WNT Therefore be imitators of God, as His dear children. And live and act lovingly, as Christ also loved you and gave Himself up to death on our behalf as an offering and sacrifice to God, yielding a fragrant odor.

James 1:26 NLT If you claim to be religious but don't control your tongue, you are just fooling yourself, and your religion is worthless.

James 3:9-11 NCV We use our tongues to praise our Lord and Father, but then we curse people, whom God made like himself. Praises and curses come from the same mouth! My brothers and sisters, this should not happen. Do good and bad water flow from the same spring?

Isaiah 53:4-5 NKJV Surely He has borne our griefs and carried our sorrows; yet we esteemed Him stricken, smitten by God, and afflicted. But He was wounded for our transgressions, He was bruised for our iniquities; the chastisement for our peace was upon Him, and by His stripes we are healed.

Mark 14:35-36 WEB He went forward a little, and fell on the ground, and prayed that, if it were possible, the hour might pass away from him. He said, "Abba, Father, all things are possible to you. Please remove this cup from me. However, not what I desire, but what you desire."

Romans 6:5-6 NIV If we have been united with him like this in his death, we will certainly also be united with him in his resurrection. For we know that our old self was crucified with him so that the body of sin might be done away with, that we should no longer be slaves to sin.

1 Corinthians 1:17-18 NIV For Christ did not send me to baptize, but to preach the gospel—not with words of human wisdom, lest the cross of Christ be emptied of its power. For the message of the cross is foolishness to those who are perishing, but to us who are being saved it is the power of God.

1 Corinthians 1:22-25 WEB For Jews ask for signs, Greeks seek after wisdom, but we preach Christ crucified; a stumbling block to Jews, and foolishness to Greeks, but to those who are called, both Jews and Greeks, Christ is the power of God and the wisdom of God. Because the foolishness of God is wiser than men, and the weakness of God is stronger than men.

Galatians 2:20 WEB I have been crucified with Christ, and it is no longer I that live, but Christ living in me. That life which I now live in the flesh, I live by faith in the Son of God, who loved me, and gave himself up for me.

Galatians 6:14–15 NIV May I never boast except in the cross of our Lord Jesus Christ, through which the world has been crucified to me, and I to the world. Neither circumcision nor uncircumcision means anything; what counts is a new creation.

Ephesians 1:7–9 WNT It is in Him, and through the shedding of His blood, that we have our deliverance—the forgiveness of our offences—so abundant was God's grace, the grace which He, the possessor of all wisdom and understanding, lavished upon us, when He made known to us the secret of His will. And this is in harmony with God's merciful purpose.

Ephesians 2:14–18 NRSV For he is our peace; in his flesh he has made both groups into one and has broken down the dividing wall, that is, the hostility between us. He has abolished the law with its commandments and ordinances, that he might create in himself one new humanity in place of the two, thus making peace, and might reconcile both groups to God in one body through the cross, thus putting to death that hostility through it. So he came and proclaimed peace to you who were far off and peace to those who were near; for through him both of us have access in one Spirit to the Father.

2 Timothy 1:8–9 NLT So you must never be ashamed to tell others about our Lord. And don't be ashamed of me, either, even though I'm in prison for Christ. With the strength God gives you, be ready to suffer with me for the proclamation of the Good News. It is God who saved us and chose us to live a holy life. He did this not because we deserved it, but because that was his plan long before the world began—to show his love and kindness to us through Christ Jesus.

Hebrews 2:14–16 NKJV As the children have partaken of flesh and blood, He Himself likewise shared in the same, that through death He might destroy him who had the power of death, that is, the devil, and release those who through fear of death were all their lifetime subject to bondage. For indeed He does not give aid to angels, but He does give aid to the seed of Abraham.

Psalm 65:11 NCV You give the year a good harvest, and you load the wagons with many crops.

Isaiah 35:10 WEB The Yahweh's ransomed ones will return, and come with singing to Zion; and everlasting joy will be on their heads. They shall obtain gladness and joy, and sorrow and sighing will flee away.

1 Corinthians 9:24–27 WEB Don't you know that those who run in a race all run, but one receives the prize? Run like that, that you may win. Every man who strives in the games exercises self-control in all things. Now they do it to receive a corruptible crown, but we an incorruptible. I therefore run like that, as not uncertainly. I fight like that, as not beating the air, but I beat my body and bring it into submission, lest by any means, after I have preached to others, I myself should be rejected.

2 Timothy 4:7–8 NCV I have fought the good fight, I have finished the race, I have kept the faith. Now, a crown is being held for me—a crown for being right with God. The Lord, the judge who judges rightly, will give the crown to me on that day—not only to me but to all those who have waited with love for him to come again.

James 1:12 NLT God blesses the people who patiently endure testing. Afterward they will receive the crown of life that God has promised to those who love him.

Revelation 3:11 WEB I am coming quickly! Hold firmly that which you have, so that no one takes your crown.

Revelation 4:10–11 NKJV The twenty four elders fall down before Him who sits on the throne and worship Him who lives forever and ever, and cast their crowns before the throne, saying: "You are worthy, O Lord, to receive glory and honor and power; for You created all things, and by Your will they exist and were created."

Deuteronomy 5:29 NASB Oh that they had such a heart in them, that they would fear Me and keep all My commandments always, that it may be well with them and with their sons forever!

Deuteronomy 6:6–9 NRSV Keep these words that I am commanding you today in your heart. Recite them to your children and talk about them when you are at home and when you are away, when you lie down and when you rise. Bind them as a sign on your hand, fix them as an emblem on your forehead, and write them on the doorposts of your house and on your gates.

Psalm 127:3–5 NKJV Behold, children are a heritage from the LORD, the fruit of the womb is a reward. Like arrows in the hand of a warrior, so are the children of one's youth. Happy is the man who has his quiver full of them; they shall not be ashamed, but shall speak with their enemies in the gate.

Psalm 128:3–5 NIV Your sons will be like olive shoots around your table. Thus is the man blessed who fears the LORD. May the LORD bless you from Zion all the days of your life . . . may you live to see your children's children.

Proverbs 13:22 NLT Good people leave an inheritance to their grandchildren, but the sinner's wealth passes to the godly.

Proverbs 20:6–7 NKJV Most men will proclaim each his own goodness, but who can find a faithful man? The righteous man walks in his integrity; his children are blessed after him.

Proverbs 23:13–14 NIV Do not withhold discipline from a child; if you punish him with the rod, he will not die. Punish him with the rod and save his soul from death.

Proverbs 29:17 NASB Correct your son, and he will give you comfort; he will also delight your soul.

Isaiah 44:3-4 NIV For I will pour water on the thirsty land, and streams on the dry ground; I will pour out my Spirit on your offspring, and my blessing on your descendants. They will spring up like grass in a meadow, like poplar trees by flowing streams.

Isaiah 54:13 NCV All your children shall be taught by the LORD, and they will have much peace.

Acts 2:38-39 NCV Peter said to them, "Change your hearts and lives and be baptized, each one of you, in the name of Jesus Christ for the forgiveness of your sins. And you will receive the gift of the Holy Spirit. This promise is for you, for your children."

Acts 16:31 NASB They said, "Believe in the Lord Jesus, and you will be saved, you and your household."

Ephesians 6:4 NLT And now a word to you fathers. Don't make your children angry by the way you treat them. Rather, bring them up with the discipline and instruction approved by the Lord.

Colossians 3:21 NASB Fathers, do not exasperate your children, so that they will not lose heart.

1 Thessalonians 2:10-12 NKJV You are witnesses, and God also, how devoutly and justly and blamelessly we behaved ourselves among you who believe; as you know how we exhorted, and comforted, and charged every one of you, as a father does his own children, that you would walk worthy of God who calls you into His own kingdom and glory.

Psalm 18:28-30 NKJV For You will light my lamp; the LORD my God will enlighten my darkness. For by You I can run against a troop, by my God I can leap over a wall. As for God, His way is perfect; the word of the LORD is proven; He is a shield to all who trust in Him.

Ephesians 5:8-11 NCV In the past you were full of darkness, but now you are full of light in the LORD. So live like children who belong to the light. Light brings every kind of goodness, right living, and truth. Try to learn what pleases the LORD. Have nothing to do with the things done in darkness, which are not worth anything. But show that they are wrong.

Colossians 1:13-14 WEB Who delivered us out of the power of darkness, and translated us into the Kingdom of the Son of his love; in whom we have our redemption through his blood, the forgiveness of our sins.

Colossians 2:15 TMB And having despoiled principalities and powers, He made a show of them openly, triumphing over them in it.

2 Timothy 4:18 NIV The Lord will rescue me from every evil attack and will bring me safely to his heavenly kingdom. To him be glory for ever and ever. Amen.

1 John 1:5-7 WEB This is the message which we have heard from him and announce to you, that God is light, and in him is no darkness at all. If we say that we have fellowship with him and walk in the darkness, we lie, and don't tell the truth. But if we walk in the light, as he is in the light, we have fellowship with one another, and the blood of Jesus Christ, his Son, cleanses us from all sin.

1 John 2:9-11 NKJV He who says he is in the light, and hates his brother, is in darkness until now. He who loves his brother abides in the light, and there is no cause for stumbling in him. But he who hates his brother is in darkness and walks in darkness, and does not know where he is going, because the darkness has blinded his eyes.

Jeremiah 48:10 NKJV Cursed is he who does the work of the LORD deceitfully.

Matthew 7:14–17 NASB For the gate is small and the way is narrow that leads to life, and there are few who find it. Beware of the false prophets, who come to you in sheep's clothing, but inwardly are ravenous wolves. You will know them by their fruits. Grapes are not gathered from thorn bushes nor figs from thistles, are they? So every good tree bears good fruit, but the bad tree bears bad fruit.

Matthew 24:24–27 WNT For there will rise up false Christs and false prophets, displaying wonderful signs and prodigies, so as to deceive, were it possible, even God's own People. Remember, I have forewarned you. If therefore they should say to you, 'See, He is in the Desert!' do not go out there: or 'See, He is indoors in the room!' do not believe it. For just as the lightning flashes in the east and is seen to the very west, so will be the Coming of the Son of Man.

Colossians 2:6–8 NRSV As you therefore have received Christ Jesus the Lord, continue to live your lives in him, rooted and built up in him and established in the faith, just as you were taught, abounding in thanksgiving. See to it that no one takes you captive through philosophy and empty deceit, according to human tradition, according to the elemental spirits of the universe, and not according to Christ.

Hebrews 4:13 NASB And there is no creature hidden from His sight, but all things are open and laid bare to the eyes of Him with whom we have to do.

1 John 4:1–3 WEB Beloved, don't believe every spirit, but test the spirits, whether they are of God, because many false prophets have gone out into the world. By this you know the Spirit of God: every spirit who confesses that Jesus Christ has come in the flesh is of God, and every spirit who doesn't confess that Jesus Christ has come in the flesh is not of God, and this is the spirit of the Antichrist, of whom you have heard that it comes. Now it is in the world already.

DEPRESSION

Psalm 42:5-6 NLT Why am I discouraged? Why so sad? I will put my hope in God! I will praise him again—my Savior and my God! Now I am deeply discouraged, but I will remember your kindness.

Psalm 143:1-12 NRSV Hear my prayer, O LORD; give ear to my supplications in your faithfulness; answer me in your righteousness. Do not enter into judgment with your servant, for no one living is righteous before you. For the enemy has pursued me, crushing my life to the ground, making me sit in darkness like those long dead. Therefore my spirit faints within me; my heart within me is appalled. I remember the days of old, I think about all your deeds, I meditate on the works of your hands. I stretch out my hands to you; my soul thirsts for you like a parched land. Answer me quickly, O LORD; my spirit fails. Do not hide your face from me, or I shall be like those who go down to the Pit. Let me hear of your steadfast love in the morning, for in you I put my trust. Teach me the way I should go, for to you I lift up my soul. Save me, O LORD, from my enemies; I have fled to you for refuge. Teach me to do your will, for you are my God. Let your good spirit lead me on a level path. For your name's sake, O LORD, preserve my life. In your righteousness bring me out of trouble. In your steadfast love cut off my enemies, and destroy all my adversaries, for I am your servant.

Isaiah 41:10 NIV So do not fear, for I am with you; do not be dismayed, for I am your God. I will strengthen you and help you; I will uphold you with my righteous right hand.

Lamentations 3:21-26 NRSV But this I call to mind, and therefore I have hope: The steadfast love of the LORD never ceases, his mercies never come to an end; they are new every morning; great is your faithfulness. "The LORD is my portion," says my soul, "therefore I will hope in him." The LORD is good to those who wait for him, to the soul that seeks him. It is good that one should wait quietly for the salvation of the LORD.

Psalm 10:17 NKJV LORD, You have heard the desire of the humble; You will prepare their heart; You will cause Your ear to hear.

Psalm 20:4 NIV May he give you the desire of your heart and make all your plans succeed.

Psalm 21:1–4 NRSV In your strength the king rejoices, O LORD, and in your help how greatly he exults! You have given him his heart's desire, and have not withheld the request of his lips. For you meet him with rich blessings; you set a crown of fine gold on his head. He asked you for life; you gave it to him—length of days forever and ever.

Psalm 51:6 NLT But you desire honesty from the heart, so you can teach me to be wise in my inmost being.

Psalm 73:25-26 NIV Whom have I in heaven but you? And earth has nothing I desire besides you. My flesh and my heart may fail, but God is the strength of my heart and my portion forever.

Psalm 145:18-19 NLT The LORD is close to all who call on him, yes, to all who call on him sincerely. He fulfills the desires of those who fear him; he hears their cries for help and rescues them.

Song of Solomon 7:10 TMB I am my beloved's, and his desire is toward me.

Matthew 5:6 NASB Blessed are those who hunger and thirst for righteousness, for they shall be satisfied.

1 Corinthians 14:1 NLT Let love be your highest goal, but also desire the special abilities the Spirit gives, especially the gift of prophecy.

Psalm 119:105 TMB Thy word is a lamp unto my feet, and a light unto my path.

John 14:16-17 NIV And I will ask the Father, and he will give you another Counselor to be with you forever—the Spirit of truth. The world cannot accept him, because it neither sees him nor knows him. But you know him, for he lives with you and will be in you.

1 Corinthians 2:14-16 WEB Now the natural man doesn't receive the things of God's Spirit, for they are foolishness to him, and he can't know them, because they are spiritually discerned. But he who is spiritual discerns all things, and he himself is judged by no one. "For who has known the mind of the Lord, that he should instruct him?" But we have Christ's mind.

Philippians 1:9-11 NCV This is my prayer for you: that your love will grow more and more; that you will have knowledge and understanding with your love; that you will see the difference between good and bad and will choose the good; that you will be pure and without wrong for the coming of Christ; that you will do many good things with the help of Christ to bring glory and praise to God.

Colossians 1:9-11 NKJV For this reason we also, since the day we heard it, do not cease to pray for you, and to ask that you may be filled with the knowledge of His will in all wisdom and spiritual understanding; that you may walk worthy of the Lord, fully pleasing Him, being fruitful in every good work and increasing in the knowledge of God; strengthened with all might, according to His glorious power, for all patience and longsuffering with joy.

Hebrews 4:12 NIV For the word of God is living and active. Sharper than any double-edged sword, it penetrates even to dividing soul and spirit, joints and marrow; it judges the thoughts and attitudes of the heart.

Psalm 119:33-38 NRSV Teach me, O LORD, the way of your statutes, and I will observe it to the end. Give me understanding, that I may keep your law and observe it with my whole heart. Lead me in the path of your commandments, for I delight in it. Turn my heart to your decrees, and not to selfish gain. Turn my eyes from looking at vanities; give me life in your ways. Confirm to your servant your promise, which is for those who fear you.

Psalm 119:49-50 NIV Remember your word to your servant, for you have given me hope. My comfort in my suffering is this: Your promise preserves my life.

Matthew 19:20-21 WEB The young man said to him, "All these things I have observed from my youth. What do I still lack?" Jesus said to him, "If you want to be perfect, go, sell what you have, and give to the poor, and you will have treasure in heaven; and come, follow me."

1 Corinthians 3:9-11 NKJV For we are God's fellow workers; you are God's field, you are God's building. According to the grace of God which was given to me, as a wise master builder I have laid the foundation, and another builds on it. But let each one take heed how he builds on it. For no other foundation can anyone lay than that which is laid, which is Jesus Christ.

Galatians 5:24-26 WEB Those who belong to Christ have crucified the flesh with its passions and lusts. If we live by the Spirit, let's also walk by the Spirit. Let's not become conceited, provoking one another, and envying one another.

Ephesians 4:1-3 WEB I therefore, the prisoner in the Lord, beg you to walk worthily of the calling with which you were called, with all lowliness and humility, with patience, bearing with one another in love; being eager to keep the unity of the Spirit in the bond of peace.

Ephesians 4:29-32 WEB Let no corrupt speech proceed out of your mouth, but such as is good for building up as the need may be, that it may give grace to those who hear. Don't grieve the Holy Spirit of God, in whom you were sealed for the day of redemption. Let all bitterness, wrath, anger, outcry, and slander, be put away from you, with all malice. And be kind to one another, tenderhearted, forgiving each other, just as God also in Christ forgave you.

Philippians 1:9-11 WEB This I pray, that your love may abound yet more and more in knowledge and all discernment; so that you may approve the things that are excellent; that you may be sincere and without offense to the day of Christ; being filled with the fruits of righteousness.

Colossians 1:9-12 NKJV We . . . pray for you . . . to ask that you may be filled with the knowledge of His will in all wisdom and spiritual understanding; that you may walk worthy of the Lord, fully pleasing Him, being fruitful in every good work and increasing in the knowledge of God; strengthened with all might, according to His glorious power, for all patience and longsuffering with joy; giving thanks to the Father who has qualified us to be partakers of the inheritance of the saints in the light.

James 2:15-17 WNT Suppose a Christian brother or sister is poorly clad or lacks daily food, and one of you says to them, "I wish you well; keep yourselves warm and well fed," and yet you do not give them what they need; what is the use of that? So also faith, if it is unaccompanied by obedience, has no life in it—so long as it stands alone.

1 John 2:4-6 WEB One who says, "I know him," and doesn't keep his commandments, is a liar, and the truth isn't in him. But whoever keeps his word, God's love has most certainly been perfected in him. This is how we know that we are in him: he who says he remains in him ought himself also to walk just like he walked.

Psalm 31:24 NKJV Be of good courage, and He shall strengthen your heart, all you who hope in the LORD.

Psalm 51:7-11 NRSV Purge me with hyssop, and I shall be clean; wash me, and I shall be whiter than snow. Let me hear joy and gladness; let the bones that you have crushed rejoice. Hide your face from my sins, and blot out all my iniquities. Create in me a clean heart, O God, and put a new and right spirit within me. Do not cast me away from your presence, and do not take your holy spirit from me.

Psalm 61:1-4 WEB Hear my cry, God. Listen to my prayer. From the end of the earth, I will call to you, when my heart is overwhelmed. Lead me to the rock that is higher than I. For you have been a refuge for me, a strong tower from the enemy. I will dwell in your tent forever. I will take refuge in the shelter of your wings.

Psalm 86:5 NLT O Lord, you are so good, so ready to forgive, so full of unfailing love for all who ask your aid.

Malachi 2:14-16 NKJV The LORD has been witness between you and the wife of your youth, with whom you have dealt treacherously; yet she is your companion and your wife by covenant. But did He not make them one, having a remnant of the Spirit? And why one? He seeks godly offspring. Therefore take heed to your spirit, and let none deal treacherously with the wife of his youth. "For the LORD God of Israel says that He hates divorce, for it covers one's garment with violence," says the LORD of hosts. "Therefore take heed to your spirit, that you do not deal treacherously."

Matthew 5:31-32 NIV It has been said, "Anyone who divorces his wife must give her a certificate of divorce." But I tell you that anyone who divorces his wife, except for marital unfaithfulness, causes her to become an adulteress, and anyone who marries the divorced woman commits adultery.

Mark 10:4-9 WEB They said, "Moses allowed a certificate of divorce to be written, and to divorce her." But Jesus said to them, "For your hardness of heart, he wrote you this commandment. But from the beginning of the creation, God made them male and female. For this cause a man will leave his father and mother, and will join to his wife, and the two will become one flesh, so that they are no longer two, but one flesh. What therefore God has joined together, let no man separate."

Mark 11:25-26 WEB Whenever you stand praying, forgive, if you have anything against anyone; so that your Father, who is in heaven, may also forgive your transgressions. But if you do not forgive, neither will your Father in heaven forgive your transgressions.

Romans 12:10-14 WEB In love of the brothers be tenderly affectionate one to another; in honor preferring one another; not lagging in diligence; fervent in spirit; serving the Lord; rejoicing in hope; enduring in troubles; continuing steadfastly in prayer; contributing to the needs of the saints; given to hospitality. Bless those who persecute you; bless, and don't curse.

1 Corinthians 7:10-15 NRSV To the married I give this command—not I but the Lord—that the wife should not separate from her husband (but if she does separate, let her remain unmarried or else be reconciled to her husband), and that the husband should not divorce his wife. To the rest I say—I and not the Lord—that if any believer has a wife who is an unbeliever, and she consents to live with him, he should not divorce her. And if any woman has a husband who is an unbeliever, and he consents to live with her, she should not divorce him. For the unbelieving husband is made holy through his wife, and the unbelieving wife is made holy through her husband. Otherwise, your children would be unclean, but as it is, they are holy. But if the unbelieving partner separates, let it be so; in such a case the brother or sister is not bound. It is to peace that God has called you.

Psalm 73:24-26 NKJV You will guide me with Your counsel, and afterward receive me to glory. Whom have I in heaven but You? And there is none upon earth that I desire besides You. My flesh and my heart fail; but God is the strength of my heart and my portion forever.

Matthew 21:21-22 NIV Jesus replied, "I tell you the truth, if you have faith and do not doubt, not only can you do what was done to the fig tree, but also you can say to this mountain, 'Go, throw yourself into the sea,' and it will be done. If you believe, you will receive whatever you ask for in prayer."

Luke 8:14-15 NIV The seed that fell among thorns stands for those who hear, but as they go on their way they are choked by life's worries, riches and pleasures, and they do not mature. But the seed on good soil stands for those with a noble and good heart, who hear the word, retain it, and by persevering produce a crop.

John 14:1-3 NCV Jesus said, "Don't let your hearts be troubled. Trust in God, and trust in me. There are many rooms in my Father's house; I would not tell you this if it were not true. I am going there to prepare a place for you. After I go and prepare a place for you, I will come back and take you to be with me so that you may be where I am."

Romans 10:8-11 WNT But what does it say? "The Message is close to you, in your mouth and in your heart;" that is, the Message which we are publishing about the faith—that if with your mouth you confess Jesus as Lord and in your heart believe that God brought Him back to life, you shall be saved. For with the heart men believe and obtain righteousness, and with the mouth they make confession and obtain salvation. The Scripture says, "No one who believes in Him shall have reason to feel ashamed."

1 Peter 5:6-7 NCV Be humble under God's powerful hand so he will lift you up when the right time comes. Give all your worries to him, because he cares about you.

Psalm 71:8-9, 12, 14-15 NRSV My mouth is filled with your praise, and with your glory all day long. Do not cast me off in the time of old age; do not forsake me when my strength is spent. . . . O God, do not be far from me; O my God, make haste to help me! . . . But I will hope continually, and will praise you yet more and more. My mouth will tell of your righteous acts, of your deeds of salvation all day long, though their number is past my knowledge.

Psalm 71:17-18 WEB God, you have taught me from my youth. Until now, I have declared your wondrous works. Yes, even when I am old and gray-haired, God, don't forsake me, until I have declared your strength to the next generation, your might to everyone who is to come.

Psalm 92:12-15 NKJV The righteous shall flourish like a palm tree, he shall grow like a cedar in Lebanon. Those who are planted in the house of the LORD shall flourish in the courts of God. They shall still bear fruit in old age; they shall be fresh and flourishing, to declare that the LORD is upright; He is my rock, and there is no unrighteousness in Him.

Proverbs 13:22 WEB A good man leaves an inheritance to his children's children, but the wealth of the sinner is stored for the righteous.

Proverbs 17:6 NIV Children's children are a crown to the aged, and parents are the pride of their children.

Isaiah 46:4 NIV Even to your old age and gray hairs I am he, I am he who will sustain you. I have made you and I will carry you; I will sustain you and I will rescue you.

Luke 2:37-38 NLT She was now eighty-four years old. She never left the Temple but stayed there day and night, worshiping God with fasting and prayer. . . . and she began praising God. She talked about Jesus to everyone who had been waiting for the promised King to come and deliver Jerusalem.

Psalm 37:23-25 NRSV Our steps are made firm by the Lord, when he delights in our way; though we stumble, we shall not fall headlong, for the Lord holds us by the hand. I have been young, and now am old, yet I have not seen the righteous forsaken or their children begging bread.

Isaiah 33:2 WEB Yahweh, be gracious to us. We have waited for you. Be our strength every morning, our salvation also in the time of trouble.

Isaiah 35:2-4 NKJV They shall see the glory of the Lord, the excellency of our God. Strengthen the weak hands, and make firm the feeble knees. Say to those who are fearful-hearted, "Be strong, do not fear!"

Isaiah 40:28-29 NKJV Have you not known? Have you not heard? The everlasting God, the Lord, the Creator of the ends of the earth, neither faints nor is weary. His understanding is unsearchable. He gives power to the weak, and to those who have no might He increases strength.

Ephesians 1:3 NKJV Blessed be the God and Father of our Lord Jesus Christ, who has blessed us with every spiritual blessing in the heavenly places in Christ.

Philippians 4:19-20 NKJV And my God shall supply all your need according to His riches in glory by Christ Jesus. Now to our God and Father be glory forever. Amen.

2 Thessalonians 2:16-17 NASB Now may our Lord Jesus Christ Himself and God our Father, who has loved us and given us eternal comfort and good hope by grace, comfort and strengthen your hearts in every good work and word.

2 Timothy 4:8 NCV Now, a crown is being held for me—a crown for being right with God. The Lord, the judge who judges rightly, will give the crown to me on that day.

Isaiah 35:3-4 NCV Make the weak hands strong and the weak knees steady. Say to people who are frightened, "Be strong. Don't be afraid. Look, your God will come, and he will punish your enemies. He will make them pay for the wrongs they did, but he will save you."

Matthew 10:22 NIV All men will hate you because of me, but he who stands firm to the end will be saved.

Galatians 6:9-10 NASB Let us not lose heart in doing good, for in due time we will reap if we do not grow weary. So then, while we have opportunity, let us do good to all people, and especially to those who are of the household of the faith.

Ephesians 6:10-11 NCV Finally, be strong in the Lord and in his great power. Put on the full armor of God so that you can fight against the devil's evil tricks.

2 Thessalonians 3:3-5 NKJV But the Lord is faithful, who will establish you and guard you from the evil one. And we have confidence in the Lord concerning you, both that you do and will do the things we command you. Now may the Lord direct your hearts into the love of God and into the patience of Christ.

2 Timothy 2:1-7 WEB You therefore, my child, be strengthened in the grace that is in Christ Jesus. The things which you have heard from me among many witnesses, commit the same to faithful men, who will be able to teach others also. You therefore must endure hardship, as a good soldier of Christ Jesus. No soldier on duty entangles himself in the affairs of life, that he may please him who enrolled him as a soldier. Also, if anyone competes in athletics, he isn't crowned unless he has competed by the rules. The farmers who labor must be the first to get a share of the crops. Consider what I say, and may the Lord give you understanding in all things.

2 Timothy 2:10-12 NIV Therefore I endure everything for the sake of the elect, that they too may obtain the salvation that is in Christ Jesus, with eternal glory. Here is a trustworthy saying: If we died with him, we will also live with him; if we endure, we will also reign with him.

2 Timothy 4:1-5 WEB I command you therefore before God and the Lord Jesus Christ, who will judge the living and the dead at his appearing and his Kingdom: preach the word; be urgent in season and out of season; reprove, rebuke, and exhort, with all patience and teaching. For the time will come when they will not listen to the sound doctrine, but, having itching ears, will heap up for themselves teachers after their own lusts; and will turn away their ears from the truth, and turn aside to fables. But you be sober in all things, suffer hardship, do the work of an evangelist, and fulfill your ministry.

Hebrews 6:10-12 WEB For God is not unrighteous, so as to forget your work and the labor of love which you showed toward his name, in that you served the saints, and still do serve them. We desire that each one of you may show the same diligence to the fullness of hope even to the end, that you won't be sluggish, but imitators of those who through faith and patience inherited the promises.

Hebrews 10:36 NLT Patient endurance is what you need now, so you will continue to do God's will. Then you will receive all that he has promised.

2 Peter 1:5-9 WEB Yes, and for this very cause adding on your part all diligence, in your faith supply moral excellence; and in moral excellence, knowledge; and in knowledge, self-control; and in self-control patience; and in patience godliness; and in godliness brotherly affection; and in brotherly affection, love. For if these things are yours and abound, they make you to be not idle nor unfruitful to the knowledge of our Lord Jesus Christ. For he who lacks these things is blind, seeing only what is near, having forgotten the cleansing from his old sins.

Deuteronomy 28:7 NLT The Lord will conquer your enemies when they attack you. They will attack you from one direction, but they will scatter from you in seven!

Psalm 60:12 TMB Through God we shall do valiantly, for He it is that shall tread down our enemies.

Acts 18:9–10 WEB The Lord said to Paul in the night by a vision, "Don't be afraid, but speak and don't be silent; for I am with you, and no one will attack you to harm you, for I have many people in this city."

1 Corinthians 15:24–26 WEB Then the end comes, when he will deliver up the Kingdom to God, even the Father; when he will have abolished all rule and all authority and power. For he must reign until he has put all his enemies under his feet. The last enemy that will be abolished is death.

Ephesians 6:10–12 NKJV Finally, my brethren, be strong in the Lord and in the power of His might. Put on the whole armor of God, that you may be able to stand against the wiles of the devil. For we do not wrestle against flesh and blood, but against principalities, against powers, against the rulers of the darkness of this age, against spiritual hosts of wickedness in the heavenly places.

Ephesians 6:14–16 WNT Stand therefore, first fastening round you the girdle of truth and putting on the breastplate of uprightness as well as the shoes of the Good News of peace—a firm foundation for your feet. And besides all these take the great shield of faith, on which you will be able to quench all the flaming darts of the Wicked one.

2 Thessalonians 3:1–3 WEB Finally, brothers, pray for us, that the word of the Lord may spread rapidly and be glorified, even as also with you; and that we may be delivered from unreasonable and evil men; for not all have faith. But the Lord is faithful, who will establish you, and guard you from the evil one.

Daniel 12:2-3 NIV Multitudes who sleep in the dust of the earth will awake: some to everlasting life, others to shame and everlasting contempt. Those who are wise will shine like the brightness of the heavens, and . . . lead many to righteousness.

John 6:47-48 NKJV Most assuredly, I say to you, he who believes in Me has everlasting life. I am the bread of life.

John 10:27-28 NIV My sheep listen to my voice; I know them, and they follow me. I give them eternal life, and they shall never perish; no one can snatch them out of my hand.

2 Corinthians 5:1-5 WEB For we know that if the earthly house of our tent is dissolved, we have a building from God, a house not made with hands, eternal, in the heavens. For most certainly in this we groan, longing to be clothed with our habitation which is from heaven; if so be that being clothed we will not be found naked. For indeed we who are in this tent do groan, being burdened; not that we desire to be unclothed, but that we desire to be clothed, that what is mortal may be swallowed up by life. Now he who made us for this very thing is God, who also gave to us the down payment of the Spirit.

Galatians 6:7-9 NKJV Do not be deceived, God is not mocked; for whatever a man sows, that he will also reap. For he who sows to his flesh will of the flesh reap corruption, but he who sows to the Spirit will of the Spirit reap everlasting life. And let us not grow weary while doing good, for in due season we shall reap if we do not lose heart.

1 John 5:13 NKJV These things I have written to you who believe in the name of the Son of God, that you may know that you have eternal life, and that you may continue to believe in the name of the Son of God.

Psalm 5:12 NLT For you bless the godly, O Lord, surrounding them with your shield of love.

Matthew 9:36–38 WEB But when he saw the multitudes, he was moved with compassion for them, because they were weary and scattered, like sheep without a shepherd. Then he said to his disciples, "The harvest indeed is plentiful, but the laborers are few. Pray therefore that the Lord of the harvest will send out laborers into his harvest."

Acts 8:5–7 NASB Philip went down to the city of Samaria and began proclaiming Christ to them. The crowds with one accord were giving attention to what was said by Philip, as they heard and saw the signs which he was performing. For in the case of many who had unclean spirits, they were coming out of them shouting with a loud voice; and many who had been paralyzed and lame were healed.

Colossians 2:6–7 WEB As therefore you received Christ Jesus, the Lord, walk in him, rooted and built up in him, and established in the faith, even as you were taught, abounding in it in thanksgiving.

1 Thessalonians 5:24 WEB He who calls you is faithful, who will also do it.

2 Timothy 4:1–5 WEB I charge you therefore before God and the Lord Jesus Christ, who will judge the living and the dead at his appearing and his Kingdom: preach the word; be urgent in season and out of season; reprove, rebuke, and exhort, with all patience and teaching. For the time will come when they will not listen to the sound doctrine, but, having itching ears, will heap up for themselves teachers after their own lusts; and will turn away their ears from the truth, and turn aside to fables. But you be sober in all things, suffer hardship, do the work of an evangelist, and fulfill your ministry.

Mark 11:22-24 NKJV So Jesus answered and said to them, "Have faith in God. For assuredly, I say to you, whoever says to this mountain, 'Be removed and be cast into the sea,' and does not doubt in his heart, but believes that those things he says will be done, he will have whatever he says. Therefore I say to you, whatever things you ask when you pray, believe that you receive them."

Luke 17:5-6 NLT One day the apostles said to the Lord, "We need more faith; tell us how to get it." "Even if you had faith as small as a mustard seed," the Lord answered, "you could say to this mulberry tree, 'May God uproot you and throw you into the sea,' and it would obey you!"

Romans 10:17 NCV So faith comes from hearing the Good News, and people hear the Good News when someone tells them about Christ.

1 Corinthians 16:13 NIV Be on your guard; stand firm in the faith; be men of courage; be strong.

2 Corinthians 5:7 TMB For we walk by faith, not by sight.

Galatians 3:26 NKJV For you are all sons of God through faith in Christ Jesus.

Ephesians 2:8-10 NKJV For by grace you have been saved through faith, and that not of yourselves; it is the gift of God, not of works, that no one would boast. For we are His workmanship, created in Christ Jesus for good works, which God prepared beforehand that we would walk in them.

Ephesians 6:16 NIV In addition to all this, take up the shield of faith, with which you can extinguish all the flaming arrows of the evil one.

Hebrews 11:1 NIV Now faith is being sure of what we hope for and certain of what we do not see.

Hebrews 11:6-9 NKJV But without faith it is impossible to please Him, for he who comes to God must believe that He is, and that He is a rewarder of those who diligently seek Him. By faith Noah, being divinely warned of things not yet seen, moved with godly fear, prepared an ark for the saving of his household, by which he condemned the world and became heir of the righteousness which is according to faith. By faith Abraham obeyed when he was called to go out . . . not knowing where he was going. By faith he dwelt in the land of promise as in a foreign country.

Hebrews 11:13 NKJV These all died in faith, not having received the promises, but having seen them afar off were assured of them, embraced them and confessed that they were strangers and pilgrims on the earth.

Hebrew 11:32-35 NKJV For the time would fail me if I tell of Gideon and Barak and Samson and Jephthah, also of David and Samuel, and the prophets, who through faith subdued kingdoms, worked righteousness, obtained promises, stopped the mouths of lions, quenched the violence of fire, escaped the edge of the sword, out of weakness were made strong, became valiant in battle, turned to flight the armies of the aliens. Women received their dead raised to life again. Others were tortured, not accepting deliverance, that they might obtain a better resurrection.

Hebrews 12:1-2 WEB Therefore let us also, seeing we are surrounded by so great a cloud of witnesses, lay aside every weight and the sin which so easily entangles us, and let us run with patience the race that is set before us, looking to Jesus, the author and perfecter of faith.

1 John 5:4 NASB For whatever is born of God overcomes the world; and this is the victory that has overcome the world—our faith.

Genesis 12:1-3 NKJV Now the Lord had said to Abram: "Get out of your country, from your family and from your father's house, to a land that I will show you. I will make you a great nation; I will bless you and make your name great; and you shall be a blessing. I will bless those who bless you, and I will curse him who curses you; and in you all the families of the earth shall be blessed."

Joshua 6:27 NASB So the Lord was with Joshua, and his fame was in all the land.

1 Kings 4:29-34 NRSV God gave Solomon very great wisdom, discernment, and breadth of understanding as vast as the sand on the seashore, so that Solomon's wisdom surpassed the wisdom of all the people of the east, and all the wisdom of Egypt. He was wiser than anyone else . . . his fame spread throughout all the surrounding nations. He composed three thousand proverbs, and his songs numbered a thousand and five. . . . People came from all the nations to hear the wisdom of Solomon; they came from all the kings of the earth who had heard of his wisdom.

Matthew 23:11-12 NIV The greatest among you will be your servant. For whoever exalts himself will be humbled, and whoever humbles himself will be exalted.

Luke 14:10-11 NIV But when you are invited, take the lowest place, so that when your host comes, he will say to you, "Friend, move up to a better place." Then you will be honored in the presence of all your fellow guests. For everyone who exalts himself will be humbled, and he who humbles himself will be exalted.

Acts 10:25-26 NASB When Peter entered, Cornelius met him, and fell at his feet and worshiped him. But Peter raised him up, saying, "Stand up; I too am just a man."

Joshua 24:14-15 NKJV Now therefore, fear the LORD, serve Him in sincerity and in truth, and put away the gods which your fathers served on the other side of the River and in Egypt. Serve the LORD! And if it seems evil to you to serve the LORD, choose for yourselves this day whom you will serve, whether the gods which your fathers served that were on the other side of the River, or the gods of the Amorites, in whose land you dwell. But as for me and my house, we will serve the LORD.

Psalm 115:13-16 NLT He will bless those who fear the LORD, both great and small. May the LORD richly bless both you and your children. May you be blessed by the LORD, who made heaven and earth . . . he has given the earth to all humanity.

Proverbs 24:3-4 WEB Through wisdom a house is built; by understanding it is established; by knowledge the rooms are filled with all rare and beautiful treasure.

Proverbs 31:27-31 NRSV She looks well to the ways of her household, and does not eat the bread of idleness. Her children rise up and call her happy; her husband too, and he praises her: "Many women have done excellently, but you surpass them all." Charm is deceitful, and beauty is vain, but a woman who fears the LORD is to be praised. Give her a share in the fruit of her hands, and let her works praise her in the city gates.

Matthew 10:36-39 WEB A man's foes will be those of his own household. He who loves father or mother more than me isn't worthy of me; and he who loves son or daughter more than me is not worthy of me. He who doesn't take his cross and follow after me, isn't worthy of me. He who seeks his life will lose it; and he who loses his life for my sake will find it.

Luke 6:37-38 NKJV Judge not, and you shall not be judged. Condemn not, and you shall not be condemned. Forgive, and you will be forgiven. Give, and it will be given to you: good measure, pressed down, shaken together, and running over will be put into your bosom. For with the same measure that you use, it will be measured back to you.

Acts 16:31-33 WEB They said, "Believe in the Lord Jesus Christ, and you will be saved, you and your household." They spoke the word of the Lord to him, and to all who were in his house. He took them the same hour of the night, and washed their stripes, and was immediately baptized, he and all his household.

1 Corinthians 1:10 NLT Now, dear brothers and sisters, I appeal to you by the authority of the Lord Jesus Christ to stop arguing among yourselves. Let there be real harmony so there won't be divisions in the church. I plead with you, be of one mind, united in thought and purpose.

2 Corinthians 5:14-15 NKJV For the love of Christ compels us . . . those who live should live no longer for themselves, but for Him.

Ephesians 4:31-32 WEB Let all bitterness, wrath, anger, outcry, and slander, be put away from you, with all malice. And be kind to one another, tenderhearted, forgiving each other, just as God also in Christ forgave you.

1 Timothy 3:4-5 NCV He must be a good family leader, having children who cooperate with full respect. (If someone does not know how to lead the family, how can that person take care of God's church?)

1 Timothy 5:8 NLT But those who won't care for their own relatives, especially those living in the same household, have denied what we believe. Such people are worse than unbelievers.

1 Peter 3:8-9 WEB Finally, be all like-minded, compassionate, loving as brothers, tenderhearted, courteous, not rendering evil for evil, or insult for insult; but instead blessing; knowing that to this were you called, that you may inherit a blessing.

Ezra 8:22–23 NLT We had told the king, "Our God protects all those who worship him, but his fierce anger rages against those who abandon him." So we fasted and earnestly prayed that our God would take care of us, and he heard our prayer.

Isaiah 58:6–7 NRSV Is not this the fast that I choose: to loose the bonds of injustice, to undo the thongs of the yoke, to let the oppressed go free, and to break every yoke? Is it not to share your bread with the hungry, and bring the homeless poor into your house; when you see the naked, to cover them, and not to hide yourself from your own kin?

Joel 1:13–14 NIV Put on sackcloth, O priests, and mourn; wail, you who minister before the altar. Come, spend the night in sackcloth, you who minister before my God; for the grain offerings and drink offerings are withheld from the house of your God. Declare a holy fast; call a sacred assembly. Summon the elders and all who live in the land to the house of the LORD your God, and cry out to the LORD.

Zechariah 7:5 NIV Ask all the people of the land and the priests, "When you fasted and mourned in the fifth and seventh months for the past seventy years, was it really for me that you fasted?"

Matthew 6:17–18 WEB But you, when you fast, anoint your head, and wash your face; so that you are not seen by men to be fasting, but by your Father who is in secret, and your Father, who sees in secret, will reward you.

Matthew 17:19–21 WEB Then the disciples came to Jesus privately, and said, "Why were we not able to cast it out?" He said to them, "Because of your unbelief. For most certainly I tell you, if you have faith as a grain of mustard seed, you will tell this mountain, 'Move from here to there,' and it will move; and nothing will be impossible to you. But this kind doesn't go out except by prayer and fasting."

Deuteronomy 32:10-12 NKJV He found him in a desert land and in the wasteland, a howling wilderness; He encircled him, He instructed him, He kept him as the apple of His eye. As an eagle stirs up its nest, hovers over its young, spreading out its wings, taking them up, carrying them on its wings so the LORD alone led him, and there was no foreign god with him.

1 Samuel 2:7-8 NIV The LORD sends poverty and wealth; he humbles and he exalts. He raises the poor from the dust and lifts the needy from the ash heap; he seats them with princes and has them inherit a throne of honor.

Psalm 17:6-8 NLT I am praying to you because I know you will answer, O God. Bend down and listen as I pray. Show me your unfailing love in wonderful ways. You save with your strength those who seek refuge from their enemies. Guard me as the apple of your eye. Hide me in the shadow of your wings.

Psalm 23:5-6 NIV You prepare a table before me in the presence of my enemies. You anoint my head with oil; my cup overflows. Surely goodness and love will follow me all the days of my life, and I will dwell in the house of the LORD forever.

Psalm 106:4-5 NLT Remember me, too, LORD, when you show favor to your people; come to me with your salvation. Let me share in the prosperity of your chosen ones. Let me rejoice in the joy of your people; let me praise you with those who are your heritage.

Proverbs 8:32-36 NRSV And now, my children, listen to me: happy are those who keep my ways. Hear instruction and be wise, and do not neglect it. Happy is the one who listens to me, watching daily at my gates, waiting beside my doors. For whoever finds me finds life and obtains favor from the LORD ; but those who miss me injure themselves; all who hate me love death.

2 Kings 17:33-39 NKJV They feared the Lord, yet served their own gods—according to the rituals of the nations from among whom they were carried away. To this day they continue practicing the former rituals; they do not fear the Lord, nor do they follow their statutes or their ordinances, or the law and commandment which the Lord had commanded the children of Jacob . . . "You shall not fear other gods, nor bow down to them nor serve them nor sacrifice to them; but the Lord who brought you up from the land of Egypt with great power and an outstretched arm, Him you shall fear, Him you shall worship, and to Him you shall offer sacrifice. And the statutes, the ordinances, the law, and the commandment which He wrote for you, you shall be careful to observe forever; you shall not fear other gods . . . But the Lord your God you shall fear; and He will deliver you from the hand of all your enemies."

Psalm 25:14 NASB The secret of the Lord is for those who fear Him, and He will make them know His covenant.

Psalm 86:11 WEB Teach me your way, Yahweh. I will walk in your truth. Make my heart undivided to fear your name.

Proverbs 1:28-33 NRSV Then they will call upon me, but I will not answer; they will seek me diligently, but will not find me. Because they hated knowledge and did not choose the fear of the Lord, would have none of my counsel, and despised all my reproof, therefore they shall eat the fruit of their way and be sated with their own devices. For waywardness kills the simple, and the complacency of fools destroys them; but those who listen to me will be secure and will live at ease, without dread of disaster.

Proverbs 14:26-27 NASB In the fear of the Lord there is strong confidence, and his children will have refuge. The fear of the Lord is a fountain of life, that one may avoid the snares of death.

Acts 2:42–47 NASB They were continually devoting themselves to the apostles' teaching and to fellowship, to the breaking of bread and to prayer. Everyone kept feeling a sense of awe; and many wonders and signs were taking place through the apostles. And all those who had believed were together and had all things in common; and they began selling their property and possessions and were sharing them with all, as anyone might have need. Day by day continuing with one mind in the temple, and breaking bread from house to house, they were taking their meals together with gladness and sincerity of heart, praising God and having favor with all the people. And the Lord was adding to their number day by day those who were being saved.

Romans 12:10–16 WEB In love of the brothers be tenderly affectionate one to another; in honor preferring one another; not lagging in diligence; fervent in spirit; serving the Lord; rejoicing in hope; enduring in troubles; continuing steadfastly in prayer; contributing to the needs of the saints; given to hospitality.... Rejoice with those who rejoice. Weep with those who weep. Be of the same mind one toward another.

2 Corinthians 6:14 NASB Do not be bound together with unbelievers; for what partnership have righteousness and lawlessness, or what fellowship has light with darkness?

Galatians 6:10 NLT Whenever we have the opportunity, we should do good to everyone, especially to our Christian brothers and sisters.

Philippians 2:1–4 WEB If there is therefore any exhortation in Christ, if any consolation of love, if any fellowship of the Spirit, if any tender mercies and compassion, make my joy full, by being like-minded, having the same love, being of one accord, of one mind; doing nothing through rivalry or through conceit, but in humility, each counting others better than himself; each of you not just looking to his own things, but each of you also to the things of others.

Psalm 23:1 TMB The LORD is my shepherd; I shall not want.

Proverbs 3:9-10 NCV Honor the LORD with your wealth and the firstfruits from all your crops. Then your barns will be full, and your wine barrels will overflow with new wine.

Proverbs 22:7 NCV The rich rule over the poor, and borrowers are servants to lenders.

Mark 9:23 WEB Jesus said to him, "If you can believe, all things are possible to him who believes."

John 10:10 NIV The thief comes only to steal and kill and destroy; I have come that they may have life, and have it to the full.

2 Corinthians 9:8-11 WEB And God is able to make all grace abound to you, that you, always having all sufficiency in everything, may abound to every good work. As it is written, "He has scattered abroad, he has given to the poor. His righteousness remains forever." Now may he who supplies seed to the sower and bread for food, supply and multiply your seed for sowing, and increase the fruits of your righteousness; you being enriched in everything to all liberality, which works through us thanksgiving to God.

Philippians 4:19 NIV And my God will meet all your needs according to his glorious riches in Christ Jesus.

1 Timothy 6:10 WEB For the love of money is a root of all kinds of evil. Some have been led astray from the faith in their greed, and have pierced themselves through with many sorrows.

Psalm 84:1-2 NIV How lovely is your dwelling place, O Lord Almighty! My soul yearns, even faints, for the courts of the Lord; my heart and my flesh cry out for the living God.

Psalm 119:103-105 NCV Your promises are sweet to me, sweeter than honey in my mouth! Your orders give me understanding, so I hate lying ways. Your word is like a lamp for my feet and a light for my path.

Song of Solomon 8:6 NLT Place me like a seal over your heart, or like a seal on your arm. For love is as strong as death, and its jealousy is as enduring as the grave.

Joel 2:12-13 NIV "Even now," declares the Lord, "return to me with all your heart, with fasting and weeping and mourning." Rend your heart and not your garments. Return to the Lord your God, for he is gracious and compassionate, slow to anger and abounding in love, and he relents from sending calamity.

Philippians 1:9-11 NKJV And this I pray, that your love may abound still more and more in knowledge and all discernment, that you may approve the things that are excellent, that you may be sincere and without offense till the day of Christ, being filled with the fruits of righteousness which are by Jesus Christ, to the glory and praise of God.

1 John 4:19 NCV We love because God first loved us.

Revelation 2:2-5 WEB I know your works, and your toil and perseverance, and that you can't tolerate evil men, and have tested those who call themselves apostles, and they are not, and found them false. You have perseverance and have endured for my name's sake, and have not grown weary. But I have this against you, that you left your first love. Remember therefore from where you have fallen, and repent and do the first works; or else I am coming to you swiftly, and will move your lampstand out of its place, unless you repent.

Micah 7:18-19 NRSV Who is a God like you, pardoning iniquity and passing over transgression for the remnant of your possession? He does not retain his anger forever because he delights in showing clemency. He will again have compassion upon us; he will tread our iniquities under foot. You will cast all our sins into the depths of the sea.

Psalm 32:5 NCV Then I confessed my sins to you and didn't hide my guilt. I said, "I will confess my sins to the LORD," and you forgave my guilt.

Psalm 79:8-9 NLT Oh, do not hold us guilty for our former sins! Let your tenderhearted mercies quickly meet our needs, for we are brought low to the dust. Help us, O God of our salvation! Help us for the honor of your name. Oh, save us and forgive our sins for the sake of your name.

Psalm 86:5-7 NIV You are forgiving and good, O Lor d, abounding in love to all who call to you. Hear my prayer, O Lor d; listen to my cry for mercy. In the day of my trouble I will call to you, for you will answer me.

Psalm 99:8-9 NLT O LORD our God, you answered them. You were a forgiving God, but you punished them when they went wrong. Exalt the LORD our God and worship at his holy mountain in Jerusalem, for the LORD our God is holy!

Psalm 103:11-12 WEB For as the heavens are high above the earth, so great is his loving kindness toward those who fear him. As far as the east is from the west, so far has he removed our transgressions from us.

Matthew 5:44-45 NKJV But I say to you, love your enemies, bless those who curse you, do good to those who hate you, and pray for those who spitefully use you and persecute you, that you may be sons of your Father in heaven; for He makes His sun rise on the evil and on the good, and sends rain on the just and on the unjust.

Matthew 6:9–15 WEB Pray like this. "Our Father in heaven, may your name be kept holy. Let your Kingdom come. Let your will be done, as in heaven, so on earth. Give us today our daily bread. Forgive us our debts, as we also forgive our debtors. Bring us not into temptation, but deliver us from the evil one. For yours is the Kingdom, the power, and the glory forever. Amen." For if you forgive men their trespasses, your heavenly Father will also forgive you. But if you don't forgive men their trespasses, neither will your Father forgive your trespasses."

Mark 11:25–26 WEB Whenever you stand praying, forgive, if you have anything against anyone; so that your Father, who is in heaven, may also forgive you your transgressions. But if you do not forgive, neither will your Father in heaven forgive your transgressions.

Luke 6:37–38 NKJV Judge not, and you shall not be judged. Condemn not, and you shall not be condemned. Forgive, and you will be forgiven. Give, and it will be given to you: good measure, pressed down, shaken together, and running over will be put into your bosom. For with the same measure that you use, it will be measured back to you.

Luke 23:34–37 WEB Jesus said, "Father, forgive them, for they don't know what they are doing." Dividing his garments among them, they cast lots. The people stood watching. The rulers with them also scoffed at him, saying, "He saved others. Let him save himself, if this is the Christ of God, his chosen one! The soldiers also mocked him, . . . saying, "If you are the King of the Jews, save yourself!"

Ephesians 4:32 NIV Be kind and compassionate to one another, forgiving each other, just as in Christ God forgave you.

1 John 1:9 NIV If we confess our sins, he is faithful and just to forgive us our sins and purify us from all unrighteousness.

Isaiah 61:1-3 NRSV The spirit of the Lord GOD is upon me, because the LORD has anointed me; he has sent me to bring good news to the oppressed, to bind up the brokenhearted, to proclaim liberty to the captives, and release to the prisoners; to proclaim the year of the LORD's favor, and the day of vengeance of our God; to comfort all who mourn; to provide for those who mourn in Zion— to give them a garland instead of ashes, the oil of gladness instead of mourning, the mantle of praise instead of a faint spirit. They will be called oaks of righteousness.

John 8:31-32 NIV To the Jews who had believed him, Jesus said, "If you hold to my teaching, you are really my disciples. Then you will know the truth, and the truth will set you free."

John 8:34-36 WEB Jesus answered them, "Most certainly I tell you, everyone who commits sin is the bondservant of sin. A bondservant doesn't live in the house forever. A son remains forever. If therefore the Son makes you free, you will be free indeed."

Romans 6:7-10 WEB For he who has died has been freed from sin. But if we died with Christ, we believe that we will also live with him; knowing that Christ, being raised from the dead, dies no more. Death no more has dominion over him! For the death that he died, he died to sin one time; but the life that he lives, he lives to God.

Galatians 5:13 NIV You, my brothers, were called to be free. But do not use your freedom to indulge the sinful nature; rather, serve one another in love.

1 Peter 2:15-16 WEB For this is the will of God, that by well-doing you should put to silence the ignorance of foolish men: as free, and not using your freedom for a cloak of wickedness, but as bondservants of God.

Psalm 119:63 NKJV I am a companion of all who fear You, and of those who keep Your precepts.

Proverbs 12:25-26 WEB Anxiety in a man's heart weighs it down, but a kind word makes it glad. A righteous person is cautious in friendship, but the way of the wicked leads them astray.

Proverbs 13:20 WEB One who walks with wise men grows wise, but a companion of fools suffers harm.

Proverbs 18:24 NIV A man of many companions may come to ruin, but there is a friend who sticks closer than a brother.

Proverbs 27:5-6 NIV Better is open rebuke than hidden love. Wounds from a friend can be trusted, but an enemy multiplies kisses.

Proverbs 27:9 WEB Perfume and incense bring joy to the heart; so does earnest counsel from a man's friend.

Proverbs 27:17 TMB Iron sharpeneth iron; so a man sharpeneth the countenance of his friend.

Ecclesiastes 4:9-10 NCV Two people are better than one, because they get more done by working together. If one falls down, the other can help him up. But it is bad for the person who is alone and falls, because no one is there to help.

John 15:12-13 WEB "This is my commandment, that you love one another, even as I have loved you. Greater love has no one than this, that someone lay down his life for his friends.

John 15:14–15 NIV You are my friends if you do what I command. I no longer call you servants, because a servant does not know his master's business. Instead, I have called you friends, for everything that I learned from my Father I have made known to you.

Romans 12:10–13 WEB In love of the brothers be tenderly affectionate one to another; in honor preferring one another; not lagging in diligence; fervent in spirit; serving the Lord; rejoicing in hope; enduring in troubles; continuing steadfastly in prayer; contributing to the needs of the saints; given to hospitality.

Romans 12:16–18 WNT Have full sympathy with one another. Do not give your mind to high things, but let humble ways content you. Do not be wise in your own conceits. Pay back to no man evil for evil. If you can, so far as it depends on you, live at peace with all the world.

1 Corinthians 10:24 NLT Don't think only of your own good. Think of other Christians and what is best for them.

2 Corinthians 6:14 WEB Don't be unequally yoked with unbelievers, for what fellowship have righteousness and iniquity?

Ephesians 4:32 NIV Be kind and compassionate to one another, forgiving each other, just as in Christ God forgave you.

Hebrews 10:24–25 NIV And let us consider how we may spur one another on toward love and good deeds. Let us not give up meeting together, as some are in the habit of doing, but let us encourage one another—and all the more as you see the Day approaching.

James 2:23 NKJV The Scripture was fulfilled which says, "Abraham believed God, and it was accounted to him for righteousness." And he was called the friend of God.

Psalm 1:1-3 NASB How blessed is the man who does not walk in the counsel of the wicked, nor stand in the path of sinners, nor sit in the seat of scoffers! But his delight is in the law of the LORD, and in His law he meditates day and night. He will be like a tree firmly planted by streams of water, which yields its fruit in its season and its leaf does not wither; and in whatever he does, he prospers.

John 15:16 WEB You didn't choose me, but I chose you, and appointed you, that you should go and bear fruit, and that your fruit should remain.

Galatians 5:22-26 WEB But the fruit of the Spirit is love, joy, peace, patience, kindness, goodness, faithfulness, gentleness, and self-control. Against such things there is no law. Those who belong to Christ have crucified the flesh with its passions and lusts. If we live by the Spirit, let's also walk by the Spirit. Let's not become conceited, provoking one another, and envying one another.

Colossians 1:9-11 WEB For this cause, we also, since the day we heard this, don't cease praying and making requests for you, that you may be filled with the knowledge of his will in all spiritual wisdom and understanding, that you may walk worthily of the Lord, to please him in all respects, bearing fruit in every good work, and increasing in the knowledge of God; strengthened with all power, according to the might of his glory, for all endurance and perseverance with joy.

Hebrews 12:11 NASB All discipline for the moment seems not to be joyful, but sorrowful; yet to those who have been trained by it, afterwards it yields the peaceful fruit of righteousness.

James 3:17-18 WEB But the wisdom that is from above is first pure, then peaceful, gentle, reasonable, full of mercy and good fruits, without partiality, and without hypocrisy. Now the fruit of righteousness is sown in peace by those who make peace.

Psalm 23:6 WEB Surely goodness and loving kindness shall follow me all the days of my life, and I shall dwell in Yahweh's house forever.

Psalm 31:24 NASB Be strong and let your heart take courage, all you who hope in the Lord.

Psalm 37:5-7 NASB Commit your way to the Lord, trust also in Him, and He will do it. He will bring forth your righteousness as the light and your judgment as the noonday. Rest in the Lord and wait patiently for Him.

Psalm 37:37 NLT Look at those who are honest and good, for a wonderful future lies before those who love peace.

Isaiah 46:3-4 NKJV Listen to Me, O house of Jacob, and all the remnant of the house of Israel, who have been upheld by Me from birth, who have been carried from the womb: even to your old age, I am He, and even to gray hairs I will carry you! I have made, and I will bear; even I will carry, and will deliver you.

Isaiah 58:11 WEB And Yahweh will guide you continually, and satisfy your soul in dry places, and make strong your bones; and you shall be like a watered garden, and like a spring of water, whose waters don't fail.

Jeremiah 29:11-14 NRSV For surely I know the plans I have for you, says the Lord, plans for your welfare and not for harm, to give you a future with hope. Then when you call upon me and come and pray to me, I will hear you. When you search for me, you will find me; if you seek me with all your heart, I will let you find me, says the Lord.

Jeremiah 31:17 NCV "So there is hope for you in the future," says the Lord.

Psalm 37:21 NASB The wicked borrows and does not pay back, but the righteous is gracious and gives.

Proverbs 11:24–25 NCV Some people give much but get back even more. Others don't give what they should and end up poor. Whoever gives to others will get richer; those who help others will themselves be helped.

Proverbs 22:9 NASB He who is generous will be blessed, for he gives some of his food to the poor.

Isaiah 32:8 NKJV But a generous man devises generous things, and by generosity he shall stand.

2 Corinthians 9:6–8 WEB He who sows sparingly will also reap sparingly. He who sows bountifully will also reap bountifully. Let each man give according as he has determined in his heart; not grudgingly, or under compulsion; for God loves a cheerful giver. And God is able to make all grace abound to you, that you, always having all sufficiency in everything, may abound to every good work.

1 Timothy 6:17–19 NKJV Command those who are rich in this present age not to be haughty, nor to trust in uncertain riches but in the living God, who gives us richly all things to enjoy. Let them do good, that they be rich in good works, ready to give, willing to share, storing up for themselves a good foundation for the time to come, that they may lay hold on eternal life.

1 John 3:16–17 NIV This is how we know what love is: Jesus Christ laid down his life for us. And we ought to lay down our lives for our brothers. If anyone has material possessions and sees his brother in need but has no pity on him, how can the love of God be in him?

Psalm 22:23 NASB You who fear the LORD, praise Him; all you descendants of Jacob, glorify Him, and stand in awe of Him, all you descendants of Israel.

Matthew 5:16 WEB Even so, let your light shine before men; that they may see your good works, and glorify your Father who is in heaven.

Matthew 15:31 NASB So the crowd marveled as they saw the mute speaking, the crippled restored, and the lame walking, and the blind seeing; and they glorified the God of Israel.

John 15:7-8 WEB If you remain in me, and my words remain in you, you will ask whatever you desire, and it will be done for you. In this is my Father glorified, that you bear much fruit; and so you will be my disciples.

John 17:4-5 WEB I glorified you on the earth. I have accomplished the work which you have given me to do. Now, Father, glorify me with your own self with the glory which I had with you before the world existed.

Romans 8:30 NCV God planned for them to be like his Son; and those he planned to be like his Son, he also called; and those he called, he also made right with him; and those he made right, he also glorified.

1 Corinthians 6:20 NASB For you have been bought with a price: therefore glorify God in your body.

1 Peter 4:11 NKJV If anyone speaks, let him speak as the oracles of God. If anyone ministers, let him do it as with the ability which God supplies, that in all things God may be glorified through Jesus Christ, to whom belong the glory and the dominion forever and ever. Amen.

Exodus 34:6-7 NLT He passed in front of Moses and said, "I am the LORD, I am the LORD, the merciful and gracious God. I am slow to anger and rich in unfailing love and faithfulness. I show this unfailing love to many thousands by forgiving every kind of sin and rebellion."

Psalm 16:2 NIV I said to the LORD, "You are my LORD; apart from you I have no good thing."

Psalm 31:19 NLT Your goodness is so great! You have stored up great blessings for those who honor you. You have done so much for those who come to you for protection, blessing them before the watching world.

Psalm 33:4-5 NASB For the word of the LORD is upright, and all His work is done in faithfulness. He loves righteousness and justice; the earth is full of the lovingkindness of the LORD.

Psalm 65:9-11 NKJV You visit the earth and water it, You greatly enrich it; the river of God is full of water; You provide their grain, for so You have prepared it. You water its ridges abundantly, You make it soft with showers, You bless its growth. You crown the year with Your goodness, and Your paths drip with abundance.

Psalm 107:31-32 NCV Let them give thanks to the LORD for his love and for the miracles he does for people. Let them praise his greatness in the meeting of the people; let them praise him in the meeting of the older leaders.

Galatians 5:22-23 NLT But when the Holy Spirit controls our lives, he will produce this kind of fruit in us: love, joy, peace, patience, kindness, goodness, faithfulness, gentleness, and self-control. Here there is no conflict with the law.

Psalm 34:13 WEB Keep your tongue from evil, and your lips from speaking lies.

Psalm 141:3 NCV LORD, help me control my tongue; help me be careful about what I say.

Proverbs 8:6-8 NRSV Hear, for I will speak noble things, and from my lips will come what is right; for my mouth will utter truth; wickedness is an abomination to my lips. All the words of my mouth are righteous; there is nothing twisted or crooked in them.

Proverbs 11:13 NLT A gossip goes around revealing secrets, but those who are trustworthy can keep a confidence.

Proverbs 21:23 WEB Whoever guards his mouth and his tongue keeps his soul from troubles.

Proverbs 29:20 NKJV Do you see a man hasty in his words? There is more hope for a fool than for him.

Galatians 5:22–26 WEB But the fruit of the Spirit is love, joy, peace, patience, kindness, goodness, faithfulness, gentleness, and self-control. Against such things there is no law. Those who belong to Christ have crucified the flesh with its passions and lusts. If we live by the Spirit, let's also walk by the Spirit. Let's not become conceited, provoking one another, and envying one another.

Philippians 4:8 NKJV Finally, brethren, whatever things are true, whatever things are noble, whatever things are just, whatever things are pure, whatever things are lovely, whatever things are of good report, if there is any virtue and if there is anything praiseworthy—meditate on these things.

Colossians 4:6 NASB Let your speech always be with grace, as though seasoned with salt, so that you will know how you should respond to each person.

Titus 3:1–2 NKJV Remind them to be subject to rulers and authorities, to obey, to be ready for every good work, to speak evil of no one, to be peaceable, gentle, showing all humility to all men.

James 1:19 NIV My dear brothers, take note of this: Everyone should be quick to listen, slow to speak and slow to become angry.

James 1:26 NLT If you claim to be religious but don't control your tongue, you are just fooling yourself, and your religion is worthless.

James 3:5-6 NASB So also the tongue is a small part of the body, and yet it boasts of great things. See how great a forest is set aflame by such a small fire! And the tongue is a fire, the very world of iniquity; the tongue is set among our members as that which defiles the entire body, and sets on fire the course of our life, and is set on fire by hell.

James 3:8-10 WEB But nobody can tame the tongue. It is a restless evil, full of deadly poison. With it we bless our God and Father, and with it we curse men, who are made in the image of God. Out of the same mouth comes forth blessing and cursing. My brothers, these things ought not to be so.

James 4:11 NIV Brothers, do not slander one another. Anyone who speaks against his brother or judges him speaks against the law and judges it. When you judge the law, you are not keeping it, but sitting in judgment on it.

1 Peter 2:1-3 WEB Putting away therefore all wickedness, all deceit, hypocrisies, envies, and all evil speaking, as newborn babies, long for the pure milk of the Word, that you may grow thereby, if indeed you have tasted that the Lord is gracious.

Psalm 9:15-16 WEB The nations have sunk down in the pit that they made; in the net which they hid, their own foot is taken. Yahweh has made himself known. He has executed judgment. The wicked is snared by the work of his own hands.

Psalm 67:3-7 NRSV Let the peoples praise you, O God; let all the peoples praise you. Let the nations be glad and sing for joy, for you judge the peoples with equity and guide the nations upon earth. Let the peoples praise you, O God; let all the peoples praise you. The earth has yielded its increase; God, our God, has blessed us. May God continue to bless us; let all the ends of the earth revere him.

Romans 13:1-4 WEB Let every soul be in subjection to the higher authorities, for there is no authority except from God, and those who exist are ordained by God. Therefore he who resists the authority, withstands the ordinance of God; and those who withstand will receive to themselves judgment. For rulers are not a terror to the good work, but to the evil. Do you desire to have no fear of the authority? Do that which is good, and you will have praise from the same, for he is a servant of God to you for good. But if you do that which is evil, be afraid, for he doesn't bear the sword in vain; for he is a servant of God.

1 Timothy 2:1-4 NKJV Therefore I exhort first of all that supplications, prayers, intercessions, and giving of thanks be made for all men, for kings and all who are in authority, that we may lead a quiet and peaceable life in all godliness and reverence. For this is good and acceptable in the sight of God our Savior, who desires all men to be saved and to come to the knowledge of the truth.

Colossians 1:9-11 WEB For this cause, we also, since the day we heard this, don't cease praying and making requests for you, that you may be filled with the knowledge of his will in all spiritual wisdom and understanding, that you may walk worthily of the Lord, to please him in all respects, bearing fruit in every good work, and increasing in the knowledge of God; strengthened with all power.

Psalm 45:1-2 NIV My heart is stirred by a noble theme as I recite my verses for the king; my tongue is the pen of a skillful writer. You are the most excellent of men and your lips have been anointed with grace, since God has blessed you forever.

Psalm 84:11 WEB For Yahweh God is a sun and a shield. Yahweh will give grace and glory. He withholds no good thing from those who walk blamelessly.

Acts 4:33 WEB With great power, the apostles gave their testimony of the resurrection of the Lord Jesus. Great grace was on them all.

Romans 1:7 NKJV Beloved of God, called to be saints: Grace to you and peace from God our Father and the Lord Jesus Christ.

Romans 5:17 NIV For if, by the trespass of the one man, death reigned through that one man, how much more will those who receive God's abundant provision of grace and of the gift of righteousness reign in life through the one man, Jesus Christ.

Romans 11:5-6 WEB Even so then at this present time also there is a remnant according to the election of grace. And if by grace, then it is no longer of works; otherwise grace is no longer grace. But if it is of works, it is no longer grace; otherwise work is no longer work.

1 Corinthians 15:10 NIV But by the grace of God I am what I am, and his grace to me was not without effect. No, I worked harder than all of them—yet not I, but the grace of God that was with me.

2 Corinthians 12:9 NIV But he said to me, "My grace is sufficient for you, for my power is made perfect in weakness." Therefore I will boast all the more gladly about my weaknesses, so that Christ's power may rest on me.

Galatians 5:4-6 NASB You have been severed from Christ, you who are seeking to be justified by law; you have fallen from grace. For we through the Spirit, by faith, are waiting for the hope of righteousness. For in Christ Jesus neither circumcision nor uncircumcision means anything, but faith working through love.

Ephesians 1:7-9 NCV In Christ we are set free by the blood of his death, and so we have forgiveness of sins. How rich is God's grace, which he has given to us so fully and freely. God, with full wisdom and understanding, let us know his secret purpose. This was what God wanted, and he planned to do it through Christ.

Ephesians 2:4-9 WEB But God, being rich in mercy, for his great love . . . made us alive together with Christ (by grace have you been saved) . . . and made us to sit with him in the heavenly places in Christ Jesus . . . He might show the exceeding riches of his grace in kindness toward us in Christ Jesus; for by grace you have been saved through faith, and that not of yourselves; it is the gift of God, not of works, that no one would boast.

Ephesians 4:7-8 NLT However, he has given each one of us a special gift according to the generosity of Christ. That is why the Scriptures say, "When he ascended to the heights, he led a crowd of captives and gave gifts to his people."

1 Timothy 1:14 WEB The grace of our Lord abounded exceedingly with faith and love which is in Christ Jesus.

Hebrews 12:28-29 NASB Therefore, since we receive a kingdom which cannot be shaken, let us show gratitude, by which we may offer to God an acceptable service with reverence and awe; for our God is a consuming fire.

James 4:6 WEB But he gives more grace. Therefore it says, "God resists the proud, but gives grace to the humble."

Psalm 10:12-14 NRSV Rise up, O LORD; O God, lift up your hand; do not forget the oppressed. Why do the wicked renounce God, and say in their hearts, "You will not call us to account"? But you do see! Indeed you note trouble and grief, that you may take it into your hands; the helpless commit themselves to you; you have been the helper of the orphan.

Ephesians 1:7-9 NCV In Christ we are set free by the blood of his death, and so we have forgiveness of sins. How rich is God's grace, which he has given to us so fully and freely. God, with full wisdom and understanding, let us know his secret purpose. This was what God wanted, and he planned to do it through Christ.

Psalm 32:7 NKJV You are my hiding place; You shall preserve me from trouble; You shall surround me with songs of deliverance.

Isaiah 51:11 WEB The ransomed of Yahweh shall return, and come with singing to Zion; and everlasting joy shall be on their heads: they shall obtain gladness and joy; and sorrow and sighing shall flee away.

Isaiah 53:3-5 NKJV He is despised and rejected by men, a Man of sorrows and acquainted with grief. And we hid, as it were, our faces from Him; He was despised, and we did not esteem Him. Surely He has borne our griefs, and carried our sorrows; yet we esteemed Him stricken, smitten by God, and afflicted. But He was wounded for our transgressions, He was bruised for our iniquities; the chastisement for our peace was upon Him, and by His stripes we are healed.

2 Corinthians 12:9-10 NKJV And He said to me, "My grace is sufficient for you, for My strength is made perfect in weakness." Therefore most gladly I will rather boast in my infirmities, that the power of Christ may rest upon me. Therefore I take pleasure in infirmities, in reproaches, in needs, in persecutions, in distresses, for Christ's sake. For when I am weak, then I am strong.

Deuteronomy 5:33 NASB You shall walk in all the way which the LORD your God has commanded you, that you may live and that it may be well with you, and that you may prolong your days in the land which you will possess.

Psalm 103:2-3 NIV Praise the LORD, O my soul, and forget not all his benefits—who forgives all your sins and heals all your diseases.

Psalm 107:19-22 NRSV Then they cried to the LORD in their trouble, and he saved them from their distress; he sent out his word and healed them, and delivered them from destruction. Let them thank the LORD for his steadfast love, for his wonderful works to humankind. And let them offer thanksgiving sacrifices, and tell of his deeds with songs of joy.

Proverbs 3:7-8 WEB Don't be wise in your own eyes. Fear Yahweh, and depart from evil. It will be health to your body, and nourishment to your bones.

Isaiah 53:4-5 NASB Surely our griefs He Himself bore, and our sorrows He carried; yet we ourselves esteemed Him stricken, smitten of God, and afflicted. But He was pierced through for our transgressions, He was crushed for our iniquities; the chastening for our well-being fell upon Him, and by His scourging we are healed.

Isaiah 61:1-2 NKJV The Spirit of the Lord GOD is upon Me, because the LORD has anointed Me to preach good tidings to the poor; He has sent Me to heal the brokenhearted, to proclaim liberty to the captives, and the opening of the prison to those who are bound; to proclaim the acceptable year of the LORD.

Jeremiah 17:14-15 NASB Heal me, O LORD, and I will be healed; save me and I will be saved, for You are my praise. Look, they keep saying to me, "Where is the word of the LORD? Let it come now!"

Matthew 9:22 WEB But Jesus, turning around and seeing her, said, "Daughter, cheer up! Your faith has made you well." And the woman was made well from that hour.

Mark 16:17-18 NKJV And these signs will follow those who believe: In My name they will cast out demons; they will speak with new tongues; they will take up serpents; and if they drink anything deadly, it will by no means hurt them; they will lay hands on the sick, and they will recover.

John 14:12-14 NASB "Truly, truly, I say to you, he who believes in Me, the works that I do, he will do also; and greater works than these he will do; because I go to the Father." Whatever you ask in My name, that will I do, so that the Father may be glorified in the Son. "If you ask Me anything in My name, I will do it."

Acts 3:16 NKJV And His name, through faith in His name, has made this man strong, whom you see and know. Yes, the faith which comes through Him has given him this perfect soundness in the presence of all.

1 Corinthians 12:27-28 WEB Now you are the body of Christ, and members individually. God has set some in the assembly: first apostles, secondly prophets, thirdly teachers, then miracle workers, then gifts of healings, helps, governments, and various kinds of languages.

James 5:13-16 WEB Is any among you suffering? Let him pray. Is any cheerful? Let him sing praises. Is any among you sick? Let him call for the elders of the assembly, and let them pray over him, anointing him with oil in the name of the Lord, and the prayer of faith will heal him who is sick, and the Lord will raise him up. If he has committed sins, he will be forgiven. Confess your offenses one to another, and pray one for another, that you may be healed.

Psalm 36:7-9 NKJV How precious is Your loving kindness, O God! Therefore the children of men put their trust under the shadow of Your wings. . . . You give them drink from the river of Your pleasures. For with You is the fountain of life; in Your light we see light.

Psalm 139:14 WEB I will give thanks to you, for I am fearfully and wonderfully made. Your works are wonderful. My soul knows that very well.

Proverbs 16:24 NASB Pleasant words are a honeycomb, sweet to the soul and healing to the bones.

Jeremiah 30:17 NASB "For I will restore you to health and I will heal you of your wounds," declares the LORD.

Acts 9:34 NASB "Aeneas, Jesus Christ heals you; get up and make your bed." Immediately he got up.

1 Corinthians 6:19-20 WEB Or don't you know that your body is a temple of the Holy Spirit which is in you, which you have from God? You are not your own, for you were bought with a price. Therefore glorify God in your body and in your spirit, which are God's.

1 Timothy 4:8 NIV For physical training is of some value, but godliness has value for all things, holding promise for both the present life and the life to come.

2 Timothy 1:7 NKJV God has not given us a spirit of fear, but of power and of love and of a sound mind.

3 John 2 NKJV Beloved, I pray that you may prosper in all things and be in health, just as your soul prospers.

Proverbs 18:15 WEB The heart of the discerning gets knowledge. The ear of the wise seeks knowledge.

Matthew 7:24–27 WEB Everyone therefore who hears these words of mine, and does them, I will liken him to a wise man, who built his house on a rock. The rain came down, the floods came, and the winds blew, and beat on that house; and it didn't fall, for it was founded on the rock. Everyone who hears these words of mine, and doesn't do them will be like a foolish man, who built his house on the sand. The rain came down, the floods came, and the winds blew, and beat on that house; and it fell—and great was its fall.

Matthew 13:14–15 NKJV Hearing you will hear and shall not understand, and seeing you will see and not perceive, for the hearts of this people have grown dull. Their ears are hard of hearing, and their eyes they have closed, lest they should see with their eyes and hear with their ears, lest they should understand with their hearts and turn, so that I should heal them.

Matthew 17:5 NCV While Peter was talking, a bright cloud covered them. A voice came from the cloud and said, "This is my Son, whom I love, and I am very pleased with him. Listen to him!"

Mark 4:24 NCV Think carefully about what you hear. The way you give to others is the way God will give to you, but God will give you even more.

John 8:47 NKJV He who is of God hears God's words.

John 18:37 WEB Jesus answered, "You say that I am a king. For this reason I have been born, and for this reason I have come into the world, that I should testify to the truth. Everyone who is of the truth listens to my voice."

1 Samuel 16:7 NKJV But the Lord said to Samuel, "Do not look at his appearance or at his physical stature, because I have refused him. For the Lord does not see as man sees; for man looks at the outward appearance, but the Lord looks at the heart."

1 Chronicles 28:9 NASB As for you, my son Solomon, know the God of your father, and serve Him with a whole heart and a willing mind; for the Lord searches all hearts, and understands every intent of the thoughts. If you seek Him, He will let you find Him; but if you forsake Him, He will reject you forever.

Psalm 16:7-9 NASB I will bless the Lord who has counseled me; indeed, my mind instructs me in the night. I have set the Lord continually before me; because He is at my right hand, I will not be shaken. Therefore my heart is glad and my glory rejoices; my flesh also will dwell securely.

Psalm 33:13-15 NLT The Lord looks down from heaven and sees the whole human race. From his throne he observes all who live on the earth. He made their hearts, so he understands everything they do.

Psalm 37:4 NLT Take delight in the Lord, and he will give you your heart's desires.

Psalm 51:10-12 NRSV Create in me a clean heart, O God, and put a new and right spirit within me. Do not cast me away from your presence, and do not take your holy spirit from me. Restore to me the joy of your salvation, and sustain in me a willing spirit.

Proverbs 4:20-23 NRSV My child, be attentive to my words; incline your ear to my sayings. Do not let them escape from your sight; keep them within your heart. For they are life to those who find them, and healing to all their flesh. Keep your heart with all vigilance, for from it flow the springs of life.

Proverbs 15:13-15 NKJV A merry heart makes a cheerful countenance, but by sorrow of the heart the spirit is broken. The heart of him who has understanding seeks knowledge, but the mouth of fools feeds on foolishness. All the days of the afflicted are evil, but he who is of a merry heart has a continual feast.

Ezekiel 36:26 NLT And I will give you a new heart with new and right desires, and I will put a new spirit in you. I will take out your stony heart of sin and give you a new, obedient heart.

Matthew 6:19-21 WEB Don't lay up treasures for yourselves on the earth, where moth and rust consume, and where thieves break through and steal; but lay up for yourselves treasures in heaven, where neither moth nor rust consume, and where thieves don't break through and steal; for where your treasure is, there your heart will be also.

John 7:37-39 NKJV On the last day, that great day of the feast, Jesus stood and cried out, saying, "If anyone thirsts, let him come to Me and drink. He who believes in Me, as the Scripture has said, out of his heart will flow rivers of living water." But this He spoke concerning the Spirit, whom those believing in Him would receive; for the Holy Spirit was not yet given, because Jesus was not yet glorified.

Colossians 3:14-16 WEB Above all these things, walk in love, which is the bond of perfection. And let the peace of God rule in your hearts, to which also you were called in one body; and be thankful. Let the word of Christ dwell in you richly; in all wisdom teaching and admonishing one another . . . with grace in your heart to the Lord.

1 John 3:17-19 WEB But whoever has the world's goods, and sees his brother in need, and closes his heart of compassion against him, how does the love of God remain in him? My little children, let's not love in word only, neither with the tongue only, but in deed and truth. And by this we know that we are of the truth, and persuade our hearts before him.

Deuteronomy 26:14–15 NRSV I have obeyed the LORD my God, doing just as you commanded me. Look down from your holy habitation, from heaven, and bless your people Israel and the ground that you have given us, as you swore to our ancestors—a land flowing with milk and honey.

Psalm 19:1 TMB The heavens declare the glory of God; and the firmament showeth His handiwork.

Isaiah 66:1 NASB Thus says the LORD, "Heaven is My throne and the earth is My footstool. Where then is a house you could build for Me? And where is a place that I may rest?"

Matthew 6:19–21 WEB Don't lay up treasures for yourselves on the earth, where moth and rust consume, and where thieves break through and steal; but lay up for yourselves treasures in heaven, where neither moth nor rust consume, and where thieves don't break through and steal; for where your treasure is, there your heart will be also.

John 6:32–33 NASB Jesus then said to them, "Truly, truly, I say to you, it is not Moses who has given you the bread out of heaven, but it is My Father who gives you the true bread out of heaven. For the bread of God is that which comes down out of heaven, and gives life to the world."

2 Corinthians 5:1 WEB For we know that if the earthly house of our tent is dissolved, we have a building from God, a house not made with hands, eternal, in the heavens.

Revelation 4:2–3 NKJV Immediately I was in the Spirit; and behold, a throne set in heaven, and One sat on the throne. And He who sat there was like a jasper and a sardius stone in appearance; and there was a rainbow around the throne, in appearance like an emerald.

Genesis 12:1–3 NRSV Now the LORD said to Abram, "Go from your country and your kindred and your father's house to the land that I will show you. I will make of you a great nation, and I will bless you, and make your name great, so that you will be a blessing. I will bless those who bless you, and the one who curses you I will curse; and in you all the families of the earth shall be blessed."

Deuteronomy 4:9–10 NKJV Only take heed to yourself, and diligently keep yourself, lest you forget the things your eyes have seen, and lest they depart from your heart all the days of your life. And teach them to your children and your grandchildren. The LORD said to me, "Gather the people to Me, and I will let them hear My words, that they may learn to fear Me all the days they live on the earth, and that they may teach their children."

Psalm 37:25–26 WEB I have been young, and now am old, yet I have not seen the righteous forsaken, nor his children begging for bread. All day long he deals graciously, and lends. His seed is blessed.

Psalm 102:17–20 NLT He will listen to the prayers of the destitute. He will not reject their pleas. Let this be recorded for future generations, so that a nation yet to be created will praise the LORD. Tell them the LORD looked down from his heavenly sanctuary. He looked to the earth from heaven to hear the groans of the prisoners, to release those condemned to die.

Psalm 119:111–112 WEB I have taken your testimonies as a heritage forever, for they are the joy of my heart. I have set my heart to perform your statutes forever, even to the end.

Isaiah 54:17 NASB "No weapon that is formed against you will prosper; and every tongue that accuses you in judgment you will condemn. This is the heritage of the servants of the LORD, and their vindication is from Me," declares the LORD.

1 Corinthians 10:4-6 NKJV For they drank of that spiritual Rock that followed them, and that Rock was Christ. But with most of them God was not well pleased, for their bodies were scattered in the wilderness. Now these things became our examples, to the intent that we should not lust after evil things as they also lusted.

Ephesians 3:8-12 NKJV To me, who am less than the least of all the saints, this grace was given, that I should preach among the Gentiles the unsearchable riches of Christ, and to make all see what is the fellowship of the mystery, which from the beginning of the ages has been hidden in God who created all things through Jesus Christ; to the intent that now the manifold wisdom of God might be made known by the church to the principalities and powers in the heavenly places, according to the eternal purpose which He accomplished in Christ Jesus our Lord, in whom we have boldness and access with confidence through faith in Him.

2 Timothy 1:3-6 WEB I thank God, whom I serve as my forefathers did, with a pure conscience. How unceasing is my memory of you in my petitions, night and day longing to see you, remembering your tears, that I may be filled with joy; having been reminded of the sincere faith that is in you; which lived first in your grandmother Lois, and your mother Eunice, and, I am persuaded, in you also. For this cause, I remind you that you should stir up the gift of God which is in you through the laying on of my hands.

2 Timothy 3:14-15 WNT But you must cling to the things which you have learnt and have been taught to believe, knowing who your teachers were, and that from infancy you have known the sacred writings which are able to make you wise to obtain salvation through faith in Christ Jesus.

James 2:5 NASB Did not God choose the poor of this world to be rich in faith and heirs of the kingdom which He promised to those who love Him?

Exodus 15:11 NASB Who is like You among the gods, O Lord? Who is like You, majestic in holiness, awesome in praises, working wonders?

Romans 12:1-2 WEB Present your bodies a living sacrifice, holy, acceptable to God, which is your spiritual service. Don't be conformed to this world, but be transformed by the renewing of your mind, so that you may prove what is the good, well-pleasing, and perfect will of God.

1 Corinthians 3:16-17 NCV Don't you know that you are God's temple and that God's Spirit lives in you? If anyone destroys God's temple, God will destroy that person, because God's temple is holy and you are that temple.

2 Corinthians 6:16-7:1 NKJV You are the temple of the living God. As God has said: "I will dwell in them and walk among them. I will be their God, and they shall be My people." Therefore "Come out from among them and be separate," says the Lord. Do not touch what is unclean, and I will receive you. I will be a Father to you, and you shall be My sons and daughters," says the Lord Almighty. Therefore, having these promises, beloved, let us cleanse ourselves from all filthiness of the flesh and spirit, perfecting holiness in the fear of God.

2 Timothy 1:3-6 WEB I thank God, whom I serve as my forefathers did, with a pure conscience. How unceasing is my memory of you in my petitions, night and day longing to see you, remembering your tears, that I may be filled with joy; having been reminded of the sincere faith that is in you; which lived first in your grandmother Lois, and your mother Eunice, and, I am persuaded, in you also. For this cause, I remind you that you should stir up the gift of God which is in you through the laying on of my hands.

1 Thessalonians 4:7-8 NASB For God has not called us for the purpose of impurity, but in sanctification. So, he who rejects this is not rejecting man but the God who gives His Holy Spirit to you.

Hebrews 12:14-16 NKJV Pursue peace with all people, and holiness, without which no one will see the Lord: looking carefully lest anyone fall short of the grace of God; lest any root of bitterness springing up cause trouble, and by this many become defiled; lest there be any fornicator or profane person like Esau, who for one morsel of food sold his birthright.

1 Peter 1:13-16 WEB Therefore, prepare your minds for action, be sober and set your hope fully on the grace that will be brought to you at the revelation of Jesus Christ—as children of obedience, not conforming yourselves according to your former lusts as in your ignorance, but just as he who called you is holy, you yourselves also be holy in all of your behavior; because it is written, "You shall be holy; for I am holy."

1 Peter 1:23 NCV You have been born again, and this new life did not come from something that dies, but from something that cannot die. You were born again through God's living message that continues forever.

1 Peter 2:1-5 WEB Putting away therefore all wickedness, all deceit, hypocrisies, envies, and all evil speaking, as newborn babies, long for the pure milk of the Word, that you may grow thereby, if indeed you have tasted that the Lord is gracious: coming to him, a living stone, rejected indeed by men, but chosen by God, precious. You also, as living stones, are built up as a spiritual house, to be a holy priesthood, to offer up spiritual sacrifices, acceptable to God through Jesus Christ.

1 Peter 3:15-17 WEB But sanctify the Lord God in your hearts: and always be ready to give an answer to everyone who asks you a reason concerning the hope that is in you, with humility and fear: having a good conscience; that, while you are spoken against as evildoers, they may be disappointed who curse your good way of life in Christ. For it is better, if it is God's will, that you suffer for doing well than for doing evil.

Mark 1:7-8 NASB After me One is coming who is mightier than I, and I am not fit to stoop down and untie the thong of His sandals. I baptized you with water; but He will baptize you with the Holy Spirit.

John 7:37-39 WEB "If anyone is thirsty, let him come to me and drink! He who believes in me, as the Scripture has said, from within him will flow rivers of living water." But he said this about the Spirit, which those believing in him were to receive. For the Holy Spirit was not yet given, because Jesus wasn't yet glorified.

John 14:25-27 NCV I have told you all these things while I am with you. But the Helper will teach you everything and will cause you to remember all that I told you. This Helper is the Holy Spirit whom the Father will send in my name. I leave you peace; my peace I give you. I do not give it to you as the world does. So don't let your hearts be troubled or afraid.

Acts 1:7-8 WEB He said to them, "It isn't for you to know times or seasons which the Father has set within his own authority. But you will receive power when the Holy Spirit has come upon you. You will be witnesses to me in Jerusalem, in all Judea and Samaria, and to the uttermost parts of the earth."

Acts 2:38-39 NKJV Then Peter said to them, "Repent, and let every one of you be baptized in the name of Jesus Christ for the remission of sins; and you shall receive the gift of the Holy Spirit. For the promise is to you and to your children, and to all who are afar off, as many as the Lord our God will call."

Romans 5:5-6 WEB And hope doesn't disappoint us, because God's love has been poured out into our hearts through the Holy Spirit who was given to us. For while we were yet weak, at the right time Christ died for the ungodly.

Romans 8:13-17 WEB For if you live after the flesh, you must die; but if by the Spirit you put to death the deeds of the body, you will live. For as many as are led by the Spirit of God, these are children of God. For you didn't receive the spirit of bondage again to fear, but you received the spirit of adoption, by whom we cry, "Abba! Father!" The Spirit himself testifies with our spirit that we are children of God; and if children, then heirs; heirs of God, and joint heirs with Christ; if indeed we suffer with him, that we may also be glorified with him.

Romans 8:26-27 NKJV Likewise the Spirit also helps in our weaknesses. For we do not know what we should pray for as we ought, but the Spirit Himself makes intercession for us with groanings which cannot be uttered. Now He who searches the hearts knows what the mind of the Spirit is, because He makes intercession for the saints according to the will of God.

1 Corinthians 2:9-10 NIV "No eye has seen, no ear has heard, no mind has conceived what God has prepared for those who love him"—but God has revealed it to us by his Spirit. The Spirit searches all things, even the deep things of God.

1 Corinthians 6:19-20 NIV Do you not know that your body is a temple of the Holy Spirit, who is in you, whom you have received from God? You are not your own; you were bought at a price. Therefore honor God with your body.

1 Corinthians 12:7-8 WEB But to each one is given the manifestation of the Spirit for the profit of all. For to one is given through the Spirit the word of wisdom, and to another the word of knowledge, according to the same Spirit.

Galatians 5:24-25 NIV Those who belong to Christ Jesus have crucified the sinful nature with its passions and desires. Since we live by the Spirit, let us keep in step with the Spirit.

Psalm 24:3-5 NKJV Who may ascend into the hill of the LORD? Or who may stand in His holy place? He who has clean hands and a pure heart, who has not lifted up his soul to an idol, nor sworn deceitfully. He shall receive blessing from the LORD.

Psalm 25:21 NLT May integrity and honesty protect me, for I put my hope in you.

Psalm 101:6-7 NASB He who walks in a blameless way is the one who will minister to me. He who practices deceit shall not dwell within my house; he who speaks falsehood shall not maintain his position before me.

Proverbs 12:17-22 NRSV Whoever speaks the truth gives honest evidence, but a false witness speaks deceitfully. Rash words are like sword thrusts, but the tongue of the wise brings healing. Truthful lips endure forever, but a lying tongue lasts only a moment. Deceit is in the mind of those who plan evil, but those who counsel peace have joy. No harm happens to the righteous, but the wicked are filled with trouble. Lying lips are an abomination to the LORD, but those who act faithfully are his delight.

Proverbs 28:18 NCV Innocent people will be kept safe, but those who are dishonest will suddenly be ruined.

2 Corinthians 1:12 NCV I can say it with a clear conscience: In everything we have done in the world, and especially with you, we have had an honest and sincere heart from God. We did this by God's grace, not by the kind of wisdom the world has.

Colossians 3:9-10 WNT Do not speak falsehoods to one another, for you have stripped off the old self with its doings, and have clothed yourselves with the new self which is being remoulded into full knowledge so as to become like Him who created it.

Deuteronomy 20:2-4 NRSV Before you engage in battle, the priest shall come forward and speak to the troops, and shall say to them: "Hear, O Israel! Today you are drawing near to do battle against your enemies. Do not lose heart, or be afraid, or panic, or be in dread of them; for it is the LORD your God who goes with you, to fight for you against your enemies, to give you victory."

Job 19:23-27 NRSV O that my words were written down! O that they were inscribed in a book! O that with an iron pen and with lead they were engraved on a rock forever! For I know that my Redeemer lives, and that at the last he will stand upon the earth; and after my skin has been thus destroyed, then in my flesh I shall see God, whom I shall see on my side, and my eyes shall behold, and not another. My heart faints within me!

Psalm 16:9-11 NRSV Therefore my heart is glad, and my soul rejoices; my body also rests secure. For you do not give me up to Sheol, or let your faithful one see the Pit. You show me the path of life. In your presence there is fullness of joy; in your right hand are pleasures forevermore.

Psalm 119:147 WEB I rise before dawn and cry for help. I put my hope in your words.

Romans 4:20-22 NCV He never doubted that God would keep his promise, and he never stopped believing. He grew stronger in his faith and gave praise to God. Abraham felt sure that God was able to do what he had promised. So "God accepted Abraham's faith, and that faith made him right with God."

Romans 5:3-5 NASB And not only this, but we also exult in our tribulations, knowing that tribulation brings about perseverance; and perseverance, proven character; and proven character, hope; and hope does not disappoint, because the love of God has been poured out within our hearts through the Holy Spirit who was given to us.

Romans 8:23-26 WEB We ourselves groan within ourselves, waiting for adoption, the redemption of our body. For we were saved in hope, but hope that is seen is not hope. For who hopes for that which he sees? But if we hope for that which we don't see, we wait for it with patience. In the same way, the Spirit also helps our weaknesses.

Romans 15:4-5 NKJV For whatever things were written before were written for our learning, that we through the patience and comfort of the Scriptures might have hope. Now may the God of patience and comfort grant you to be like-minded toward one another, according to Christ Jesus.

Romans 15:13 NCV I pray that the God who gives hope will fill you with much joy and peace while you trust in him. Then your hope will overflow by the power of the Holy Spirit.

Hebrews 6:19-20 TMB This hope we have as an anchor of the soul, both sure and steadfast, and which entereth into that within the veil, where the Forerunner has entered for us, even Jesus, who is made a high priest forever.

1 Peter 1:3-5 WEB Blessed be the God and Father of our Lord Jesus Christ, who according to his great mercy became the father of us again to a living hope by the resurrection of Jesus Christ from the dead, to an incorruptible and undefiled inheritance, that doesn't fade away, reserved in Heaven for you, who by the power of God are guarded through faith for a salvation ready to be revealed in the last time.

1 John 3:2-3 NIV Dear friends, now we are children of God, and what we will be has not yet been made known. But we know that when he appears, we shall be like him, for we shall see him as he is. Everyone who has this hope in him purifies himself, just as he is pure.

Deuteronomy 10:17-19 NRSV For the LORD your God is God of gods
. . . who executes justice for the orphan and the widow, and who loves
the strangers, providing them food and clothing. You shall also love the
stranger, for you were strangers in the land of Egypt.

Matthew 25:37-40 WEB Then the righteous will answer him, saying,
"Lord, when did we see you hungry, and feed you; or thirsty, and give
you a drink? When did we see you as a stranger, and take you in; or
naked, and clothe you? When did we see you sick, or in prison, and come
to you?" The King will answer them, "Most assuredly I tell you, inasmuch
as you did it to one of the least of these my brothers, you did it to me."

Luke 14:12-14 NASB When you give a luncheon or a dinner, do not
invite your friends or your brothers or your relatives or rich neighbors,
otherwise they may also invite you in return and that will be your
repayment. But when you give a reception, invite the poor, the crippled,
the lame, the blind, and you will be blessed, since they do not have the
means to repay you; for you will be repaid at the resurrection of the
righteous.

Romans 12:9-13 WEB Let love be without hypocrisy. Abhor that which
is evil. Cling to that which is good. In love of the brothers be tenderly
affectionate one to another; in honor preferring one another; not
lagging in diligence; fervent in spirit; serving the Lord; rejoicing in hope;
enduring in troubles; continuing steadfastly in prayer; contributing to
the needs of the saints; given to hospitality.

Hebrews 13:1-2 NLT Continue to love each other with true Christian
love. Don't forget to show hospitality to strangers, for some who have
done this have entertained angels without realizing it!

1 Peter 4:8-9 NASB Above all, keep fervent in your love for one another,
because love covers a multitude of sins. Be hospitable to one another
without complaint.

Psalm 25:8-9 NRSV Good and upright is the LORD; therefore he instructs sinners in the way. He leads the humble in what is right, and teaches the humble his way.

Psalm 145:14-16 NLT The LORD helps the fallen and lifts up those bent beneath their loads. All eyes look to you for help; you give them their food as they need it. When you open your hand, you satisfy the hunger and thirst of every living thing.

Proverbs 16:18-19 WEB Pride goes before destruction, and a haughty spirit before a fall. It is better to be of a lowly spirit with the poor, than to divide the plunder with the proud.

Proverbs 27:2 WEB Let another man praise you, and not your own mouth; a stranger, and not your own lips.

Isaiah 29:19 NIV Once more the humble will rejoice in the LORD; the needy will rejoice in the Holy One of Israel.

Isaiah 57:15 NKJV For thus says the High and Lofty One who inhabits eternity, whose name is Holy: "I dwell in the high and holy place, with him who has a contrite and humble spirit, to revive the spirit of the humble, and to revive the heart of the contrite ones."

Matthew 18:4 NCV The greatest person in the kingdom of heaven is the one who makes himself humble like this child.

John 3:30 TMB He must increase, but I must decrease.

Romans 12:16 NASB Be of the same mind toward one another; do not be haughty in mind, but associate with the lowly. Do not be wise in your own estimation.

Psalm 25:12-13 NKJV Who is the man that fears the LORD? Him shall He teach in the way He chooses. He himself shall dwell in prosperity.

Psalm 128:2-4 NRSV You shall eat the fruit of the labor of your hands; you shall be happy, and it shall go well with you. Your wife will be like a fruitful vine within your house; your children will be like olive shoots around your table. Thus shall the man be blessed who fears the LORD.

Proverbs 5:18-22 NRSV Let your fountain be blessed, and rejoice in the wife of your youth, a lovely deer, a graceful doe. May her breasts satisfy you at all times; may you be intoxicated always by her love. Why should you be intoxicated, my son, by another woman and embrace the bosom of an adulteress? For human ways are under the eyes of the LORD, and he examines all their paths. The iniquities of the wicked ensnare them, and they are caught in the toils of their sin.

Proverbs 18:22 WEB Whoever finds a wife finds a good thing, and obtains favor of Yahweh.

Proverbs 21:22 NASB A wise man scales the city of the mighty and brings down the stronghold in which they trust.

Proverbs 22:29 NASB Do you see a man skilled in his work? He will stand before kings; he will not stand before obscure men.

Proverbs 27:8 WEB As a bird that wanders from her nest, so is a man who wanders from his home.

Proverbs 27:19 WEB As water reflects a face, so a man's heart reflects the man.

Isaiah 54:5 WEB For your Maker is your husband; Yahweh of Armies is his name: and the Holy One of Israel is your Redeemer.

1 Corinthians 7:2-5 WEB Because of sexual immoralities, let each man have his own wife, and let each woman have her own husband. Let the husband render to his wife the affection owed her, and likewise also the wife to her husband. The wife doesn't have authority over her own body, but the husband. Likewise also the husband doesn't have authority over his own body, but the wife. Don't deprive one another, unless it is by consent for a season, that you may give yourselves to fasting and prayer.

Ephesians 5:25-28 WEB Husbands, love your wives, even as Christ also loved the assembly, and gave himself up for it; that he might sanctify it, having cleansed it by the washing of water with the word, that he might present the assembly to himself gloriously, not having spot or wrinkle or any such thing; but that it should be holy and without blemish. Even so husbands also ought to love their own wives as their own bodies. He who loves his own wife loves himself.

Colossians 3:19 NCV Husbands, love your wives and be gentle with them.

Titus 2:1-2, 6-8 WEB Say the things which fit the sound doctrine, that older men should be temperate, sensible, sober minded, sound in faith, in love, and in patience. . . . Likewise, exhort the younger men to be sober minded; in all things showing yourself an example of good works; in your teaching showing integrity, seriousness, incorruptibility, and soundness of speech that can't be condemned.

1 Peter 3:7 WEB You husbands, in the same way, live with your wives according to knowledge, giving honor to the woman, as to the weaker vessel, as being also joint heirs of the grace of life; that your prayers may not be hindered.

Exodus 20:4-6 NKJV You shall not make for yourself a carved image—any likeness of anything that is in heaven above, or that is in the earth beneath, or that is in the water under the earth; you shall not bow down to them nor serve them. For I, the Lord your God, am a jealous God, visiting the iniquity of the fathers upon the children to the third and fourth generations of those who hate Me, but showing mercy to thousands, to those who love Me and keep My commandments.

Deuteronomy 4:23-24 NIV Be careful not to forget the covenant of the Lord your God that he made with you; do not make for yourselves an idol in the form of anything the Lord your God has forbidden. For the Lord your God is a consuming fire, a jealous God.

Psalm 135:15-18 NRSV The idols of the nations are silver and gold, the work of human hands. They have mouths, but they do not speak; they have eyes, but they do not see; they have ears, but they do not hear, and there is no breath in their mouths. Those who make them and all who trust them shall become like them.

1 Corinthians 8:4-6 WEB We know that no idol is anything in the world, and that there is no other God but one. For though there are things that are called "gods," whether in the heavens or on earth; as there are many "gods" and many "lords;" yet to us there is one God, the Father, of whom are all things, and we for him; and one Lord, Jesus Christ, through whom are all things, and we live through him.

2 Corinthians 6:16-18 NRSV What agreement has the temple of God with idols? For we are the temple of the living God. Even as God said, "I will live in them, and walk among them; and I will be their God, and they shall be my people. Therefore come out from them, and be separate, says the Lord, and touch nothing unclean; then I will welcome you, and I will be your father, and you shall be my sons and daughters, says the Lord Almighty.

Romans 6:8-12 WEB But if we died with Christ, we believe that we will also live with him; knowing that Christ, being raised from the dead, dies no more. Death no more has dominion over him! For the death that he died, he died to sin one time; but the life that he lives, he lives to God. Thus consider yourselves also to be dead to sin, but alive to God in Christ Jesus our Lord. Therefore don't let sin reign in your mortal body, that you should obey it in its lusts.

2 Corinthians 5:17 NASB Therefore if anyone is in Christ, he is a new creature; the old things passed away; behold, new things have come.

Galatians 2:20-21 NIV I have been crucified with Christ and I no longer live, but Christ lives in me. The life I live in the body, I live by faith in the Son of God, who loved me and gave himself for me. I do not set aside the grace of God, for if righteousness could be gained through the law, Christ died for nothing!

Ephesians 2:4-7 NCV But God's mercy is great, and he loved us very much. Though we were spiritually dead because of the things we did against God, he gave us new life with Christ. You have been saved by God's grace. And he raised us up with Christ and gave us a seat with him in the heavens. He did this for those in Christ Jesus so that for all future time he could show the very great riches of his grace by being kind to us in Christ Jesus.

Ephesians 2:19-22 WEB So then you are no longer strangers and foreigners, but you are fellow citizens with the saints, and of the household of God, being built on the foundation of the apostles and prophets, Christ Jesus himself being the chief cornerstone; in whom the whole building, fitted together, grows into a holy temple in the Lord; in whom you also are built together for a habitation of God in the Spirit.

Psalm 16:5-7 NRSV The LORD is my chosen portion and my cup; you hold my lot. The boundary lines have fallen for me in pleasant places; I have a goodly heritage. I bless the LORD who gives me counsel; in the night also my heart instructs me.

Psalm 25:12-14 WEB What man is he who fears Yahweh? He shall instruct him in the way that he shall choose. His soul shall dwell at ease. His seed shall inherit the land. The friendship of Yahweh is with those who fear him. He will show them his covenant.

Psalm 37:18-19 WEB Yahweh knows the days of the perfect. Their inheritance shall be forever. They shall not be disappointed in the time of evil. In the days of famine they shall be satisfied.

Acts 20:32 NASB And now I commend you to God and to the word of His grace, which is able to build you up and to give you the inheritance among all those who are sanctified.

Ephesians 1:11-14 WEB In whom also we were assigned an inheritance, having been foreordained according to the purpose of him who works all things after the counsel of his will; to the end that we should be to the praise of his glory, we who had before hoped in Christ: in whom you also, having heard the word of the truth, the Good News of your salvation,— in whom, having also believed, you were sealed with the Holy Spirit of promise, who is a pledge of our inheritance, to the redemption of God's own possession, to the praise of his glory.

Hebrews 11:8 NIV By faith Abraham, when called to go to a place he would later receive as his inheritance, obeyed and went, even though he did not know where he was going.

Psalm 7:8-10 NRSV The LORD judges the peoples; judge me, O LORD, according to my righteousness and according to the integrity that is in me. O let the evil of the wicked come to an end, but establish the righteous, you who test the minds and hearts, O righteous God. God is my shield, who saves the upright in heart.

Proverbs 11:1-3 WEB A false balance is an abomination to Yahweh, but accurate weights are his delight. When pride comes, then comes shame, but with humility comes wisdom. The integrity of the upright shall guide them, but the perverseness of the treacherous shall destroy them.

Ephesians 4:1-3 NKJV I, therefore, the prisoner of the Lord, beseech you to walk worthy of the calling with which you were called, with all lowliness and gentleness, with longsuffering, bearing with one another in love, endeavoring to keep the unity of the Spirit in the bond of peace.

Ephesians 4:25-30 WEB Therefore, putting away falsehood, speak truth each one with his neighbor. For we are members one of another. "Be angry, and don't sin." Don't let the sun go down on your wrath, neither give place to the devil. Let him who stole steal no more; but rather let him labor, working with his hands the thing that is good, that he may have something to give to him who has need. Let no corrupt speech proceed out of your mouth, but such as is good for building up as the need may be, that it may give grace to those who hear. Don't grieve the Holy Spirit of God, in whom you were sealed to the day of redemption.

Titus 2:6-8 NLT In the same way, encourage the young men to live wisely in all they do. And you yourself must be an example to them by doing good deeds of every kind. Let everything you do reflect the integrity and seriousness of your teaching. Let your teaching be so correct that it can't be criticized. Then those who want to argue will be ashamed because they won't have anything bad to say about us.

Deuteronomy 4:23-24 NRSV So be careful not to forget the covenant that the LORD your God made with you, and not to make for yourselves an idol in the form of anything that the LORD your God has forbidden you. For the LORD your God is a devouring fire, a jealous God.

Psalm 73:1-3 NLT Truly God is good to Israel, to those whose hearts are pure. But as for me, I came so close to the edge of the cliff! My feet were slipping, and I was almost gone. For I envied the proud when I saw them prosper despite their wickedness.

Proverbs 14:30 NCV Peace of mind means a healthy body, but jealousy will rot your bones.

Proverbs 23:17-18 NIV Do not let your heart envy sinners, but always be zealous for the fear of the LORD. There is surely a future hope for you, and your hope will not be cut off.

Song of Solomon 8:6 NCV Put me like a seal on your heart, like a seal on your arm. Love is as strong as death; jealousy is as strong as the grave. Love bursts into flames and burns like a hot fire.

1 Corinthians 13:4-7 WEB Love is patient and is kind; love doesn't envy. Love doesn't brag, is not proud, doesn't behave itself inappropriately, doesn't seek its own way, is not provoked, takes no account of evil; doesn't rejoice in unrighteousness, but rejoices with the truth; bears all things, believes all things, hopes all things, endures all things.

Galatians 6:3-5 WEB For if a man thinks himself to be something when he is nothing, he deceives himself. But let each man test his own work, and then he will take pride in himself and not in his neighbor. For each man will bear his own burden.

John 1:14-18 WEB The Word became flesh, and lived among us. We saw his glory, such glory as of the one and only Son of the Father, full of grace and truth. John testified about him. He cried out, saying, "This was he of whom I said, 'He who comes after me has surpassed me, for he was before me.'" From his fullness we all received grace upon grace. For the law was given through Moses. Grace and truth were realized through Jesus Christ. No one has seen God at any time. The one and only Son, who is in the bosom of the Father, he has declared him.

John 1:29 NASB The next day he saw Jesus coming to him and said, "Behold, the Lamb of God who takes away the sin of the world!"

John 3:35-36 NKJV The Father loves the Son, and has given all things into His hand. He who believes in the Son has everlasting life; and he who does not believe the Son shall not see life, but the wrath of God abides on him.

John 6:32-35 WEB Jesus therefore said to them, "Most certainly, I tell you, it wasn't Moses who gave you the bread out of heaven, but my Father gives you the true bread out of heaven. For the bread of God is that which comes down out of heaven, and gives life to the world." They said therefore to him, "Lord, always give us this bread." Jesus said to them, "I am the bread of life. He who comes to me will not be hungry, and he who believes in me will never be thirsty."

John 8:12 NIV When Jesus spoke again to the people, he said, "I am the light of the world. Whoever follows me will never walk in darkness, but will have the light of life."

John 10:9-10 NIV I am the gate; whoever enters through me will be saved. He will come in and go out, and find pasture. The thief comes only to steal and kill and destroy; I have come that they may have life, and have it to the full.

Romans 8:9-10 NKJV But you are not in the flesh but in the Spirit, if indeed the Spirit of God dwells in you. Now if anyone does not have the Spirit of Christ, he is not His. And if Christ is in you, the body is dead because of sin, but the Spirit is life because of righteousness.

2 Corinthians 1:20 NLT For all of God's promises have been fulfilled in him. That is why we say "Amen" when we give glory to God through Christ.

Philippians 4:12-13 NLT I know how to live on almost nothing or with everything. I have learned the secret of living in every situation, whether it is with a full stomach or empty, with plenty or little. For I can do everything with the help of Christ who gives me the strength I need.

Colossians 2:6-7 NIV So then, just as you received Christ Jesus as Lord, continue to live in him, rooted and built up in him, strengthened in the faith as you were taught, and overflowing with thankfulness.

Colossians 3:1-4 WEB If then you were raised together with Christ, seek the things that are above, where Christ is, seated on the right hand of God. Set your mind on the things that are above, not on the things that are on the earth. For you died, and your life is hidden with Christ in God. When Christ, our life, is revealed, then you will also be revealed with him in glory.

Hebrews 12:2 WEB Looking to Jesus, the author and perfecter of faith, who for the joy that was set before him endured the cross, despising its shame, and has sat down at the right hand of the throne of God.

Hebrews 13:8 NCV Jesus Christ is the same yesterday, today, and forever.

1 John 5:1 NIV Everyone who believes that Jesus is the Christ is born of God, and everyone who loves the father loves his child as well.

1 Samuel 2:1-2 NCV Hannah prayed: "The LORD has filled my heart with joy; I feel very strong in the LORD. I can laugh at my enemies; I am glad because you have helped me! There is no one holy like the LORD. There is no God but you; there is no Rock like our God."

Psalm 4:7 NLT You have given me greater joy than those who have abundant harvests of grain and wine.

Psalm 16:11 NIV You have made known to me the path of life; you will fill me with joy in your presence, with eternal pleasures at your right hand.

Psalm 51:12 NASB Restore to me the joy of Your salvation and sustain me with a willing spirit.

Psalm 89:15-16 NLT Happy are those who hear the joyful call to worship, for they will walk in the light of your presence, LORD. They rejoice all day long in your wonderful reputation. They exult in your righteousness.

Psalm 100:1-3 NRSV Make a joyful noise to the LORD, all the earth. Worship the LORD with gladness; come into his presence with singing. Know that the LORD is God. It is he that made us, and we are his; we are his people, and the sheep of his pasture.

Proverbs 12:20 WEB Deceit is in the heart of those who plot evil, but joy comes to the promoters of peace.

Isaiah 55:12 NKJV For you shall go out with joy, and be led out with peace; the mountains and the hills shall break forth into singing before you, and all the trees of the field shall clap their hands.

Psalm 7:6-8 NKJV Arise, O LORD, in Your anger; lift Yourself up because of the rage of my enemies; rise up for me to the judgment You have commanded! So the congregation of the peoples shall surround You; for their sakes, therefore, return on high. The LORD shall judge the peoples; judge me, O LORD, according to my righteousness, and according to my integrity within me.

Psalm 119:17-20 NRSV Deal bountifully with your servant, so that I may live and observe your word. Open my eyes, so that I may behold wondrous things out of your law. I live as an alien in the land; do not hide your commandments from me. My soul is consumed with longing for your ordinances at all times.

Isaiah 26:7-9 NRSV The way of the righteous is level; O Just One, you make smooth the path of the righteous. In the path of your judgments, O LORD, we wait for you; your name and your renown are the soul's desire. My soul yearns for you in the night, my spirit within me earnestly seeks you. For when your judgments are in the earth, the inhabitants of the world learn righteousness.

John 5:30 NIV By myself I can do nothing; I judge only as I hear, and my judgment is just, for I seek not to please myself but him who sent me.

John 12:47-48 NKJV And if anyone hears My words and does not believe, I do not judge him; for I did not come to judge the world but to save the world. He who rejects Me, and does not receive My words, has that which judges him—the word that I have spoken will judge him in the last day.

Romans 2:1 NCV If you think you can judge others, you are wrong. When you judge them, you are really judging yourself guilty, because you do the same things they do.

Romans 2:5-6 WEB But according to your hardness and unrepentant heart you are treasuring up for yourself wrath in the day of wrath, revelation, and of the righteous judgment of God; who "will pay back to everyone according to their works."

Romans 11:33 WEB Oh the depth of the riches both of the wisdom and the knowledge of God! How unsearchable are his judgments, and his ways past tracing out!

1 Corinthians 11:31-32 WNT If, however, we estimated ourselves aright, we should not be judged. But when we are judged by the Lord, chastisement follows, to save us from being condemned along with the world.

Hebrews 4:13 NLT Nothing in all creation can hide from him. Everything is naked and exposed before his eyes. This is the God to whom we must explain all that we have done.

Hebrews 10:30-31 NIV For we know him who said, "It is mine to avenge; I will repay," and again, "The Lord will judge his people." It is a dreadful thing to fall into the hands of the living God.

James 2:10-13 WEB For whoever shall keep the whole law, and yet stumble in one point, he has become guilty of all. For he who said, "Do not commit adultery," also said, "Do not commit murder." Now if you do not commit adultery, but murder, you have become a transgressor of the law. So speak, and so do, as men who are to be judged by a law of freedom. For judgment is without mercy to him who has shown no mercy. Mercy triumphs over judgment.

James 4:11-12 NKJV Do not speak evil of one another, brethren. He who speaks evil of a brother and judges his brother, speaks evil of the law and judges the law. But if you judge the law, you are not a doer of the law but a judge. There is one Lawgiver, who is able to save and to destroy. Who are you to judge another?

1 Samuel 24:10 NIV This day you have seen with your own eyes how the Lord delivered you into my hands in the cave. Some urged me to kill you, but I spared you; I said, "I will not lift my hand against my master, because he is the Lord's anointed."

Psalm 7:9-12 NRSV O let the evil of the wicked come to an end, but establish the righteous, you who test the minds and hearts, O righteous God. God is my shield, who saves the upright in heart. God is a righteous judge, and a God who has indignation every day. If one does not repent, God will whet his sword; he has bent and strung his bow.

Psalm 89:14 WEB Righteousness and justice are the foundation of your throne.

John 5:22-23 WEB For the Father judges no one, but he has given all judgment to the Son, that all may honor the Son, even as they honor the Father.

1 Corinthians 6:1-5 WEB Dare any of you, having a matter against his neighbor, go to law before the unrighteous, and not before the saints? Don't you know that the saints will judge the world? And if the world is judged by you, are you unworthy to judge the smallest matters? Don't you know that we will judge angels? How much more, things that pertain to this life? If then, you have to judge things pertaining to this life, do you set them to judge who are of no account in the assembly? I say this to move you to shame. Isn't there even one wise man among you who would be able to decide between his brothers?

1 Peter 1:17-19 NKJV And if you call on the Father, who without partiality judges according to each one's work, conduct yourselves . . . in fear; knowing that you were not redeemed with corruptible things, like silver or gold, from your aimless conduct received by tradition from your fathers, but with the precious blood of Christ, as of a lamb without blemish and without spot.

Psalm 31:21 NKJV Blessed be the LORD, for He has shown me His marvelous kindness in a strong city!

Matthew 25:34-36 WEB Come, blessed of my Father, inherit the kingdom prepared for you from the foundation of the world; for I was hungry, and you gave me food to eat; I was thirsty, and you gave me drink; I was a stranger, and you took me in; I was naked, and you clothed me; I was sick, and you visited me; I was in prison, and you came to me.

Luke 6:35-36 NIV But love your enemies, do good to them, and lend to them without expecting to get anything back. Then your reward will be great, and you will be sons of the Most High, because he is kind to the ungrateful and wicked. Be merciful, just as your Father is merciful.

Romans 12:10-13 NASB Be devoted to one another in brotherly love; give preference to one another in honor; not lagging behind in diligence, fervent in spirit, serving the Lord; rejoicing in hope, persevering in tribulation, devoted to prayer, contributing to the needs of the saints, practicing hospitality.

1 Corinthians 13:4 WNT Love is patient and kind. Love knows neither envy nor jealousy. Love is not forward and self-assertive, nor boastful and conceited.

Ephesians 4:32 NLT Be kind to each other, tenderhearted, forgiving one another, just as God through Christ has forgiven you.

Colossians 3:12-13 WEB Put on therefore, as God's chosen ones, holy and beloved, a heart of compassion, kindness, lowliness, humility, and perseverance; bearing with one another, and forgiving each other, if any man has a complaint against any; even as Christ forgave you, so you also do.

Proverbs 6:6-9 NRSV Go to the ant, you lazybones; consider its ways, and be wise. Without having any chief or officer or ruler, it prepares its food in summer, and gathers its sustenance in harvest. How long will you lie there, O lazybones? When will you rise from your sleep?

Proverbs 14:23 NIV All hard work brings a profit, but mere talk leads only to poverty.

Proverbs 18:9 WEB One who is slack in his work is brother to him who is a master of destruction.

Proverbs 26:13-16 NLT The lazy person is full of excuses, saying, "I can't go outside because there might be a lion on the road! Yes, I'm sure there's a lion out there!" As a door turns back and forth on its hinges, so the lazy person turns over in bed. Some people are so lazy that they won't lift a finger to feed themselves. Lazy people consider themselves smarter than seven wise counselors.

2 Thessalonians 3:7-12 WEB For you know how you ought to imitate us. For we didn't behave ourselves rebelliously among you, neither did we eat bread from one's hand without paying for it, but in labor and travail, worked night and day, that we might not burden any of you; not because we don't have the right, but to make ourselves an example to you, that you should imitate us. For even when we were with you, we commanded you this: "If anyone will not work, neither let him eat." For we hear of some who walk among you in rebellion, who don't work at all, but are busybodies. Now those who are that way, we command and exhort in the Lord Jesus Christ, that with quietness they work, and eat their own bread.

Hebrews 6:11-12 NASB And we desire that each one of you show the same diligence so as to realize the full assurance of hope until the end, so that you will not be sluggish, but imitators of those who through faith and patience inherit the promises.

Acts 1:24–25 WEB They prayed, and said, "You, Lord, who know the hearts of all men, show which one of these two you have chosen to take part in this ministry and apostleship."

Acts 20:28 NASB Be on guard for yourselves and for all the flock, among which the Holy Spirit has made you overseers, to shepherd the church of God which He purchased with His own blood.

1 Corinthians 12:28–31 NRSV And God has appointed in the church first apostles, second prophets, third teachers; then deeds of power, then gifts of healing, forms of assistance, forms of leadership, various kinds of tongues. Are all apostles? Are all prophets? Are all teachers? Do all work miracles? Do all possess gifts of healing? Do all speak in tongues? Do all interpret? But strive for the greater gifts.

Ephesians 4:11–13 WEB He gave some to be apostles; and some, prophets; and some, evangelists; and some, shepherds and teachers; for the perfecting of the saints, to the work of serving, to the building up of the body of Christ; until we all attain to the unity of the faith, and of the knowledge of the Son of God, to a full grown man, to the measure of the stature of the fullness of Christ.

Titus 1:7–9 WNT For, as God's steward, a minister must be of blameless life, not over-fond of having his own way, not a man of a passionate temper nor a hard drinker, not given to blows nor greedy of gain, but hospitable to strangers, a lover of goodness, sober-minded, upright, saintly, self-controlled; holding fast to the faithful Message.

1 Peter 5:2–4 NKJV Shepherd the flock of God which is among you, serving as overseers, not by compulsion but willingly, not for dishonest gain but eagerly; nor as being lords over those entrusted to you, but being examples to the flock; and when the Chief Shepherd appears, you will receive the crown of glory that does not fade away.

Exodus 3:11-12 NASB But Moses said to God, "Who am I, that I should go to Pharaoh, and that I should bring the sons of Israel out of Egypt?" And He said, "Certainly I will be with you, and this shall be the sign to you that it is I who have sent you: when you have brought the people out of Egypt, you shall worship God at this mountain."

Exodus 4:10-12 NRSV Moses said to the LORD, "O my LORD, I have never been eloquent, neither in the past nor even now that you have spoken to your servant; but I am slow of speech and slow of tongue." Then the LORD said to him, "Who gives speech to mortals? Who makes them mute or deaf, seeing or blind? Is it not I, the LORD? Now go, and I will be with your mouth and teach you what you are to speak."

2 Samuel 23:3-4 NKJV He who rules over men must be just, ruling in the fear of God. And he shall be like the light of the morning when the sun rises, a morning without clouds, like the tender grass springing out of the earth, by clear shining after rain.

Psalm 84:10 WEB For a day in your courts is better than a thousand. I would rather be a doorkeeper in the house of my God, than to dwell in the tents of wickedness.

Proverbs 11:14 NLT Without wise leadership, a nation falls; with many counselors, there is safety.

Jeremiah 5:30-31 NRSV An appalling and horrible thing has happened in the land: the prophets prophesy falsely, and the priests rule as the prophets direct; my people love to have it so.

Jeremiah 42:4 NASB I have heard you. Behold, I am going to pray to the LORD your God in accordance with your words; and I will tell you the whole message which the LORD will answer you. I will not keep back a word from you.

Mark 10:42-45 WEB Jesus summoned them, and said to them, "You know that they who are recognized as rulers over the nations lord it over them, and their great ones exercise authority over them. But it shall not be so among you, but whoever wants to become great among you shall be your servant. Whoever of you wants to become first among you, shall be bondservant of all. For the Son of Man also came not to be served, but to serve, and to give his life as a ransom for many."

John 13:14-17 WEB If I then, the Lord and the Teacher, have washed your feet, you also ought to wash one another's feet. For I have given you an example, that you also should do as I have done to you. Most certainly I tell you, a servant is not greater than his lord, neither one who is sent greater than he who sent him. If you know these things, blessed are you if you do them.

Romans 12:6-8 NKJV Having then gifts differing according to the grace that is given to us, let us use them: if prophecy, let us prophesy in proportion to our faith; or ministry, let us use it in our ministering; he who teaches, in teaching; he who exhorts, in exhortation; he who gives, with liberality; he who leads, with diligence; he who shows mercy, with cheerfulness.

1 Thessalonians 5:12-13 NASB But we request of you, brethren, that you appreciate those who diligently labor among you, and have charge over you in the Lord and give you instruction, and that you esteem them very highly in love because of their work.

1 Timothy 3:8-13 WEB Deacons, in the same way, must be reverent, not double-tongued, not addicted to much wine, not greedy for money; holding the mystery of the faith in a pure conscience. Let them also first be tested; then let them serve as deacons, if they are blameless. Their wives in the same way must be reverent, not slanderers, temperate, faithful in all things. Let deacons be husbands of one wife, ruling their children and their own houses well. For those who have served well as deacons gain for themselves a good standing, and great boldness in the faith which is in Christ Jesus.

Psalm 119:45-47 WEB I will walk in liberty, for I have sought your precepts. I will also speak of your statutes before kings, and will not be disappointed. I will delight myself in your commandments, because I love them.

Isaiah 61:1-3 NRSV The spirit of the Lord GOD is upon me, because the LORD has anointed me; he has sent me to bring good news to the oppressed, to bind up the brokenhearted, to proclaim liberty to the captives, and release to the prisoners; to proclaim the year of the LORD's favor, and the day of vengeance of our God; to comfort all who mourn; to provide for those who mourn in Zion— to give them a garland instead of ashes, the oil of gladness instead of mourning, the mantle of praise instead of a faint spirit. They will be called oaks of righteousness, the planting of the LORD, to display his glory.

Romans 7:6 NLT But now we have been released from the law, for we died with Christ, and we are no longer captive to its power. Now we can really serve God, not in the old way by obeying the letter of the law, but in the new way, by the Spirit.

1 Corinthians 6:12 NASB All things are lawful for me, but not all things are profitable. All things are lawful for me, but I will not be mastered by anything.

1 Corinthians 8:9 NLT But you must be careful with this freedom of yours. Do not cause a brother or sister with a weaker conscience to stumble.

2 Corinthians 3:17 WEB Now the Lord is the Spirit and where the spirit of the Lord is, there is liberty.

Galatians 4:6-7 WEB And because you are children, God sent out the Spirit of his Son into your hearts, crying, "Abba, Father!" So you are no longer a bondservant, but a son; and if a son, then an heir of God through Christ.

Psalm 27:1 NCV The LORD is my light and the one who saves me. I fear no one.

Psalm 36:9 NKJV For with You is the fountain of life; in Your light we see light.

Psalm 43:3 WEB Oh, send out your light and your truth. Let them lead me.

Psalm 119:105 TMB Thy word is a lamp unto my feet, and a light unto my path.

Psalm 119:129-130 NASB Your testimonies are wonderful; therefore my soul observes them. The unfolding of Your words gives light; it gives understanding to the simple.

Proverbs 6:23 NLT For these commands and this teaching are a lamp to light the way ahead of you. The correction of discipline is the way to life.

Isaiah 58:8 NKJV Then your light shall break forth like the morning, your healing shall spring forth speedily, and your righteousness shall go before you; the glory of the LORD shall be your rear guard.

Isaiah 60:19-20 NRSV The sun shall no longer be your light by day, nor for brightness shall the moon give light to you by night; but the LORD will be your everlasting light, and your God will be your glory. Your sun shall no more go down, or your moon withdraw itself; for the LORD will be your everlasting light, and your days of mourning shall be ended.

Matthew 5:14-16 NRSV You are the light of the world. A city built on a hill cannot be hid. No one after lighting a lamp puts it under the bushel basket, but on the lampstand, and it gives light to all in the house. In the same way, let your light shine before others, so that they may see your good works and give glory to your Father in heaven.

John 1:4–9 WEB In him was life, and the life was the light of men. The light shines in the darkness, and the darkness hasn't overcome it. There came a man, sent from God, whose name was John. The same came as a witness, that he might testify about the light, that all might believe through him. He was not the light, but was sent that he might testify about the light. The true light that enlightens everyone was coming into the world.

John 3:19–21 WEB This is the judgment, that the light has come into the world, and men loved the darkness rather than the light; for their works were evil. For everyone who does evil hates the light, and doesn't come to the light, lest his works would be exposed. But he who does the truth comes to the light, that his works may be revealed, that they have been done in God.

John 8:12 NLT Jesus said to the people, "I am the light of the world. If you follow me, you won't be stumbling through the darkness, because you will have the light that leads to life."

Ephesians 5:14 NIV For it is light that makes everything visible. This is why it is said: "Wake up, O sleeper, rise from the dead, and Christ will shine on you."

Philippians 2:14–16 WEB Do all things without murmurings and disputes, that you may become blameless and harmless, children of God without blemish in the midst of a crooked and perverse generation, among whom you are seen as lights in the world, holding up the word of life.

1 John 1:5–7 NASB This is the message we have heard from Him and announce to you, that God is Light, and in Him there is no darkness at all. If we say that we have fellowship with Him and yet walk in the darkness, we lie and do not practice the truth; but if we walk in the Light as He Himself is in the Light, we have fellowship with one another, and the blood of Jesus His Son cleanses us from all sin.

Deuteronomy 31:8 NIV The LORD himself goes before you and will be with you; he will never leave you nor forsake you. Do not be afraid; do not be discouraged.

Job 19:13-14, 17, 19, 23-25 NRSV He has put my family far from me, and my acquaintances are wholly estranged from me. My relatives and my close friends have failed me. . . . My breath is repulsive to my wife; I am loathsome to my own family. . . . All my intimate friends abhor me, and those whom I loved have turned against me. . . . O that my words were written down! O that they were inscribed in a book! O that with an iron pen and with lead they were engraved on a rock forever! For I know that my Redeemer lives, and that at the last he will stand upon the earth."

Psalm 31:12-15 NRSV I have passed out of mind like one who is dead; I have become like a broken vessel. For I hear the whispering of many— terror all around!—as they scheme together against me, as they plot to take my life. But I trust in you, O LORD; I say, "You are my God." My times are in your hand.

Psalm 68:5-6 NIV A father to the fatherless, a defender of widows, is God in his holy dwelling. God sets the lonely in families, he leads forth the prisoners with singing; but the rebellious live in a sun-scorched land.

Psalm 142:4-7 NASB There is no one who regards me; there is no escape for me; no one cares for my soul. I cried out to You, O LORD; I said, "You are my refuge, my portion in the land of the living. Give heed to my cry, for I am brought very low; deliver me from my persecutors, for they are too strong for me. Bring my soul out of prison."

John 16:32 NKJV And yet I am not alone, because the Father is with Me.

2 Timothy 4:16-17 WEB No one came to help me, but all left me. May it not be held against them. But the Lord stood by me, and strengthened me.

Exodus 15:3 TMB The Lord is a man of war; the Lord is His name.

2 Chronicles 16:9 NKJV For the eyes of the Lord run to and fro throughout the whole earth, to show Himself strong on behalf of those whose heart is loyal to Him.

Nehemiah 9:6 WEB You are Yahweh, even you alone. You have made heaven, the heaven of heavens, with all their army, the earth and all things that are on it, the seas and all that is in them, and you preserve them all. The army of heaven worships you.

Psalm 33:13-15 NCV The Lord looks down from heaven and sees every person. From his throne he watches all who live on earth. He made their hearts and understands everything they do.

Psalm 33:18-20 NRSV Truly the eye of the Lord is on those who fear him, on those who hope in his steadfast love, to deliver their soul from death, and to keep them alive in famine. Our soul waits for the Lord; he is our help and shield.

Psalm 107:21-22 NLT Let them praise the Lord for his great love and for all his wonderful deeds to them. Let them offer sacrifices of thanksgiving and sing joyfully about his glorious acts.

Psalm 138:1-5 NRSV I give you thanks, O Lord, with my whole heart; before the gods I sing your praise; I bow down toward your holy temple and give thanks to your name for your steadfast love and your faithfulness; for you have exalted your name and your word above everything On the day I called, you answered me, you increased my strength of soul. All the kings of the earth shall praise you, O Lord, for they have heard the words of your mouth. They shall sing of the ways of the Lord, for great is the glory of the Lord.

Psalm 149:1-5 NRSV Praise the LORD! Sing to the LORD a new song, his praise in the assembly of the faithful. Let Israel be glad in its Maker; let the children of Zion rejoice in their King. Let them praise his name with dancing, making melody to him with tambourine and lyre. For the LORD takes pleasure in his people; he adorns the humble with victory. Let the faithful exult in glory; let them sing for joy on their couches.

Isaiah 45:11-13 NRSV Thus says the LORD, the Holy One of Israel, and its Maker: Will you question me about my children, or command me concerning the work of my hands? I made the earth, and created humankind upon it; it was my hands that stretched out the heavens, and I commanded all their host. I have aroused Cyrus in righteousness, and I will make all his paths straight; he shall build my city and set my exiles free, not for price or reward, says the LORD of hosts.

Isaiah 30:18 NASB Therefore the LORD longs to be gracious to you, and therefore He waits on high to have compassion on you. For the LORD is a God of justice; how blessed are all those who long for Him.

Daniel 4:2-3 NKJV I thought it good to declare the signs and wonders that the Most High God has worked for me. How great are His signs, and how mighty His wonders! His kingdom is an everlasting kingdom, and His dominion is from generation to generation.

2 Thessalonians 2:16-17 NIV May our Lord Jesus Christ himself and God our Father, who loved us and by his grace gave us eternal encouragement and good hope, encourage your hearts and strengthen you in every good deed and word.

Revelation 4:11 NASB Worthy are You, our Lord and our God, to receive glory and honor and power; for You created all things, and because of Your will they existed, and were created.

Deuteronomy 6:5 NLT And you must love the LORD your God with all your heart, all your soul, and all your strength.

Deuteronomy 32:10-12 NRSV He sustained him in a desert land, in a howling wilderness waste; he shielded him, cared for him, guarded him as the apple of his eye. As an eagle stirs up its nest, and hovers over its young; as it spreads its wings, takes them up, and bears them aloft on its pinions, the LORD alone guided him; no foreign god was with him.

Proverbs 15:16-17 NASB Better is a little with the fear of the LORD than great treasure and turmoil with it. Better is a dish of vegetables where love is than a fattened ox served with hatred.

Song of Solomon 8:6-7 TMB Set me as a seal upon thine heart, as a seal upon thine arm; for love is strong as death; jealousy is cruel as the grave; the coals thereof are coals of fire, which hath a most vehement flame. Many waters cannot quench love, neither can the floods drown it; if a man would give all the substance of his house for love, it would utterly be contemned.

Ezekiel 16:7-9 NRSV "Like a plant of the field." You grew up and became tall and arrived at full womanhood; your breasts were formed, and your hair had grown; yet you were naked and bare. I passed by you again and looked on you; you were at the age for love. I spread the edge of my cloak over you, and covered your nakedness: I pledged myself to you and entered into a covenant with you, says the Lord GOD, and you became mine. Then I bathed you with water and washed off the blood from you, and anointed you with oil.

John 3:16 NCV God loved the world so much that he gave his one and only Son so that whoever believes in him may not be lost, but have eternal life.

1 Corinthians 13:1-3 NKJV Though I speak with the tongues of men and of angels, but have not love, I have become sounding brass or a clanging cymbal. And though I have the gift of prophecy, and understand all mysteries and all knowledge, and though I have all faith, so that I could remove mountains, but have not love, I am nothing. And though I bestow all my goods to feed the poor . . . but have not love, it profits me nothing.

1 Corinthians 13:4-8 WEB Love is patient and is kind; love doesn't envy. Love doesn't brag, is not proud, doesn't behave itself inappropriately, doesn't seek its own way, is not provoked, takes no account of evil; doesn't rejoice in unrighteousness, but rejoices with the truth; bears all things, believes all things, hopes all things, endures all things. Love never fails.

Ephesians 5:1-2 NCV You are God's children whom he loves, so try to be like him. Live a life of love just as Christ loved us and gave himself for us as a sweet-smelling offering and sacrifice to God.

Hebrews 13:1-3 WEB Let brotherly love continue. Don't forget to show hospitality to strangers, for in doing so, some have entertained angels without knowing it. Remember those who are in bonds, as bound with them; and those who are ill-treated, since you are also in the body.

1 Peter 4:8-9 NIV Above all, love each other deeply, because love covers over a multitude of sins. Offer hospitality to one another without grumbling.

1 John 3:16-17 NIV This is how we know what love is: Jesus Christ laid down his life for us. And we ought to lay down our lives for our brothers. If anyone has material possessions and sees his brother in need but has no pity on him, how can the love of God be in him?

Ecclesiastes 4:9–11 NKJV Two are better than one, because they have a good reward for their labor. For if they fall, one will lift up his companion. But woe to him who is alone when he falls, for he has no one to help him up. Again, if two lie down together, they will keep warm; but how can one be warm alone?

Matthew 12:25 WEB Knowing their thoughts, Jesus said to them, "Every kingdom divided against itself is brought to desolation, and every city or house divided against itself will not stand."

Matthew 19:4–6 NCV Jesus answered, ". . . When God made the world, 'he made them male and female.' And God said, 'So a man will leave his father and mother and be united with his wife, and the two will become one body.' So there are not two, but one. God has joined the two together, so no one should separate them."

Romans 15:5–6 NIV May the God who gives endurance and encouragement give you a spirit of unity among yourselves as you follow Christ Jesus, so that with one heart and mouth you may glorify the God and Father of our Lord Jesus Christ.

1 Corinthians 7:3–9 WEB Let the husband render to his wife the affection owed her, and likewise also the wife to her husband. The wife doesn't have authority over her own body, but the husband. Likewise also the husband doesn't have authority over his own body, but the wife. Don't deprive one another, unless it is by consent for a season, that you may give yourselves to fasting and prayer, and may be together again, that Satan doesn't tempt you because of your lack of self-control. But this I say by way of concession, not of commandment. Yet I wish that all men were like me. However each man has his own gift from God, one of this kind, and another of that kind. But I say to the unmarried and to widows, it is good for them if they remain even as I am. But if they don't have self-control, let them marry. For it's better to marry than to burn.

Ephesians 5:31–33 WNT "For this reason a man is to leave his father and his mother and be united to his wife, and the two shall be as one." That is a great truth hitherto kept secret: I mean the truth concerning Christ and the Church. Yet I insist that among you also, each man is to love his own wife as much as he loves himself, and let a married woman see to it that she treats her husband with respect.

Colossians 3:12–15 WNT Clothe yourselves therefore, as God's own people holy and dearly loved, with tender-heartedness, kindness, lowliness of mind, meekness, long-suffering; bearing with one another and readily forgiving each other, if any one has a grievance against another. Just as the Lord has forgiven you, you also must forgive. And over all these put on love, which is the perfect bond of union; and let the peace which Christ gives settle all questionings in your hearts.

1 Thessalonians 3:12–13 WEB And the Lord make you to increase and abound in love one toward another, and toward all men, even as we also do toward you, to the end he may establish your hearts blameless in holiness before our God and Father, at the coming of our Lord Jesus with all his saints.

Hebrews 13:4–5 NLT Give honor to marriage, and remain faithful to one another in marriage. God will surely judge people who are immoral and those who commit adultery. Stay away from the love of money; be satisfied with what you have. For God has said, "I will never fail you. I will never forsake you."

James 4:7–8 NCV So give yourselves completely to God. Stand against the devil, and the devil will run from you. Come near to God, and God will come near to you.

Joshua 1:8 NIV Do not let this Book of the Law depart from your mouth; meditate on it day and night, so that you may be careful to do everything written in it. Then you will be prosperous and successful.

Psalm 4:4–5 NKJV Be angry, and do not sin. Meditate within your heart on your bed, and be still. Offer the sacrifices of righteousness, and put your trust in the Lord.

Psalm 19:14 NASB Let the words of my mouth and the meditation of my heart be acceptable in Your sight, O Lord, my rock and my Redeemer.

Psalm 42:1–2 NLT As the deer pants for streams of water, so I long for you, O God. I thirst for God, the living God. When can I come and stand before him?

Psalm 63:6–8 NCV I remember you while I'm lying in bed; I think about you through the night. You are my help. Because of your protection, I sing. I stay close to you; you support me with your right hand.

Psalm 77:11–14 WEB I will remember Yah's deeds; for I will remember your wonders of old. I will also meditate on all your work, and consider your doings. Your way, God, is in the sanctuary. What god is great like God? You are the God who does wonders. You have made your strength known among the peoples.

Psalm 139:17–18 NASB How precious also are Your thoughts to me, O God! How vast is the sum of them! If I should count them, they would outnumber the sand. When I awake, I am still with You.

Philippians 4:8 NIV Finally, brothers, whatever is true, whatever is noble, whatever is right, whatever is pure, whatever is lovely, whatever is admirable— if anything is excellent or praiseworthy—think about such things.

Psalm 37:11 NIV But the meek will inherit the land and enjoy great peace.

Zephaniah 2:3 NKJV Seek the LORD, all you meek of the earth, who have upheld His justice. Seek righteousness, seek humility.

Matthew 5:3-7 WNT Blessed are the poor in spirit, for to them belongs the Kingdom of the Heavens. Blessed are the mourners, for they shall be comforted. Blessed are the meek, for they as heirs shall obtain possession of the earth. Blessed are those who hunger and thirst for righteousness, for they shall be completely satisfied. Blessed are the compassionate, for they shall receive compassion.

Matthew 11:29-30 WNT Take my yoke upon you and learn from me; for I am gentle and lowly in heart, and you will find rest for your souls. For it is good to bear my yoke, and my burden is light.

1 Corinthians 13:4-6 NCV Love is patient and kind. Love is not jealous, it does not brag, and it is not proud. Love is not rude, is not selfish, and does not get upset with others. Love does not count up wrongs that have been done. Love is not happy with evil but is happy with the truth.

2 Corinthians 10:1 NKJV Now I, Paul, myself am pleading with you by the meekness and gentleness of Christ—who in presence am lowly among you, but being absent am bold toward you.

James 3:13-17 WEB Who is wise and understanding among you? Let him show by his good conduct that his deeds are done in gentleness of wisdom. But if you have bitter jealousy and selfish ambition in your heart, don't boast and don't lie against the truth. This wisdom is not that which comes down from above, but is earthly, sensual, and demonic. For where jealousy and selfish ambition are, there is confusion and every evil deed. But the wisdom that is from above is first pure, then peaceful, gentle, reasonable, full of mercy and good fruits, without partiality, and without hypocrisy.

Numbers 14:18 NKJV The Lord is longsuffering and abundant in mercy, forgiving iniquity and transgression.

1 Kings 3:6 NKJV You have shown great mercy to Your servant David my father, because he walked before You in truth, in righteousness, and in uprightness of heart.

Psalm 23:6 TMB Surely goodness and mercy shall follow me all the days of my life; and I will dwell in the house of the Lord for ever.

Psalm 25:10 TMB All the paths of the Lord are mercy and truth, unto them that keep His covenant and His testimonies.

Psalm 36:5-6 WEB Your lovingkindness, Yahweh, is in the heavens. Your faithfulness reaches to the skies. Your righteousness is like the mountains of God.

Psalm 59:17 WEB For God is my high tower, the God of my mercy.

Psalm 85:10-13 WEB Mercy and truth meet together. Righteousness and peace have kissed each other. Truth springs out of the earth. Righteousness has looked down from heaven. Yes, Yahweh will give that which is good. Our land will yield its increase. Righteousness goes before him, and prepares the way for his steps.

Psalm 103:10-12 NRSV He does not deal with us according to our sins, nor repay us according to our iniquities. For as the heavens are high above the earth, so great is his steadfast love toward those who fear him; as far as the east is from the west, so far he removes our transgressions from us.

Psalm 116:5-6 TMB Gracious is the Lord and righteous; yea, our God is merciful. The Lord preserveth the simple; I was brought low, and He helped me.

Psalm 119:132-133 NKJV Look upon me and be merciful to me, as Your custom is toward those who love Your name. Direct my steps by Your word, and let no iniquity have dominion over me.

Psalm 123:2 WEB Behold, as the eyes of servants look to the hand of their master, as the eyes of a maid to the hand of her mistress; so our eyes look to Yahweh, our God, until he has mercy on us.

Proverbs 3:3-4 NCV Don't ever forget kindness and truth. Wear them like a necklace. Write them on your heart as if on a tablet. Then you will be respected and will please both God and people.

Micah 6:8 NLT No, O people, the LORD has already told you what is good, and this is what he requires: to do what is right, to love mercy, and to walk humbly with your God.

Micah 7:18 NKJV He does not retain His anger forever, because He delights in mercy.

Luke 6:35-36 NKJV But love your enemies, do good, and lend, hoping for nothing in return; and your reward will be great, and you will be sons of the Most High. For He is kind to the unthankful and evil. Therefore be merciful, just as your Father also is merciful.

2 Corinthians 4:1 NLT And so, since God in his mercy has given us this wonderful ministry, we never give up.

Hebrews 4:16 NASB Therefore let us draw near with confidence to the throne of grace, so that we may receive mercy and find grace to help in time of need.

Isaiah 26:3-4 NIV You will keep in perfect peace him whose mind is steadfast, because he trusts in you. Trust in the LORD forever, for the LORD, the LORD, is the Rock eternal.

Luke 12:29-31 WNT Therefore, do not be asking what you are to eat nor what you are to drink; and do not waver between hope and fear. For though the nations of the world pursue these things, as for you, your Father knows that you need them. But make His Kingdom the object of your pursuit, and these things shall be given you in addition.

Romans 11:33-34 WEB Oh the depth of the riches both of the wisdom and the knowledge of God! How unsearchable are his judgments, and his ways past tracing out! "For who has known the mind of the Lord? Or who has been his counselor?"

1 Corinthians 2:16 NCV "Who has known the mind of the Lord? Who has been able to teach him?" But we have the mind of Christ.

Philippians 2:5-8 NRSV Let the same mind be in you that was in Christ Jesus, who, though he was in the form of God, did not regard equality with God as something to be exploited, but emptied himself, taking the form of a slave, being born in human likeness. And being found in human form, he humbled himself and became obedient to the point of death—even death on a cross.

2 Timothy 1:6-7 NKJV Therefore I remind you to stir up the gift of God which is in you through the laying on of my hands. For God has not given us a spirit of fear, but of power and of love and of a sound mind.

1 Peter 1:13 NCV So prepare your minds for service and have self-control. All your hope should be for the gift of grace that will be yours when Jesus Christ is shown to you.

Acts 13:2-3 NKJV As they ministered to the Lord and fasted, the Holy Spirit said, "Now separate to me Barnabas and Saul for the work to which I have called them." Then having fasted and prayed, and laid hands on them, they sent them away.

2 Corinthians 6:3-10 WEB We give no occasion of stumbling in anything, that our service may not be blamed, but in everything commending ourselves, as servants of God, in great endurance, in afflictions, in hardships, in distresses, in beatings, in imprisonments, in riots, in labors, in watchings, in fastings; in pureness, in knowledge, in patience, in kindness, in the Holy Spirit, in sincere love, in the word of truth, in the power of God; by the armor of righteousness on the right hand and on the left, by glory and dishonor, by evil report and good report; as deceivers, and yet true; as unknown, and yet well known; as dying, and behold, we live; as punished, and not killed; as sorrowful, yet always rejoicing; as poor, yet making many rich; as having nothing, and yet possessing all things.

1 Timothy 4:6-11 WEB Be a good servant of Christ Jesus, nourished in the words of the faith, and of the good doctrine which you have followed. But refuse profane and old wives' fables. Exercise yourself toward godliness. For bodily exercise has some value, but godliness has value for all things. This saying is faithful and worthy of all acceptance. For to this end we both labor and suffer reproach, because we have set our trust in the living God, who is the Savior of all men, especially of those who believe. Command and teach these things.

1 Peter 4:10-11 WNT Whatever be the gifts which each has received, you must use them for one another's benefit, as good stewards of God's many-sided kindness. If any one preaches, let it be as uttering God's truth; if any one renders a service to others, let it be in the strength which God supplies; so that in everything glory may be given to God in the name of Jesus Christ.

Daniel 3:24-25 NKJV Then King Nebuchadnezzar was astonished; and he rose in haste and spoke, saying to his counselors, "Did we not cast three men bound into the midst of the fire?" They answered and said to the king, "True, O king." "Look!" he answered, "I see four men loose, walking in the midst of the fire; and they are not hurt, and the form of the fourth is like the Son of God."

Luke 7:20-22 WEB When the men had come to him, they said, "John the Baptizer has sent us to you, saying, 'Are you he who comes, or should we look for another?'" In that hour he cured many of diseases and plagues and evil spirits; and to many who were blind he gave sight. Jesus answered them "Go and tell John the things which you have seen and heard: that the blind receive their sight, the lame walk, the lepers are cleansed, the deaf hear, the dead are raised up, and the poor have good news preached to them."

John 20:30-31 WNT There were also a great number of other signs which Jesus performed in the presence of the disciples, which are not recorded in this book. But these have been recorded in order that you may believe that He is the Christ, the Son of God, and that, through believing, you may have Life through His name.

Acts 19:11-12 WEB God worked special miracles by the hands of Paul, so that even handkerchiefs or aprons were carried away from his body to the sick, and the evil spirits went out.

1 Corinthians 12:7-10 NCV Something from the Spirit can be seen in each person, for the common good. The Spirit gives one person the ability to speak with wisdom, and the same Spirit gives another the ability to speak with knowledge. The same Spirit gives faith to one person. And, to another, that one Spirit gives gifts of healing. The Spirit gives to another person the power to do miracles, to another the ability to prophesy. . . . The Spirit gives one person the ability to speak in different kinds of languages and to another the ability to interpret those languages.

Psalm 143:8-10 WEB Cause me to hear your lovingkindness in the morning, for I trust in you. Cause me to know the way in which I should walk, for I lift up my soul to you. Deliver me, Yahweh, from my enemies. I flee to you to hide me. Teach me to do your will, for you are my God. Your Spirit is good. Lead me in the land of uprightness.

Proverbs 18:10 NIV The name of the LORD is a strong tower; the righteous run to it and are safe.

Isaiah 6:8 NIV Then I heard the voce of the LORD, saying: "Whom shall I send, and who will go for Us?" And I said, "Here am I! Send me."

Jeremiah 1:7-8 NKJV But the LORD said to me: "Do not say, 'I am a youth,' for you shall go to all whom I send you, and whatever I command you, you shall speak. Do not be afraid of their faces, for I am with you to deliver you," says the LORD.

Matthew 9:37-38 NASB Then He said to His disciples, "The harvest is plentiful, but the workers are few. Therefore beseech the Lord of the harvest to send out workers into His harvest."

Matthew 28:18-20 NASB And Jesus came up and spoke to them, saying, "All authority has been given to Me in heaven and on earth. Go therefore and make disciples of all the nations, baptizing them in the name of the Father and the Son and the Holy Spirit, teaching them to observe all that I commanded you; and lo, I am with you always, even to the end of the age."

John 20:21-23 WEB Jesus therefore said to them again, "Peace be to you. As the Father has sent me, even so I send you." When he had said this, he breathed on them, and said to them, "Receive the Holy Spirit! Whoever's sins you forgive, they are forgiven to them. Whoever's sins you retain, they are retained."

Deuteronomy 11:18-21 NRSV You shall put these words of mine in your heart and soul, and you shall bind them as a sign on your hand, and fix them as an emblem on your forehead. Teach them to your children, talking about them when you are at home and when you are away, when you lie down and when you rise. Write them on the doorposts of your house and on your gates, so that your days and the days of your children may be multiplied in the land that the LORD swore to your ancestors to give them, as long as the heavens are above the earth.

1 Samuel 1:27-2:2 NRSV "For this child I prayed; and the LORD has granted me the petition that I made to him. Therefore I have lent him to the LORD; as long as he lives, he is given to the LORD." . . . Hannah prayed and said, "My heart exults in the LORD; my strength is exalted in my God. My mouth derides my enemies, because I rejoice in my victory. There is no Holy One like the LORD, no one besides you; there is no Rock like our God.

Psalm 71:5-6 NIV For you have been my hope, O Sovereign LORD, my confidence since my youth. From birth I have relied on you; you brought me forth from my mother's womb. I will ever praise you.

Psalm 86:16-17 NLT Look down and have mercy on me. Give strength to your servant; yes, save me, for I am your servant. Send me a sign of your favor. Then those who hate me will be put to shame, for you, O LORD, help and comfort me.

Psalm 127:3-4 NLT Children are a gift from the LORD; they are a reward from him. Children born to a young man are like sharp arrows in a warrior's hands.

Proverbs 14:1-2 NIV The wise woman builds her house, but with her own hands the foolish one tears hers down. He whose walk is upright fears the LORD, but he whose ways are devious despises him.

Proverbs 29:17 TMB Correct thy son, and he shall give thee rest; yea, he shall give delight unto thy soul.

Proverbs 31:26-29 NASB She opens her mouth in wisdom, and the teaching of kindness is on her tongue. She looks well to the ways of her household, and does not eat the bread of idleness. Her children rise up and bless her; her husband also, and he praises her, saying: "Many daughters have done nobly, but you excel them all."

Isaiah 40:10-11 NIV See, the Sovereign LORD comes with power, and his arm rules for him. See, his reward is with him, and his recompense accompanies him. He tends his flock like a shepherd: He gathers the lambs in his arms and carries them close to his heart; he gently leads those that have young.

Isaiah 40:29-31 NLT He gives power to those who are tired and worn out; he offers strength to the weak. Even youths will become exhausted, and young men will give up. But those who wait on the LORD will find new strength. They will fly high on wings like eagles. They will run and not grow weary. They will walk and not faint.

Isaiah 54:13 NIV All your sons will be taught by the LORD, and great will be your children's peace.

Acts 2:38-39 NASB Peter said to them, "Repent, and each of you be baptized in the name of Jesus Christ for the forgiveness of your sins; and you will receive the gift of the Holy Spirit."For the promise is for you and your children and for all who are far off, as many as the Lord our God will call to Himself."

3 John 4 NKJV I have no greater joy than to hear that my children walk in truth.

Genesis 22:18 NKJV In your seed all the nations of the earth shall be blessed, because you have obeyed My voice.

2 Chronicles 7:14 NKJV If My people who are called by My name will humble themselves, and pray and seek My face, and turn from their wicked ways, then I will hear from heaven, and will forgive their sin and heal their land.

Job 12:22-23 WEB He uncovers deep things out of darkness, and brings out to light the shadow of death. He increases the nations, and he destroys them. He enlarges the nations, and he leads them captive.

Psalm 2:7-8 NCV Now I will tell you what the LORD has declared: He said to me, "You are my son. Today I have become your father. If you ask me, I will give you the nations; all the people on earth will be yours."

Psalm 9:19-20 WEB Arise, Yahweh! Don't let man prevail. Let the nations be judged in your sight. Put them in fear, Yahweh. Let the nations know that they are only men.

Psalm 33:10-12 NRSV The LORD brings the counsel of the nations to nothing; he frustrates the plans of the peoples. The counsel of the LORD stands forever, the thoughts of his heart to all generations. Happy is the nation whose God is the LORD, the people whom he has chosen as his heritage.

Psalm 72:11 NCV Let all kings bow down to him and all nations serve him.

Revelation 2:26 NIV To him who overcomes and does my will to the end, I will give authority over the nations.

Leviticus 19:13 NKJV You shall not cheat your neighbor, nor rob him. The wages of him who is hired shall not remain with you all night until morning.

Psalm 15:1-5 NCV LORD, who may enter your Holy Tent? Who may live on your holy mountain? Only those who are innocent and who do what is right. Such people speak the truth from their hearts and do not tell lies about others. They do no wrong to their neighbors and do not gossip. They do not respect hateful people but honor those who honor the LORD. They keep their promises to their neighbors, even when it hurts. . . . whoever does all these things will never be destroyed.

Proverbs 3:27-29 NRSV Do not withhold good from those to whom it is due, when it is in your power to do it. Do not say to your neighbor, "Go, and come again, tomorrow I will give it"—when you have it with you. Do not plan harm against your neighbor who lives trustingly beside you.

Proverbs 26:18-19 NIV Like a madman shooting firebrands or deadly arrows is a man who deceives his neighbor and says, "I was only joking!"

Matthew 22:37-40 NRSV He said to him, "'You shall love the Lord your God with all your heart, and with all your soul, and with all your mind.' This is the greatest and first commandment. And a second is like it: 'You shall love your neighbor as yourself.' On these two commandments hang all the law and the prophets."

Romans 13:10 WEB Love doesn't harm a neighbor. Love therefore is the fulfillment of the law.

James 2:8-9 WEB However, if you fulfill the royal law, according to the Scripture, "You shall love your neighbor as yourself," you do well. But if you show partiality, you commit sin, being convicted by the law as transgressors.

Psalm 40:1–3 NRSV I waited patiently for the LORD; he inclined to me and heard my cry. He drew me up from the desolate pit, out of the miry bog, and set my feet upon a rock, making my steps secure. He put a new song in my mouth, a song of praise to our God. Many will see and fear, and put their trust in the LORD.

Isaiah 43:18–19 WEB Don't remember the former things, and don't consider the things of old. Behold, I will do a new thing. It springs forth now.

Ezekiel 36:25–27 WEB I will sprinkle clean water on you, and you shall be clean: from all your filthiness, and from all your idols, will I cleanse you. I will also give you a new heart, and I will put a new Spirit within you; and I will take away the stony heart out of your flesh, and I will give you a heart of flesh. I will put my Spirit within you, and cause you to walk in my statutes, and you shall keep my ordinances, and do them.

2 Corinthians 5:17–18 NLT What this means is that those who become Christians become new persons. They are not the same anymore, for the old life is gone. A new life has begun! All this newness of life is from God, who brought us back to himself through what Christ did.

Ephesians 4:21–24 WNT If at least you have heard His voice and in Him have been taught—and this is true Christian teaching—to put away, in regard to your former mode of life, your original evil nature which is doomed to perish as befits its misleading impulses, and to get yourselves renewed in the temper of your minds and clothe yourselves with that new and better self which has been created to resemble God in the righteousness and holiness which come from the truth.

Deuteronomy 28:1–6 NRSV If you will only obey the Lord your God, by diligently observing all his commandments that I am commanding you today, the Lord your God will set you high above all the nations of the earth; all these blessings shall come upon you and overtake you, if you obey the Lord your God: Blessed shall you be in the city, and blessed shall you be in the field. Blessed shall be the fruit of your womb, the fruit of your ground, and the fruit of your livestock, both the increase of your cattle and the issue of your flock. Blessed shall be your basket and your kneading bowl. Blessed shall you be when you come in, and blessed shall you be when you go out.

Joshua 1:8–9 NASB This book of the law shall not depart from your mouth, but you shall meditate on it day and night, so that you may be careful to do according to all that is written in it; for then you will make your way prosperous, and then you will have success. Have I not commanded you? Be strong and courageous! Do not tremble or be dismayed, for the Lord your God is with you wherever you go.

Psalm 119:2–3 NASB How blessed are those who observe His testimonies, who seek Him with all their heart. They also do no unrighteousness; they walk in His ways.

Psalm 119:65–68 NRSV You have dealt well with your servant, O Lord, according to your word. Teach me good judgment and knowledge, for I believe in your commandments. Before I was humbled I went astray, but now I keep your word. You are good and do good; teach me your statutes.

Psalm 143:8–10 NCV Tell me in the morning about your love, because I trust you. Show me what I should do, because my prayers go up to you. Lord, save me from my enemies; I hide in you. Teach me to do what you want, because you are my God. Let your good Spirit lead me on level ground.

Isaiah 48:18 NCV If you had obeyed me, you would have had peace like a full-flowing river. Good things would have flowed to you like the waves of the sea.

John 7:17 TMB If any man will do His will, he shall know of the doctrine whether it be from God, or whether I speak from Myself.

James 1:22-25 NCV Do what God's teaching says; when you only listen and do nothing, you are fooling yourselves. Those who hear God's teaching and do nothing are like people who look at themselves in a mirror. They see their faces and then go away and quickly forget what they looked like. But the truly happy people are those who carefully study God's perfect law that makes people free, and they continue to study it. They do not forget what they heard, but they obey what God's teaching says. Those who do this will be made happy.

1 John 2:4-6 NCV Anyone who says, "I know God," but does not obey God's commands is a liar, and the truth is not in that person. But if someone obeys God's teaching, then in that person God's love has truly reached its goal. This is how we can be sure we are living in God: Whoever says that he lives in God must live as Jesus lived.

1 John 3:22-24 WNT And whatever we ask for we obtain from Him, because we obey His commands and do the things which are pleasing in His sight. And this is His command—that we are to believe in His Son Jesus Christ and love one another, just as He has commanded us to do. The man who obeys His commands continues in union with God, and God continues in union with him; and through His Spirit whom He has given us we can know that He continues in union with us.

Revelation 3:10-11 NIV Since you have kept my command to endure patiently, I will also keep you from the hour of trial that is going to come upon the whole world to test those who live on the earth. I am coming soon. Hold on to what you have, so that no one will take your crown.

Deuteronomy 20:3-4 NCV He will say, "Listen, Israel! Today you are going into battle against your enemies. Don't lose your courage or be afraid. Don't panic or be frightened, because the LORD your God goes with you, to fight for you against your enemies and to save you."

Joshua 1:9 NLT I command you—be strong and courageous! Do not be afraid or discouraged. For the LORD your God is with you wherever you go.

1 Kings 8:27 NKJV But will God indeed dwell on the earth? Behold, heaven and the heaven of heavens cannot contain You. How much less this temple which I have built!

Psalm 139:7-10 WEB Where could I go from your Spirit? Or where could I flee from your presence? If I ascend up into heaven, you are there. If I make my bed in Sheol, behold, you are there! If I take the wings of the dawn, and settle in the uttermost parts of the sea; even there your hand will lead me, and your right hand will hold me.

Proverbs 15:3 NKJV The eyes of the LORD are in every place, keeping watch on the evil and the good.

Isaiah 66:1-2 WEB Thus says Yahweh, "Heaven is my throne, and the earth is my footstool: what kind of house will you build to me? and what place shall be my rest? For all these things has my hand made, and so all these things came to be," says Yahweh: but to this man will I look, even to him who is poor and of a contrite spirit, and who trembles at my word.

Jeremiah 23:23-24 NCV "I am a God who is near," says the LORD. "I am also a God who is far away. No one can hide where I cannot see him," says the LORD. "I fill all of heaven and earth," says the LORD.

Psalm 27:6 NCV My head is higher than my enemies around me. I will offer joyful sacrifices in his Holy Tent. I will sing and praise the LORD.

Psalm 56:1-7 NLT The enemy troops press in on me. My foes attack me all day long. My slanderers hound me constantly, and many are boldly attacking me. But when I am afraid, I put my trust in you. O God, I praise your word. I trust in God, so why should I be afraid? What can mere mortals do to me? . . . Don't let them get away with their wickedness; in your anger, O God, throw them to the ground.

Psalm 56:8-9 NKJV You number my wanderings, put my tears into Your bottle. . . . When I cry out to You, then my enemies will turn back; this I know, because God is for me.

Proverbs 16:7 NLT When the ways of people please the LORD, he makes even their enemies live at peace with them.

Jeremiah 1:19 NKJV "They will fight against you, but they shall not prevail against you. For I am with you," says the LORD, "to deliver you."

Jeremiah 20:11 WEB But Yahweh is with me as an awesome mighty one: therefore my persecutors shall stumble, and they shall not prevail; they shall be utterly disappointed, because they have not dealt wisely, even with an everlasting dishonor which shall never be forgotten.

Romans 8:31-34 WNT What then shall we say to this? If God is on our side, who is there to appear against us? He who did not withhold even His own Son, but gave Him up for all of us, will He not also with Him freely give us all things? Who shall impeach those whom God has chosen? God declares them free from guilt. Who is there to condemn them? Christ Jesus died, or rather has risen to life again. He is also at the right hand of God, and is interceding for us.

Romans 8:35-39 WNT Who shall separate us from Christ's love? Shall affliction or distress, persecution or hunger, nakedness or danger or the sword? As it stands written in the Scripture, "For Thy sake they are, all day long, trying to kill us. We have been looked upon as sheep destined for slaughter." Yet amid all these things we are more than conquerors through Him who has loved us. For I am convinced that neither death nor life, neither the lower ranks of evil angels nor the higher, neither things present nor things future, nor the forces of nature, nor height nor depth, nor any other created thing, will be able to separate us from the love of God which rests upon us in Christ Jesus our Lord.

Romans 12:19-21 NCV It is written: "I will punish those who do wrong; I will repay them," says the Lord. . . . Do not let evil defeat you, but defeat evil by doing good.

1 Corinthians 16:9 NKJV For a great and effective door has opened to me, and there are many adversaries.

1 Thessalonians 2:18 NKJV Therefore we wanted to come to you—even I, Paul, time and again—but Satan hindered us.

2 Timothy 3:10-12 NASB But you followed my teaching, conduct, purpose, faith, patience, love, perseverance, persecutions, and sufferings, such as happened to me at Antioch . . . what persecutions I endured, and out of them all the Lord rescued me! Indeed, all who desire to live godly in Christ Jesus will be persecuted.

1 Peter 5:8-11 WNT Curb every passion, and be on the alert. Your great accuser, the Devil, is going about like a roaring lion to see whom he can devour. Withstand him, firm in your faith; knowing that your brethren in other parts of the world are passing through just the same experiences. And God, the giver of all grace, who has called you to share His eternal glory, through Christ, after you have suffered for a short time, will Himself make you perfect, firm, and strong. To Him be all power unto the Ages of the Ages! Amen.

Exodus 22:22-24 NRSV You shall not abuse any widow or orphan. If you do abuse them, when they cry out to me, I will surely heed their cry; my wrath will burn, and I will kill you with the sword, and your wives shall become widows and your children orphans.

Deuteronomy 26:12 NIV When you have finished setting aside a tenth of all your produce in the third year, the year of the tithe, you shall give it to the Levite, the alien, the fatherless and the widow, so that they may eat in your towns and be satisfied.

Joshua 1:5-9 NIV "No one will be able to stand up against you all the days of your life. As I was with Moses, so I will be with you; I will never leave you nor forsake you. Be strong and courageous . . . for the LORD your God will be with you wherever you go."

Psalm 27:10 NLT Even if my father and my mother abandon me, the Lord will hold me close.

Psalm 68:4-5 NKJV Sing to God, sing praises to His name; extol Him who rides on the clouds, by His name Yah, and rejoice before Him. A father of the fatherless, a defender of widows, is God in His holy habitation.

Isaiah 1:17 NASB Learn to do good; seek justice, reprove the ruthless, defend the orphan, plead for the widow.

John 14:18-19 NLT No, I will not abandon you as orphans—I will come to you. In just a little while the world will not see me again, but you will. For I will live again, and you will, too.

James 1:27 NKJV Pure and undefiled religion before God and the Father is this: to visit orphans and widows in their trouble, and to keep oneself unspotted from the world.

John 16:33 NLT I have told you all this so that you may have peace in me. Here on earth you will have many trials and sorrows. But take heart, because I have overcome the world.

Romans 8:37–39 NCV But in all these things we have full victory through God who showed his love for us. Yes, I am sure that neither death, nor life, nor angels, nor ruling spirits, nothing now, nothing in the future, no powers, nothing above us, nothing below us, nor anything else in the whole world will ever be able to separate us from the love of God that is in Christ Jesus our Lord.

1 John 2:13–14 WNT I am writing to you, fathers, because you know Him who has existed from the very beginning. I am writing to you, young men, because you have overcome the Evil one. I have written to you, children, because you know the Father. I have written to you, fathers, because you know Him who has existed from the very beginning. I have written to you, young men, because you are strong and God's Message still has a place in your hearts, and you have overcome the Evil one.

1 John 4:4 NIV You, dear children, are from God and have overcome them, because the one who is in you is greater than the one who is in the world.

1 John 5:4–5 NKJV For whatever is born of God overcomes the world. And this is the victory that has overcome the world—our faith. Who is he who overcomes the world, but he who believes that Jesus is the Son of God?

Revelation 2:7 NIV He who has an ear, let him hear what the Spirit says to the churches. To him who overcomes, I will give the right to eat from the tree of life, which is in the paradise of God.

Revelation 2:11 NKJV He who has an ear, let him hear what the Spirit says to the churches. He who overcomes shall not be hurt by the second death.

Revelation 2:17 NASB To him who overcomes, to him I will give some of the hidden manna, and I will give him a white stone, and a new name written on the stone which no one knows but he who receives it.

Revelation 2:26-28 NRSV To everyone who conquers and continues to do my works to the end, I will give authority over the nations; to rule them with an iron rod, as when clay pots are shattered—even as I also received authority from my Father. To the one who conquers I will also give the morning star.

Revelation 3:5 TMB He that overcometh, the same shall be clothed in white raiment; and I will not blot out his name from the Book of Life, but I will confess his name before My Father and before His angels.

Revelation 3:10-12 WEB Because you kept my command to endure, I also will keep you from the hour of testing, which is to come on the whole world. . . . I am coming quickly. Hold firmly that which you have, so that no one takes your crown. He who overcomes, I will make him a pillar in the temple of my God, and he will go out from there no more. I will write on him the name of my God, and the name of the city of my God.

Revelation 3:21 NLT I will invite everyone who is victorious to sit with me on my throne, just as I was victorious and sat with my Father on his throne.

Revelation 17:14 NCV They will make war against the Lamb, but the Lamb will defeat them, because he is Lord of lords and King of kings. He will defeat them with his called, chosen, and faithful followers.

Revelation 21:7-8 WEB He who overcomes, I will give him these things. I will be his God, and he will be my son. But for the cowardly, unbelieving, sinners, abominable, murderers, sexually immoral, sorcerers, idolaters, and all liars, their part is in the lake that burns with fire and sulfur, which is the second death.

Psalm 78:4-8 NRSV We will not hide them from their children; we will tell to the coming generation the glorious deeds of the LORD, and his might, and the wonders that he has done. He established a decree in Jacob, and appointed a law in Israel, which he commanded our ancestors to teach to their children; that the next generation might know them, the children yet unborn, and rise up and tell them to their children, so that they should set their hope in God, and not forget the works of God, but keep his commandments; and that they should not be like their ancestors, a stubborn and rebellious generation, a generation whose heart was not steadfast, whose spirit was not faithful to God.

Psalm 115:14-16 WEB May Yahweh increase you more and more, you and your children. Blessed are you by Yahweh, who made heaven and earth. The heavens are the heavens of Yahweh; but the earth has he given to the children of men.

Psalm 127:3-5 NASB Behold, children are a gift of the LORD, the fruit of the womb is a reward. Like arrows in the hand of a warrior, so are the children of one's youth. How blessed is the man whose quiver is full of them; they will not be ashamed when they speak with their enemies in the gate.

Proverbs 4:1-9 NRSV Listen, children, to a father's instruction, and be attentive, that you may gain insight; for I give you good precepts: do not forsake my teaching. When I was a son with my father, tender, and my mother's favorite, he taught me, and said to me, "Let your heart hold fast my words; keep my commandments, and live. Get wisdom; get insight: do not forget, nor turn away from the words of my mouth. Do not forsake her, and she will keep you; love her, and she will guard you. The beginning of wisdom is this: Get wisdom, and whatever else you get, get insight. Prize her highly, and she will exalt you; she will honor you if you embrace her. She will place on your head a fair garland; she will bestow on you a beautiful crown."

Matthew 18:5-6 NCV Whoever accepts a child in my name accepts me. If one of these little children believes in me, and someone causes that child to sin, it would be better for that person to have a large stone tied around the neck and be drowned in the sea.

Proverbs 22:6 NASB Train up a child in the way he should go, even when he is old he will not depart from it.

Isaiah 54:13 NIV All your sons will be taught by the Lord, and great will be your children's peace.

Ephesians 5:1-2 NCV You are God's children whom he loves, so try to be like him. Live a life of love just as Christ loved us and gave himself for us as a sweet-smelling offering and sacrifice to God.

Ephesians 6:1, 4 WEB Children, obey your parents in the Lord, for this is right. . . . You fathers, don't provoke your children to wrath, but nurture them in the discipline and instruction of the Lord.

Ephesians 6:11-13 NCV Put on the full armor of God so that you can fight against the devil's evil tricks. Our fight is not against people on earth but against the rulers and authorities and the powers of this world's darkness, against the spiritual powers of evil in the heavenly world. That is why you need to put on God's full armor. Then on the day of evil you will be able to stand strong. And when you have finished the whole fight, you will still be standing.

Hebrews 4:16 TMB Let us therefore come boldly unto the throne of grace, that we may obtain mercy and find grace to help in time of need.

Psalm 4:7-8 NCV But you have made me very happy, happier than they are, even with all their grain and new wine. I go to bed and sleep in peace, because, LORD, only you keep me safe.

Psalm 119:165-169 NKJV Great peace have those who love Your law, and nothing causes them to stumble. LORD, I hope for Your salvation, and I do Your commandments. . . . Let my cry come before You, O LORD; give me understanding according to Your word.

Proverbs 12:20 NIV There is deceit in the hearts of those who plot evil, but joy for those who promote peace.

Proverbs 20:3 NLT Avoiding a fight is a mark of honor; only fools insist on quarreling.

Isaiah 32:17-19 NKJV The work of righteousness will be peace, and the effect of righteousness, quietness and assurance forever. My people will dwell in a peaceful habitation, in secure dwellings, and in quiet resting places, though hail comes down on the forest, and the city is brought low in humiliation.

Matthew 5:7-9 WNT Blessed are the compassionate, for they shall receive compassion. Blessed are the pure in heart, for they shall see God. Blessed are the peacemakers, for it is they who will be recognized as sons of God.

Luke 24:36-39 NKJV Now as they said these things, Jesus Himself stood in the midst of them, and said to them, "Peace to you." But they were terrified and frightened, and supposed they had seen a spirit. And He said to them, "Why are you troubled? And why do doubts arise in your hearts? Behold My hands and My feet, that it is I Myself."

John 14:27 NASB Peace I leave with you; My peace I give to you; not as the world gives do I give to you. Do not let your heart be troubled, nor let it be fearful.

John 16:33 NASB These things I have spoken to you, so that in Me you may have peace. In the world you have tribulation, but take courage; I have overcome the world.

Romans 12:17-18 NIV Do not repay anyone evil for evil. Be careful to do what is right in the eyes of everybody. If it is possible, as far as it depends on you, live at peace with everyone.

Ephesians 2:13-18 NKJV But now in Christ Jesus you who once were far off have been brought near by the blood of Christ. For He Himself is our peace, who has made both one, and has broken down the middle wall of separation, having abolished in His flesh the enmity, that is, the law of commandments contained in ordinances, so as to create in Himself one new man from the two, thus making peace, and that He might reconcile them both to God in one body through the cross, thereby putting to death the enmity. And He came and preached peace to you who were afar off and to those who were near. For through Him we both have access by one Spirit to the Father.

Philippians 4:9 NLT Keep putting into practice all you learned from me and heard from me and saw me doing, and the God of peace will be with you.

Colossians 3:15 NCV Let the peace that Christ gives control your thinking, because you were all called together in one body to have peace. Always be thankful.

James 3:17-18 NKJV But the wisdom that is from above is first pure, then peaceable, gentle, willing to yield, full of mercy and good fruits, without partiality and without hypocrisy. Now the fruit of righteousness is sown in peace by those who make peace.

Exodus 15:6–11 NASB Your right hand, O LORD, is majestic in power, Your right hand, O LORD, shatters the enemy. And in the greatness of Your excellence You overthrow those who rise up against You; You send forth Your burning anger, *and* it consumes them as chaff. At the blast of Your nostrils the waters were piled up, the flowing waters stood up like a heap; the deeps were congealed in the heart of the sea. The enemy said, "I will pursue, I will overtake, I will divide the spoil; my desire shall be gratified against them; I will draw out my sword, my hand will destroy them." You blew with Your wind, the sea covered them; they sank like lead in the mighty waters. Who is like You among the gods, O LORD? Who is like You, majestic in holiness, awesome in praises, working wonders?

Psalm 29:3–5 NLT The voice of the LORD echoes above the sea. The God of glory thunders. The LORD thunders over the mighty sea. The voice of the LORD is powerful; the voice of the LORD is full of majesty. The voice of the LORD splits the mighty cedars; the LORD shatters the cedars of Lebanon.

Psalm 62:11 NKJV God has spoken once, twice I have heard this: That power belongs to God.

Psalm 63:2 WEB So I have seen you in the sanctuary, watching your power and your glory.

Psalm 65:6–8 WEB Who by his power forms the mountains, having armed yourself with strength; who stills the roaring of the seas, the roaring of their waves, and the turmoil of the nations. They also who dwell in faraway places are afraid at your wonders. You call the morning's dawn and the evening with songs of joy.

Psalm 66:2–3 NLT Tell the world how glorious he is. Say to God, "How awesome are your deeds! Your enemies cringe before your mighty power."

Psalm 66:5-7 NKJV Come and see the works of God; He is awesome in His doing toward the sons of men. He turned the sea into dry land; they went through the river on foot. There we will rejoice in Him. He rules by His power forever; His eyes observe the nations; do not let the rebellious exalt themselves.

Psalm 68:35 NKJV O God, You are more awesome than Your holy places. The God of Israel is He who gives strength and power to His people. Blessed be God!

Jeremiah 32:26-27 NKJV Then the word of the LORD came to Jeremiah, saying, "Behold, I am the LORD, the God of all flesh. Is there anything too hard for Me?"

Acts 1:7-8 WEB He said to them, "It isn't for you to know times or seasons which the Father has set within his own authority. But you will receive power when the Holy Spirit has come on you. You will be witnesses to me in Jerusalem, in all Judea and Samaria, and to the uttermost parts of the earth."

Hebrews 4:12 NLT For the word of God is full of living power. It is sharper than the sharpest knife, cutting deep into our innermost thoughts and desires. It exposes us for what we really are.

2 Peter 1:2-3 NASB Grace and peace be multiplied to you in the knowledge of God and of Jesus our Lord; seeing that His divine power has granted to us everything pertaining to life and godliness, through the true knowledge of Him who called us by His own glory and excellence.

Revelation 5:13 WEB I heard every created thing which is in heaven, on the earth, under the earth, on the sea, and everything in them, saying, "To him who sits on the throne, and to the Lamb be the blessing, the honor, the glory, and the dominion, forever and ever! Amen."

Exodus 15:1-2 NIV Then Moses and the Israelites sang this song to the LORD: "I will sing to the LORD, for he is highly exalted. The horse and its rider he has hurled into the sea. The LORD is my strength and my song; he has become my salvation. He is my God, and I will praise him, my father's God, and I will exalt him."

Deuteronomy 32:3-4 NKJV For I proclaim the name of the LORD: Ascribe greatness to our God. He is the Rock, His work is perfect; for all His ways are justice, a God of truth and without injustice; righteous and upright is He.

Psalm 22:22-23 NLT Then I will declare the wonder of your name to my brothers and sisters. I will praise you among all your people. Praise the LORD, all you who fear him! Honor him, all you descendants of Jacob! Show him reverence, all you descendants of Israel!

Psalm 33:1-3 NCV Sing to the LORD, you who do what is right; honest people should praise him. Praise the LORD on the harp; make music for him on a ten-stringed lyre. Sing a new song to him; play well and joyfully.

Psalm 43:3-4 WEB Oh, send out your light and your truth. Let them lead me. Let them bring me to your holy hill, to your tents. Then I will go to the altar of God, to God, my exceeding joy. I will praise you on the harp, God, my God.

Psalm 56:10-12 NLT O God, I praise your word. Yes, LORD, I praise your word. I trust in God, so why should I be afraid? What can mere mortals do to me? I will fulfill my vows to you, O God, and offer a sacrifice of thanks for your help.

Psalm 59:16-17 NIV But I will sing of your strength, in the morning I will sing of your love; for you are my fortress, my refuge in times of trouble. O my Strength, I sing praise to you; you, O God, are my fortress, my loving God.

Psalm 67:5-7 WEB Let the peoples praise you, God. Let all the peoples praise you. The earth has yielded its increase. God, even our own God, will bless us. God will bless us. All the ends of the earth shall fear him.

Psalm 71:7-8 WEB I am a marvel to many, but you are my strong refuge. My mouth shall be filled with your praise, with your honor all the day.

Psalm 89:5-7 NRSV Let the heavens praise your wonders, O LORD, your faithfulness in the assembly of the holy ones. For who in the skies can be compared to the LORD? Who among the heavenly beings is like the LORD, a God feared in the council of the holy ones, great and awesome above all that are around him?

Psalm 95:1-3 WEB Oh come, let's sing to Yahweh. Let's shout aloud to the rock of our salvation! Let's come before his presence with thanksgiving. Let's extol him with songs! For Yahweh is a great God, a great King above all gods.

Psalm 95:6-7 NLT Come, let us worship and bow down. Let us kneel before the LORD our maker, for he is our God. We are the people he watches over, the sheep under his care. Oh, that you would listen to his voice today!

Psalm 96:8-9 NIV Ascribe to the LORD the glory due his name; bring an offering and come into his courts. Worship the LORD in the splendor of his holiness; tremble before him, all the earth.

Revelation 5:13-14 NKJV And every creature which is in heaven and on the earth and under the earth and such as are in the sea, and all that are in them, I heard saying: "Blessing and honor and glory and power be to Him who sits on the throne, and to the Lamb, forever and ever!" Then the four living creatures said, "Amen!"

1 Kings 8:28-30 WEB Have respect for the prayer of your servant, and for his supplication, Yahweh my God, to listen to the cry and to the prayer which your servant prays before you this day; that your eyes may be open toward this house night and day, even toward the place of which you have said, "My name shall be there;" to listen to the prayer which your servant shall pray toward this place . . . Yes, hear in heaven, your dwelling place; and when you hear, forgive.

2 Chronicles 7:14-16 WEB If my people, who are called by my name, shall humble themselves, and pray, and seek my face, and turn from their wicked ways; then will I hear from heaven, and will forgive their sin, and will heal their land. Now my eyes shall be open, and my ears attentive, to the prayer that is made in this place. For now have I chosen and made this house holy, that my name may be there forever; and my eyes and my heart shall be there perpetually.

Psalm 62:7-8 NASB On God my salvation and my glory rest; the rock of my strength, my refuge is in God. Trust in Him at all times, O people; pour out your heart before Him; God is a refuge for us.

Psalm 66:18-20 NRSV If I had cherished iniquity in my heart, the Lord would not have listened. But truly God has listened; he has given heed to the voice of my prayer. Blessed be God, because he has not rejected my prayer or removed his steadfast love from me.

Jeremiah 33:3 NIV Call to me and I will answer you and tell you great and unsearchable things you do not know.

Matthew 21:21-22 NKJV If you have faith and do not doubt, you will not only do what was done to the fig tree, but also if you say to this mountain, "Be removed and be cast into the sea," it will be done. And whatever things you ask in prayer, believing, you will receive.

Luke 11:1-3 WEB It happened, that when he finished praying in a certain place, one of his disciples said to him, "Lord, teach us to pray, just as John also taught his disciples." He said to them, "When you pray, say, 'Our Father in heaven, may your name be kept holy. May your kingdom come. May your will be done on Earth, as it is in heaven. Give us day by day our daily bread.'"

John 17:9-10 NRSV I am asking on their behalf; I am not asking on behalf of the world, but on behalf of those whom you gave me, because they are yours. All mine are yours, and yours are mine; and I have been glorified in them.

Acts 4:31 TMB And when they had prayed, the place was shaken where they were assembled together; and they were all filled with the Holy Ghost, and they spoke the Word of God with boldness.

Ephesians 6:16-19 NCV Use the shield of faith with which you can stop all the burning arrows of the Evil One. Accept God's salvation as your helmet, and take the sword of the Spirit, which is the word of God. Pray in the Spirit at all times with all kinds of prayers, asking for everything you need. To do this you must always be ready and never give up. Always pray for all God's people. Also pray for me that when I speak, God will give me words so that I can tell the secret of the Good News without fear.

1 Timothy 4:4-5 NCV Everything God made is good, and nothing should be refused if it is accepted with thanks, because it is made holy by what God has said and by prayer.

James 5:16-18 WNT Therefore confess your sins to one another, and pray for one another, so that you may be cured. The heartfelt supplication of a righteous man exerts a mighty influence. Elijah was a man with a nature similar to ours, and he earnestly prayed that there might be no rain: and no rain fell on the land for three years and six months. Again he prayed, and the sky gave rain and the land yielded its crops.

Isaiah 61:1 NIV The Spirit of the Sovereign LORD is on me, because the LORD has anointed me to preach good news to the poor. He has sent me to bind up the brokenhearted, to proclaim freedom for the captives and release from darkness for the prisoners.

Matthew 10:6-8 NCV But go to the people of Israel, who are like lost sheep. When you go, preach this: "The kingdom of heaven is near." Heal the sick, raise the dead to life again, heal those who have skin diseases, and force demons out of people. I give you these powers freely, so help other people freely.

Romans 2:21-23 NIV You, then, who teach others, do you not teach yourself? You who preach against stealing, do you steal? You who say that people should not commit adultery, do you commit adultery? You who abhor idols, do you rob temples? You who brag about the law, do you dishonor God by breaking the law?

Mark 16:15-16 WEB He said to them, "Go into all the world, and preach the Good News to the whole creation. He who believes and is baptized will be saved; but he who disbelieves will be condemned."

1 Corinthians 1:17-18 WEB For Christ sent me not to baptize, but to preach the Good News—not in wisdom of words, so that the cross of Christ wouldn't be made void. For the word of the cross is foolishness to those who are dying, but to us who are saved it is the power of God.

1 Corinthians 9:17-18 NKJV I have been entrusted with a stewardship. What is my reward then? That when I preach the gospel, I may present the gospel of Christ without charge, that I may not abuse my authority in the gospel.

2 Timothy 4:2 NKJV Preach the word! Be ready in season and out of season. Convince, rebuke, exhort, with all longsuffering and teaching.

Deuteronomy 8:11-19 NRSV Take care that you do not forget the LORD your God, by failing to keep his commandments, his ordinances, and his statutes, which I am commanding you today. When you have eaten your fill and have built fine houses and live in them, and when your herds and flocks have multiplied, and your silver and gold is multiplied, and all that you have is multiplied, then do not exalt yourself, forgetting the LORD your God, who brought you out of the land of Egypt, out of the house of slavery, who led you through the great and terrible wilderness, an arid wasteland with poisonous snakes and scorpions. He made water flow for you from flint rock, and fed you in the wilderness with manna that your ancestors did not know, to humble you and to test you, and in the end to do you good. Do not say to yourself, "My power and the might of my own hand have gotten me this wealth." But remember the LORD your God, for it is he who gives you power to get wealth, so that he may confirm his covenant that he swore to your ancestors, as he is doing today. If you do forget the LORD your God and follow other gods to serve and worship them, I solemnly warn you today that you shall surely perish.

Deuteronomy 9:5 NKJV It is not because of your righteousness or the uprightness of your heart that you go in to possess their land, but because of the wickedness of these nations that the LORD your God drives them out from before you, and that He may fulfill the word which the LORD swore to your fathers.

Psalm 34:1-3 NCV I will praise the LORD at all times; his praise is always on my lips. My whole being praises the LORD. The poor will hear and be glad. Glorify the LORD with me, and let us praise his name together.

Proverbs 16:5-6 WEB Everyone who is proud in heart is an abomination to Yahweh: they shall certainly not be unpunished. By mercy and truth iniquity is atoned for. By the fear of Yahweh men depart from evil.

Proverbs 16:18-19 NASB Pride goes before destruction, and a haughty spirit before stumbling. It is better to be humble in spirit with the lowly than to divide the spoil with the proud.

Proverbs 21:2-4 NLT People may think they are doing what is right, but the LORD examines the heart. The LORD is more pleased when we do what is just and right than when we give him sacrifices. Haughty eyes, a proud heart, and evil actions are all sin.

Proverbs 22:4 NLT True humility and fear of the LORD lead to riches, honor, and long life.

Isaiah 2:12 NKJV For the day of the LORD of hosts shall come upon everything proud and lofty, upon everything lifted up—and it shall be brought low.

Isaiah 42:8 NASB I am the LORD, that is My name; I will not give My glory to another, nor My praise to graven images.

Jeremiah 9:24 WEB But let him who glories glory in this, that he has understanding, and knows me, that I am Yahweh who exercises lovingkindness, justice, and righteousness, in the earth: for in these things I delight, says Yahweh.

Matthew 6:3-4 NCV So when you give to the poor, don't let anyone know what you are doing. Your giving should be done in secret. Your Father can see what is done in secret, and he will reward you.

Galatians 6:3-4 WEB For if a man thinks himself to be something when he is nothing, he deceives himself. But let each man test his own work, and then he will take pride in himself and not in his neighbor.

Deuteronomy 6:5 NLT And you must love the LORD your God with all your heart, all your soul, and all your strength.

Proverbs 23:4–5 NLT Don't weary yourself trying to get rich. Why waste your time? For riches can disappear as though they had the wings of a bird!

Ecclesiastes 12:13 NKJV Fear God and keep His commandments, for this is man's all.

Matthew 6:33–34 NASB But seek first His kingdom and His righteousness, and all these things will be added to you. So do not worry about tomorrow; for tomorrow will care for itself. Each day has enough trouble of its own.

Luke 16:15 NKJV And He said to them, "You are those who justify yourselves before men, but God knows your hearts. For what is highly esteemed among men is an abomination in the sight of God."

Acts 5:29 NLT But Peter and the apostles replied, "We must obey God rather than human authority."

Colossians 3:1–3 WNT If however you have risen with Christ, seek the things that are above, where Christ is, enthroned at God's right hand. Give your minds to the things that are above, not to the things that are on the earth. For you have died, and your life is hidden with Christ in God.

1 John 2:15–17 NIV Do not love the world or anything in the world. If anyone loves the world, the love of the Father is not in him. For everything in the world—the cravings of sinful man, the lust of his eyes and the boasting of what he has and does—comes not from the Father but from the world. The world and its desires pass away, but the man who does the will of God lives forever.

Psalm 9:9–10 TMB The LORD also will be a refuge for the oppressed, a refuge in times of trouble. And they that know Thy name will put their trust in Thee; for Thou, LORD, hast not forsaken them that seek Thee.

Psalm 61:1–4 NASB Hear my cry, O God; give heed to my prayer. From the end of the earth I call to You when my heart is faint; lead me to the rock that is higher than I. For You have been a refuge for me, a tower of strength against the enemy. Let me dwell in Your tent forever; let me take refuge in the shelter of Your wings.

Psalm 142:5–7 NCV LORD, I cry out to you. I say, "You are my protection. You are all I want in this life." Listen to my cry, because I am helpless. Save me from those who are chasing me, because they are too strong for me. Free me from my prison, and then I will praise your name. Then good people will surround me, because you have taken care of me.

Psalm 146:5–7 WEB Happy is he who has the God of Jacob for his help, whose hope is in Yahweh, his God: who made heaven and earth, the sea, and all that is in them; who keeps truth forever; who executes justice for the oppressed; who gives food to the hungry. Yahweh frees the prisoners.

Isaiah 61:1–2 NASB The Spirit of the Lord GOD is upon me, because the LORD has anointed me to bring good news to the afflicted; He has sent me to bind up the brokenhearted, to proclaim liberty to captives and freedom to prisoners; to proclaim the favorable year of the LORD and the day of vengeance of our God; to comfort all who mourn.

Matthew 11:1–3 NCV After Jesus finished telling these things to his twelve followers, he left there and went to the towns in Galilee to teach and preach. John the Baptist was in prison, but he heard about what Christ was doing. So John sent some of his followers to Jesus. They asked him, "Are you the One who is to come, or should we wait for someone else?"

Matthew 25:34-36 NASB Then the King will say to those on His right, "Come, you who are blessed of My Father, inherit the kingdom prepared for you from the foundation of the world. For I was hungry, and you gave Me something to eat; I was thirsty, and you gave Me something to drink; I was a stranger, and you invited Me in; naked, and you clothed Me; I was sick, and you visited Me; I was in prison, and you came to Me."

Acts 16:25-26 NKJV But at midnight Paul and Silas were praying and singing hymns to God, and the prisoners were listening to them. Suddenly there was a great earthquake, so that the foundations of the prison were shaken; and immediately all the doors were opened and everyone's chains were loosed.

Acts 24:23 NKJV So he commanded the centurion to keep Paul and to let him have liberty, and told him not to forbid any of his friends to provide for or visit him.

1 Corinthians 10:12-13 NASB Therefore let him who thinks he stands take heed that he does not fall. No temptation has overtaken you but such as is common to man; and God is faithful, who will not allow you to be tempted beyond what you are able, but with the temptation will provide the way of escape also, so that you will be able to endure it.

Hebrews 11:32-34 WNT And why need I say more? For time will fail me if I tell the story of Gideon, Barak, Samson, Jephthah, and of David and Samuel and the Prophets; men who, as the result of faith, conquered whole kingdoms, brought about true justice, obtained promises from God, stopped lions' mouths, deprived fire of its power, escaped being killed by the sword, out of weakness were made strong, became mighty in war, put to flight foreign armies.

Hebrews 13:3 NCV Remember those who are in prison as if you were in prison with them. Remember those who are suffering as if you were suffering with them.

Psalm 37:39-40 WEB But the salvation of the righteous is from Yahweh. He is their stronghold in the time of trouble. Yahweh helps them, and rescues them. He rescues them from the wicked, and saves them, because they have taken refuge in him.

Isaiah 43:1-4 NCV Now this is what the LORD says. He created you, people of Jacob; he formed you, people of Israel. He says, "Don't be afraid, because I have saved you. I have called you by name, and you are mine. When you pass through the waters, I will be with you. When you cross rivers, you will not drown. When you walk through fire, you will not be burned, nor will the flames hurt you. This is because I, the LORD, am your God, the Holy One of Israel, your Savior. I gave Egypt to pay for you, and I gave Cush and Seba to make you mine. Because you are precious to me.

Isaiah 49:25 NKJV But thus says the LORD: "Even the captives of the mighty shall be taken away, and the prey of the terrible be delivered; for I will contend with him who contends with you, and I will save your children".

Jeremiah 31:17 NASB "There is hope for your future," declares the LORD, "and your children will return to their own territory."

Luke 15:20-24 WEB He arose, and came to his father. But while he was still far off, his father saw him, and was moved with compassion, and ran, and fell on his neck, and kissed him. The son said to him, "Father, I have sinned against heaven, and in your sight. I am no more worthy to be called your son." But the father said to his servants, "Bring out the best robe, and put it on him. Put a ring on his hand, and shoes on his feet. Bring the fattened calf, kill it, and let us eat, and celebrate; for this, my son, was dead, and is alive again. He was lost, and is found." They began to celebrate.

John 16:33 NKJV These things I have spoken to you, that in Me you may have peace. In the world you will have tribulation; but be of good cheer, I have overcome the world.

2 Corinthians 5:20-21 NLT We are Christ's ambassadors, and God is using us to speak to you. We urge you, as though Christ himself were here pleading with you, "Be reconciled to God!" For God made Christ, who never sinned, to be the offering for our sin, so that we could be made right with God through Christ.

Ephesians 2:13-16 WEB But now in Christ Jesus you who once were far off are made near in the blood of Christ. For he is our peace, who made both one, and broke down the middle wall of partition, having abolished in the flesh the hostility, the law of commandments contained in ordinances, that he might create in himself one new man of the two, making peace; and might reconcile them both in one body to God through the cross, having killed the hostility thereby.

Hebrews 4:13 NKJV And there is no creature hidden from His sight, but all things are naked and open to the eyes of Him to whom we must give account.

Hebrews 12:12-13 WEB Therefore, lift up the hands that hang down and the feeble knees, and make straight paths for your feet, so that which is lame may not be dislocated, but rather be healed.

James 5:19-20 WNT My brethren, if one of you strays from the truth and some one brings him back, let him know that he who brings a sinner back from his evil ways will save the man's soul from death and throw a veil over a multitude of sins.

1 Peter 2:25 NLT Once you were wandering like lost sheep. But now you have turned to your Shepherd, the Guardian of your souls.

Genesis 9:16 NIV Whenever the rainbow appears in the clouds, I will see it and remember the everlasting covenant between God and all living creatures of every kind on the earth.

Deuteronomy 7:9 NKJV Therefore know that the LORD your God, He is God, the faithful God who keeps covenant and mercy for a thousand generations with those who love Him and keep His commandments.

1 Kings 8:56 NKJV Blessed be the LORD, who has given rest to His people Israel, according to all that He promised. There has not failed one word of all His good promise, which He promised through His servant Moses.

Psalm 84:11 NASB For the LORD God is a sun and shield; the LORD gives grace and glory; no good thing does He withhold from those who walk uprightly.

Psalm 91:14–16 NIV "Because he loves me," says the LORD, "I will rescue him; I will protect him, for he acknowledges my name. He will call upon me, and I will answer him; I will be with him in trouble, I will deliver him and honor him. With long life will I satisfy him and show him my salvation."

Isaiah 40:29–31 NRSV He gives power to the faint, and strengthens the powerless. Even youths will faint and be weary, and the young will fall exhausted; but those who wait for the LORD shall renew their strength, they shall mount up with wings like eagles, they shall run and not be weary, they shall walk and not faint.

Isaiah 41:13 NASB For I am the LORD your God, who upholds your right hand, who says to you, "Do not fear, I will help you."

Isaiah 43:1-3 NRSV Do not fear, for I have redeemed you; I have called you by name, you are mine. When you pass through the waters, I will be with you; and through the rivers, they shall not overwhelm you; when you walk through fire you shall not be burned, and the flame shall not consume you. For I am the LORD your God, the Holy One of Israel, your Savior.

Mark 10:29-30 WNT "In solemn truth I tell you," replied Jesus, "that there is no one who has forsaken house or brothers or sisters, or mother or father, or children or lands, for my sake and for the sake of the Good News, but will receive a hundred times as much now in this present life— houses, brothers, sisters, mothers, children, lands—and persecution with them—and in the coming age the Life of the Ages."

John 1:51 NCV And Jesus said to them, "I tell you the truth, you will all see heaven open and 'angels of God going up and coming down' on the Son of Man."

John 6:35 NIV Then Jesus declared, "I am the bread of life. He who comes to me will never go hungry, and he who believes in me will never be thirsty."

John 8:51 NLT I assure you, anyone who obeys my teaching will never die!

James 1:12 NKJV Blessed is the man who endures temptation; for when he has been approved, he will receive the crown of life which the Lord has promised to those who love Him.

2 Peter 1:3-4 NCV Jesus has the power of God, by which he has given us everything we need to live and to serve God. We have these things because we know him. Jesus called us by his glory and goodness. Through these he gave us the very great and precious promises. With these gifts you can share in being like God, and the world will not ruin you with its evil desires.

Genesis 39:21-23 WEB But Yahweh was with Joseph, and showed kindness to him, and gave him favor in the sight of the keeper of the prison. The keeper of the prison committed to Joseph's hand all the prisoners who were in the prison. Whatever they did there, he was responsible for it. The keeper of the prison didn't look after anything that was under his hand, because Yahweh was with him; and that which he did, Yahweh made it prosper.

Deuteronomy 8:18 WEB But you shall remember Yahweh your God, for it is he who gives you power to get wealth; that he may establish his covenant which he swore to your fathers, as at this day.

Joshua 1:7-8 NKJV Only be strong and very courageous, that you may observe to do according to all the law which Moses My servant commanded you; do not turn from it to the right hand or to the left, that you may prosper wherever you go. This Book of the Law shall not depart from your mouth, but you shall meditate in it day and night, that you may observe to do according to all that is written in it. For then you will make your way prosperous, and then you will have good success.

1 Kings 2:1-4 NRSV When David's time to die drew near, he charged his son Solomon, saying: "I am about to go the way of all the earth. Be strong, be courageous, and keep the charge of the LORD your God, walking in his ways and keeping his statutes, his commandments, his ordinances, and his testimonies, as it is written in the law of Moses, so that you may prosper in all that you do and wherever you turn. Then the LORD will establish his word that he spoke concerning me: 'If your heirs take heed to their way, to walk before me in faithfulness with all their heart and with all their soul, there shall not fail you a successor on the throne of Israel.'"

2 Chronicles 31:20-21 NKJV Thus Hezekiah did throughout all Judah, and he did what was good and right and true before the LORD his God. And in every work that he began in the service of the house of God, in the law and in the commandment, to seek his God, he did it with all his heart. So he prospered.

Job 36:11 WEB If they listen and serve him, they shall spend their days in prosperity, and their years in pleasures.

Psalm 45:3-4 NKJV Gird Your sword upon Your thigh, O Mighty One, with Your glory and Your majesty. And in Your majesty ride prosperously because of truth, humility, and righteousness; and Your right hand shall teach You awesome things.

Psalm 90:17 NIV May the favor of the Lord our God rest upon us; establish the work of our hands for us—yes, establish the work of our hands.

Psalm 128:1-4 NRSV Happy is everyone who fears the LORD, who walks in his ways. You shall eat the fruit of the labor of your hands; you shall be happy, and it shall go well with you. Your wife will be like a fruitful vine within your house; your children will be like olive shoots around your table. Thus shall the man be blessed who fears the LORD.

Proverbs 10:22 TMB The blessings of the LORD maketh rich, and He addeth no sorrow with it.

Proverbs 28:13 NLT People who cover over their sins will not prosper. But if they confess and forsake them, they will receive mercy.

Isaiah 54:17 NKJV "No weapon formed against you shall prosper, and every tongue which rises against you in judgment you shall condemn. This is the heritage of the servants of the LORD, and their righteousness is from Me," says the LORD.

3 John 2 NKJV Beloved, I pray that you may prosper in all things and be in health, just as your soul prospers.

Deuteronomy 9:1-3 NRSV Hear, O Israel! You are about to cross the Jordan today, to go in and dispossess nations larger and mightier than you, great cities, fortified to the heavens, a strong and tall people, the offspring of the Anakim, whom you know. You have heard it said of them, "Who can stand up to the Anakim?" Know then today that the LORD your God is the one who crosses over before you as a devouring fire; he will defeat them and subdue them before you, so that you may dispossess and destroy them quickly, as the LORD has promised you.

Psalm 3:1-3 NCV LORD, I have many enemies! Many people have turned against me. Many are saying about me, "God won't rescue him." But, LORD, you are my shield, my wonderful God who gives me courage.

Psalm 9:9-10 NLT The LORD is a shelter for the oppressed, a refuge in times of trouble. Those who know your name trust in you, for you, O LORD, have never abandoned anyone who searches for you.

Psalm 17:7-9 WEB Show your marvelous loving kindness, you who save those who take refuge by your right hand from their enemies. Keep me as the apple of your eye; hide me under the shadow of your wings, from the wicked who oppress me, my deadly enemies, who surround me.

Psalm 27:4-5 NKJV One thing I have desired of the LORD, that will I seek: that I may dwell in the house of the LORD all the days of my life, to behold the beauty of the LORD, and to inquire in His temple. For in the time of trouble He shall hide me in His pavilion; in the secret place of His tabernacle He shall hide me; He shall set me high upon a rock.

Psalm 56:12-13 NLT I will fulfill my vows to you, O God, and offer a sacrifice of thanks for your help. For you have rescued me from death; you have kept my feet from slipping. So now I can walk in your presence, O God, in your life-giving light.

Psalm 61:2-4 NIV From the ends of the earth I call to you, I call as my heart grows faint; lead me to the rock that is higher than I. For you have been my refuge, a strong tower against the foe. I long to dwell in your tent forever and take refuge in the shelter of your wings.

Psalm 62:5-7 WEB My soul, wait in silence for God alone, for my expectation is from him. He alone is my rock and my salvation, my fortress. I will not be shaken. With God is my salvation and my honor. The rock of my strength, and my refuge, is in God.

Psalm 84:11-12 NASB For the LORD God is a sun and shield; the LORD gives grace and glory; no good thing does He withhold from those who walk uprightly. O LORD of hosts, how blessed is the man who trusts in You!

Psalm 91:9-12 NRSV Because you have made the LORD your refuge, the Most High your dwelling place, no evil shall befall you, no scourge come near your tent. For he will command his angels concerning you to guard you in all your ways. On their hands they will bear you up, so that you will not dash your foot against a stone.

Psalm 138:7-8 WEB Though I walk in the midst of trouble, you will revive me. You will stretch forth your hand against the wrath of my enemies. Your right hand will save me. Yahweh will fulfill that which concerns me; your loving kindness, Yahweh, endures forever. Don't forsake the works of your own hands.

Psalm 140:7 TMB O GOD the Lord, the strength of my salvation, Thou hast covered my head in the day of battle.

Psalm 145:18-20 NRSV The LORD is near to all who call on him, to all who call on him in truth. He fulfills the desire of all who fear him; he also hears their cry, and saves them. The LORD watches over all who love him, but all the wicked he will destroy.

Genesis 39:21-23 NRSV But the LORD was with Joseph and showed him steadfast love; he gave him favor in the sight of the chief jailer. The chief jailer committed to Joseph's care all the prisoners who were in the prison, and whatever was done there, he was the one who did it. The chief jailer paid no heed to anything that was in Joseph's care, because the LORD was with him; and whatever he did, the LORD made it prosper.

Psalm 23:5-6 WEB You prepare a table before me in the presence of my enemies. You anoint my head with oil. My cup runs over. Surely goodness and loving kindness shall follow me all the days of my life, and I shall dwell in Yahweh's house forever.

Psalm 36:5-6 NKJV Your mercy, O LORD, is in the heavens; Your faithfulness reaches to the clouds. Your righteousness is like the great mountains; Your judgments are a great deep; O LORD, You preserve man and beast.

Psalm 36:7-9 NRSV How precious is your steadfast love, O God! All people may take refuge in the shadow of your wings. They feast on the abundance of your house, and you give them drink from the river of your delights. For with you is the fountain of life; in your light we see light.

Psalm 65:9-10 WEB You visit the earth, and water it. You greatly enrich it. The river of God is full of water. You provide them grain, for so you have ordained it. You drench its furrows. You level its ridges. You soften it with showers. You bless it with a crop.

Psalm 84:11-12 NKJV For the LORD God is a sun and shield; the LORD will give grace and glory; no good thing will He withhold from those who walk uprightly. O LORD of hosts, blessed is the man who trusts in You!

Psalm 123:1-2 NASB Unto You I lift up my eyes, O You who dwell in the heavens. Behold, as the eyes of servants look to the hand of their masters, as the eyes of a maid to the hand of her mistress, so our eyes look to the LORD our God, until He has mercy on us.

Psalm 145:14-16 NRSV The LORD upholds all who are falling, and raises up all who are bowed down. The eyes of all look to you, and you give them their food in due season. You open your hand, satisfying the desire of every living thing.

Proverbs 16:7 NLT When the ways of people please the LORD, he makes even their enemies live at peace with them.

Isaiah 45:2-3 NKJV I will go before you and make the crooked places straight; I will break in pieces the gates of bronze and cut the bars of iron. I will give you the treasures of darkness and hidden riches of secret places, that you may know that I, the LORD, who call you by your name, am the God of Israel.

Jeremiah 33:9 NKJV Then it shall be to Me a name of joy, a praise, and an honor before all nations of the earth, who shall hear all the good that I do to them; they shall fear and tremble for all the goodness and all the prosperity that I provide for it.

Matthew 6:9-11 NIV This, then, is how you should pray: "Our Father in heaven, hallowed be your name, your kingdom come, your will be done on earth as it is in heaven. Give us today our daily bread."

Philippians 4:19 NASB And my God will supply all your needs according to His riches in glory in Christ Jesus.

Revelation 7:15-17 NRSV For this reason they are before the throne of God, and worship him day and night within his temple, and the one who is seated on the throne will shelter them. They will hunger no more, and thirst no more; the sun will not strike them, nor any scorching heat; for the Lamb at the center of the throne will be their shepherd, and he will guide them to springs of the water of life, and God will wipe away every tear from their eyes.

Psalm 12:6-7 NASB The words of the Lord are pure words; as silver tried in a furnace on the earth, refined seven times. You, O Lord, will keep them; You will preserve him from this generation forever.

Psalm 24:3-5 NRSV Who shall ascend the hill of the Lord? And who shall stand in his holy place? Those who have clean hands and pure hearts, who do not lift up their souls to what is false, and do not swear deceitfully. They will receive blessing from the Lord, and vindication from the God of their salvation.

Proverbs 15:26 NLT The Lord despises the thoughts of the wicked, but he delights in pure words.

Proverbs 30:11-13 NCV Some people curse their fathers and do not bless their mothers. Some people think they are pure, but they are not really free from evil. Some people have such a proud look! They look down on others.

Isaiah 1:18-20 WEB "Come now, and let us reason together," says Yahweh: "Though your sins be as scarlet, they shall be as white as snow. Though they be red like crimson, they shall be as wool. If you are willing and obedient, you shall eat the good of the land; but if you refuse and rebel, you shall be devoured with the sword; for the mouth of Yahweh has spoken it."

Malachi 3:2-3 NKJV But who can endure the day of His coming? And who can stand when He appears? For He is like a refiner's fire and like launderers' soap. He will sit as a refiner and a purifier of silver; He will purify the sons of Levi, and purge them as gold and silver, that they may offer to the Lord an offering in righteousness.

Matthew 5:8-9 TMB Blessed are the pure in heart, for they shall see God. Blessed are the peacemakers, for they shall be called the children of God.

Philippians 4:8 NKJV Whatever things are true, whatever things are noble, whatever things are just, whatever things are pure, whatever things are lovely, whatever things are of good report, if there is any virtue and if there is anything praiseworthy—meditate on these things.

Colossians 3:5-10 WNT Therefore put to death your earthward inclinations—fornication, impurity, sensual passion, unholy desire, and all greed, for that is a form of idolatry. It is on account of these very sins that God's anger is coming, and you also were once addicted to them, while you were living under their power. But now you must rid yourselves of every kind of sin—angry and passionate outbreaks, ill-will, evil speaking, foul-mouthed abuse—so that these may never soil your lips. Do not speak falsehoods to one another, for you have stripped off the old self with its doings, and have clothed yourselves with the new self.

1 Timothy 5:22 NIV Do not be hasty in the laying on of hands, and do not share in the sins of others. Keep yourself pure.

James 4:7-8 NKJV Submit to God. Resist the devil and he will flee from you. Draw near to God and He will draw near to you. Cleanse your hands, you sinners; and purify your hearts, you double-minded.

1 Peter 2:11-12 NKJV Beloved, I beg you as sojourners and pilgrims, abstain from fleshly lusts which war against the soul, having your conduct honorable among the Gentiles, that when they speak against you as evildoers, they may, by your good works which they observe, glorify God in the day of visitation.

1 John 3:2-3 NASB We know that when He appears, we will be like Him, because we will see Him just as He is. And everyone who has this hope fixed on Him purifies himself, just as He is pure.

Psalm 16:11 NASB You will make known to me the path of life; in Your presence is fullness of joy; in Your right hand there are pleasures forever.

Psalm 20:4-5 NKJV May He grant you according to your heart's desire, and fulfill all your purpose. We will rejoice in your salvation, and in the name of our God we will set up our banners! May the LORD fulfill all your petitions.

Proverbs 16:1-3 NKJV The preparations of the heart belong to man, but the answer of the tongue is from the LORD. All the ways of a man are pure in his own eyes, but the LORD weighs the spirits. Commit your works to the LORD, and your thoughts will be established.

Ecclesiastes 3:1 NLT There is a time for everything, a season for every activity under heaven.

John 9:4 NKJV I must work the works of Him who sent Me while it is day; the night is coming when no one can work.

John 19:28-30 WEB After this, Jesus, seeing that all things were now finished, that the Scripture might be fulfilled, said, "I am thirsty." Now a vessel full of vinegar was set there; so they put a sponge full of the vinegar on hyssop, and held it at his mouth. When Jesus therefore had received the vinegar, he said "It is finished." He bowed his head, and gave up his spirit.

Acts 11:23-24 NASB Then when he arrived and witnessed the grace of God, he rejoiced and began to encourage them all with resolute heart to remain true to the LORD; for he was a good man, and full of the Holy Spirit and of faith.

Romans 8:28–29 NKJV And we know that all things work together for good to those who love God, to those who are the called according to His purpose. For whom He foreknew, He also predestined to be conformed to the image of His Son, that He might be the firstborn among many brethren.

Romans 12:6–8 NKJV Having then gifts differing according to the grace that is given to us, let us use them: if prophecy, let us prophesy in proportion to our faith; or ministry, let us use it in our ministering; he who teaches, in teaching; he who exhorts, in exhortation; he who gives, with liberality; he who leads, with diligence; he who shows mercy, with cheerfulness.

Philippians 3:12–14 WEB Not that I have already obtained, or am already made perfect; but I press on, if it is so that I may take hold of that for which also I was taken hold of by Christ Jesus. Brothers, I don't regard myself as yet having taken hold, but one thing I do. Forgetting the things which are behind, and stretching forward to the things which are before, I press on toward the goal for the prize of the high calling of God in Christ Jesus.

Colossians 3:23–25 NIV Whatever you do, work at it with all your heart, as working for the Lord, not for men, since you know that you will receive an inheritance from the Lord as a reward. It is the Lord Christ you are serving. Anyone who does wrong will be repaid for his wrong, and there is no favoritism.

2 Timothy 1:8–10 NKJV Do not be ashamed of the testimony of our Lord, nor of me His prisoner, but share with me in the sufferings for the gospel according to the power of God, who has saved us and called us with a holy calling, not according to our works, but according to His own purpose and grace which was given to us in Christ Jesus before time began, but has now been revealed by the appearing of our Savior Jesus Christ, who has abolished death and brought life and immortality to light through the gospel.

1 Samuel 15:22-23 NASB Samuel said, "Has the LORD as much delight in burnt offerings and sacrifices as in obeying the voice of the LORD? Behold, to obey is better than sacrifice, and to heed than the fat of rams. For rebellion is as the sin of divination, and insubordination is as iniquity and idolatry. Because you have rejected the word of the LORD, He has also rejected you from being king.

Job 23:10-12 NASB But He knows the way I take; when He has tried me, I shall come forth as gold. My foot has held fast to His path; I have kept His way and not turned aside. I have not departed from the command of His lips; I have treasured the words of His mouth more than my necessary food.

Psalm 81:11-14 NKJV But My people would not heed My voice, and Israel would have none of Me. So I gave them over to their own stubborn heart, to walk in their own counsels. Oh, that My people would listen to Me, that Israel would walk in My ways! I would soon subdue their enemies, and turn My hand against their adversaries.

Psalm 95:7-11 NKJV Today, if you will hear His voice: "Do not harden your hearts, as in the rebellion, as in the day of trial in the wilderness, when your fathers tested Me; they tried Me, though they saw My work. For forty years I was grieved with that generation, and said, 'It is a people who go astray in their hearts, and they do not know My ways.' So I swore in My wrath, 'They shall not enter My rest.' "

Proverbs 5:21-23 NKJV For the ways of man are before the eyes of the LORD, and He ponders all his paths. His own iniquities entrap the wicked man, and he is caught in the cords of his sin. He shall die for lack of instruction, and in the greatness of his folly he shall go astray.

Proverbs 28:18 NKJV He who is perverse in his ways will suddenly fall.

Isaiah 65:2-5 NKJV I have stretched out My hands all day long to a rebellious people, who walk in a way that is not good, according to their own thoughts; a people who provoke Me to anger continually to My face; who sacrifice in gardens, and burn incense on altars of brick; who sit among the graves, and spend the night in the tombs; who eat swine's flesh, and the broth of abominable things is in their vessels; who say, "Keep to yourself, do not come near me, for I am holier than you!" These are smoke in My nostrils, a fire that burns all the day.

Ezekiel 18:21-23 WEB But if the wicked turn from all his sins that he has committed, and keep all my statutes, and do that which is lawful and right, he shall surely live, he shall not die. None of his transgressions that he has committed shall be remembered against him: in his righteousness that he has done he shall live. Have I any pleasure in the death of the wicked? says the Lord Yahweh; and not rather that he should return from his way, and live?

Ezekiel 20:37-38 NIV I will take note of you as you pass under my rod, and I will bring you into the bond of the covenant. I will purge you of those who revolt and rebel against me. Although I will bring them out of the land where they are living, yet they will not enter the land of Israel. Then you will know that I am the LORD.

Hebrews 3:7-11 NKJV Therefore, as the Holy Spirit says: "Today, if you will hear His voice, do not harden your hearts as in the rebellion, in the day of trial in the wilderness, where your fathers tested Me, tried Me, and saw My works forty years. Therefore I was angry with that generation, and said, 'They always go astray in their heart, and they have not known My ways.' So I swore in My wrath, they shall not enter My rest."

1 Peter 2:25 WEB For you were going astray like sheep; but are now returned to the Shepherd and Overseer of your souls.

Matthew 5:23-24 NKJV Therefore if you bring your gift to the altar, and there remember that your brother has something against you, leave your gift there before the altar, and go your way. First be reconciled to your brother, and then come and offer your gift.

Luke 15:20-24 NLT So he returned home to his father. And while he was still a long distance away, his father saw him coming. Filled with love and compassion, he ran to his son, embraced him, and kissed him. His son said to him, "Father, I have sinned against both heaven and you, and I am no longer worthy of being called your son." But his father said to the servants, "Quick! Bring the finest robe in the house and put it on him. Get a ring for his finger, and sandals for his feet. And kill the calf we have been fattening in the pen. We must celebrate with a feast, for this son of mine was dead and has now returned to life. He was lost, but now he is found." So the party began.

Romans 5:11 NIV Not only is this so, but we also rejoice in God through our Lord Jesus Christ, through whom we have now received reconciliation.

2 Corinthians 5:18-19 NKJV Now all things are of God, who has reconciled us to Himself through Jesus Christ, and has given us the ministry of reconciliation, that is, that God was in Christ reconciling the world to Himself, not imputing their trespasses to them, and has committed to us the word of reconciliation.

2 Corinthians 5:20-21 WEB We beg you on behalf of Christ, be reconciled to God. For him who knew no sin he made to be sin on our behalf; so that in him we might become the righteousness of God.

Ephesians 2:13-15 NKJV But now in Christ Jesus you who once were far off have been brought near by the blood of Christ. For He Himself is our peace, who has made both one, and has broken down the middle wall of separation, having abolished in His flesh the enmity.

Psalm 25:16-21 NKJV Turn Yourself to me, and have mercy on me, for I am desolate and afflicted. The troubles of my heart have enlarged; bring me out of my distresses! Look on my affliction and my pain, and forgive all my sins. Consider my enemies, for they are many; and they hate me with cruel hatred. Keep my soul, and deliver me; let me not be ashamed, for I put my trust in You. Let integrity and uprightness preserve me, for I wait for You.

Psalm 94:14 NASB For the LORD will not abandon His people, nor will He forsake His inheritance.

Psalm 142:1-4 NKJV I cry out to the LORD with my voice; with my voice to the LORD I make my supplication. I pour out my complaint before Him; I declare before Him my trouble. When my spirit was overwhelmed within me, then You knew my path. In the way in which I walk they have secretly set a snare for me. Look on my right hand and see, for there is no one who acknowledges me; refuge has failed me; no one cares for my soul.

Jeremiah 31:3-4 NIV The LORD appeared to us in the past, saying: "I have loved you with an everlasting love; I have drawn you with loving-kindness. I will build you up again and you will be rebuilt, O Virgin Israel. Again you will take up your tambourines and go out to dance with the joyful."

Romans 8:31 NASB What then shall we say to these things? If God is for us, who is against us?

1 Peter 2:4-5 NASB And coming to Him as to a living stone which has been rejected by men, but is choice and precious in the sight of God, you also, as living stones, are being built up as a spiritual house for a holy priesthood, to offer up spiritual sacrifices acceptable to God through Jesus Christ.

2 Chronicles 7:14–16 NKJV If My people who are called by My name will humble themselves, and pray and seek My face, and turn from their wicked ways, then I will hear from heaven, and will forgive their sin and heal their land. Now My eyes will be open and My ears attentive to prayer made in this place. For now I have chosen and sanctified this house, that My name may be there forever; and My eyes and My heart will be there perpetually.

Job 11:13–15 NKJV If you would prepare your heart, and stretch out your hands toward Him; if iniquity were in your hand, and you put it far away, and would not let wickedness dwell in your tents; then surely you could lift up your face without spot; yes, you could be steadfast, and not fear.

Ezekiel 18:30–32 NIV Repent! Turn away from all your offenses; then sin will not be your downfall. Rid yourselves of all the offenses you have committed, and get a new heart and a new spirit. Why will you die, O house of Israel? For I take no pleasure in the death of anyone, declares the Sovereign Lord. Repent and live!

Joel 2:12–13 NIV "Even now," declares the Lord, "return to me with all your heart, with fasting and weeping and mourning." Rend your heart and not your garments. Return to the Lord your God, for he is gracious and compassionate, slow to anger and abounding in love, and he relents from sending calamity.

Matthew 9:12–13 NKJV When Jesus heard that, He said to them, "Those who are well have no need of a physician, but those who are sick. But go and learn what this means: 'I desire mercy and not sacrifice.' For I did not come to call the righteous, but sinners, to repentance."

Mark 1:15 NLT "At last the time has come!" he announced. "The Kingdom of God is near! Turn from your sins and believe this Good News!"

Luke 15:7 NASB There will be more joy in heaven over one sinner who repents than over ninety-nine righteous persons who need no repentance.

Acts 3:19-20 WEB Repent therefore, and turn again, that your sins may be blotted out, so that there may come times of refreshing from the presence of the Lord, and that he may send Christ Jesus, who was ordained for you before.

Acts 8:20-23 NKJV Peter said, . . . "Your heart is not right in the sight of God. Repent therefore of this your wickedness, and pray God if perhaps the thought of your heart may be forgiven you. For I see that you are poisoned by bitterness and bound by iniquity."

Acts 17:30-31 NASB God is now declaring to men that all people should repent, because He has fixed a day in which He will judge the world in righteousness through a Man whom He has appointed, having furnished proof to all men by raising Him from the dead.

Romans 2:4 NASB Or do you think lightly of the riches of His kindness and tolerance and patience, not knowing that the kindness of God leads you to repentance?

Revelation 2:21 WEB I gave her time to repent, but she refuses to repent of her sexual immorality.

Revelation 3:17-19 NKJV Because you say, "I am rich, have become wealthy, and have need of nothing"—and do not know that you are wretched, miserable, poor, blind, and naked—I counsel you to buy from Me gold refined in the fire, that you may be rich; and white garments, that you may be clothed, that the shame of your nakedness may not be revealed; and anoint your eyes with eye salve, that you may see. As many as I love, I rebuke and chasten. Therefore be zealous and repent!

Proverbs 10:12 WEB Hatred stirs up strife, but love covers all wrongs.

Isaiah 45:9 NLT Destruction is certain for those who argue with their Creator. Does a clay pot ever argue with its maker? Does the clay dispute with the one who shapes it, saying, "Stop, you are doing it wrong!" Does the pot exclaim, "How clumsy can you be!"

Galatians 5:14–16 NKJV The law is fulfilled in one word, even in this: "You shall love your neighbor as yourself." But if you bite and devour one another, beware lest you be consumed by one another! I say then: Walk in the Spirit, and you shall not fulfill the lust of the flesh.

Galatians 5:18–21 WEB But if you are led by the Spirit, you are not under the law. Now the works of the flesh are obvious, which are: adultery, sexual immorality, uncleanness, lustfulness, idolatry, sorcery, hatred, strife, jealousies, outbursts of anger, rivalries, divisions, heresies, envyings, murders, drunkenness, orgies, and things like these; of which I forewarn you, even as I also forewarned you, that those who practice such things will not inherit the Kingdom of God.

Ephesians 4:30-32 WEB Don't grieve the Holy Spirit of God, in whom you were sealed to the day of redemption. Let all bitterness, wrath, anger, outcry, and slander, be put away from you, with all malice. And be kind to one another, tenderhearted, forgiving each other, just as God also in Christ forgave you.

1 John 2:9–11 NKJV He who says he is in the light, and hates his brother, is in darkness until now. He who loves his brother abides in the light, and there is no cause for stumbling in him. But he who hates his brother is in darkness and walks in darkness, and does not know where he is going, because the darkness has blinded his eyes.

Genesis 2:3 NKJV Then God blessed the seventh day and sanctified it, because in it He rested from all His work which God had created and made.

Psalm 23:1–3 NKJV The LORD is my shepherd; I shall not want. He makes me to lie down in green pastures; He leads me beside the still waters. He restores my soul.

Psalm 37:7 NASB Rest in the LORD and wait patiently for Him; do not fret because of him who prospers in his way.

Psalm 55:22 NLT Give your burdens to the LORD, and he will take care of you. He will not permit the godly to slip and fall.

Psalm 95:7–11 NKJV Today, if you will hear His voice: "Do not harden your hearts, as in the rebellion, as in the day of trial in the wilderness, when your fathers tested Me; they tried Me, though they saw My work. For forty years I was grieved with that generation, and said, 'It is a people who go astray in their hearts, and they do not know My ways.' So I swore in My wrath, 'They shall not enter My rest.' "

Matthew 11:28–30 NIV Come to me, all you who are weary and burdened, and I will give you rest. Take my yoke upon you and learn from me, for I am gentle and humble in heart, and you will find rest for your souls. For my yoke is easy and my burden is light.

Mark 6:31 NLT Then Jesus said, "Let's get away from the crowds for a while and rest."

Hebrews 4:9–10 NKJV There remains therefore a rest for the people of God. For he who has entered His rest has himself also ceased from his works as God did from His.

2 Chronicles 7:1-2 NKJV When Solomon had finished praying, fire came down from heaven and consumed the burnt offering and the sacrifices; and the glory of the Lord filled the temple. And the priests could not enter the house of the Lord, because the glory of the Lord had filled the Lord's house.

Psalm 80:18-19 NLT Revive us so we can call on your name once more. Turn us again to yourself, O Lord God Almighty. Make your face shine down upon us. Only then will we be saved.

Psalm 85:6-7 NLT Won't you revive us again, so your people can rejoice in you? Show us your unfailing love, O Lord, and grant us your salvation.

Isaiah 64:1-2 NKJV Oh, that You would rend the heavens! That You would come down! That the mountains might shake at Your presence— as fire burns brushwood, as fire causes water to boil—to make Your name known to Your adversaries, that the nations may tremble at Your presence!

Hosea 6:1-3 NIV Come, let us return to the Lord. He has torn us to pieces but he will heal us; he has injured us but he will bind up our wounds. After two days he will revive us; on the third day he will restore us, that we may live in his presence. Let us acknowledge the Lord; let us press on to acknowledge him. As surely as the sun rises, he will appear; he will come to us like the winter rains, like the spring rains that water the earth.

Acts 3:19-21 NIV Repent, then, and turn to God, so that your sins may be wiped out, that times of refreshing may come from the Lord, and that he may send the Christ, who has been appointed for you—even Jesus. He must remain in heaven until the time comes for God to restore everything, as he promised long ago through his holy prophets.

Job 33:12-16 NKJV God is greater than man. Why do you contend with Him? For He does not give an accounting of any of His words. For God may speak in one way, or in another, yet man does not perceive it. In a dream, in a vision of the night, when deep sleep falls upon men, while slumbering on their beds, then He opens the ears of men, and seals their instruction.

Psalm 119:140 NASB Your word is very pure, therefore Your servant loves it.

Isaiah 48:6-8 NKJV I have made you hear new things from this time, even hidden things, and you did not know them. They are created now and not from the beginning; and before this day you have not heard them, lest you should say, "Of course I knew them." Surely you did not hear, surely you did not know; surely from long ago your ear was not opened.

Isaiah 55:8-11 NKJV "For My thoughts are not your thoughts, nor are your ways My ways," says the LORD. "For as the heavens are higher than the earth, so are My ways higher than your ways, and My thoughts than your thoughts. For as the rain comes down, and the snow from heaven, and do not return there, but water the earth, and make it bring forth and bud, that it may give seed to the sower and bread to the eater, so shall My word be that goes forth from My mouth; it shall not return to Me void, but it shall accomplish what I please; it shall prosper in the thing for which I sent it."

Jeremiah 33:2-3 NASB Thus says the LORD who made the earth, the LORD who formed it to establish it, the LORD is His name, "Call to Me and I will answer you, and I will tell you great and mighty things, which you do not know."

Daniel 2:19-20 NKJV Then the secret was revealed to Daniel in a night vision. So Daniel blessed the God of heaven. Daniel answered and said: "Blessed be the name of God forever and ever, for wisdom and might are His."

Amos 3:7 WEB Surely the Lord Yahweh will do nothing, unless he reveals his secret to his servants the prophets.

Amos 4:13 NLT For the LORD is the one who shaped the mountains, stirs up the winds, and reveals his every thought.

John 16:13-14 NKJV However, when He, the Spirit of truth, has come, He will guide you into all truth; for He will not speak on His own authority, but whatever He hears He will speak; and He will tell you things to come. He will glorify Me, for He will take of what is Mine and declare it to you.

1 Corinthians 1:4-8 NKJV I thank my God always concerning you for the grace of God which was given to you by Christ Jesus, that you were enriched in everything by Him in all utterance and all knowledge, even as the testimony of Christ was confirmed in you, so that you come short in no gift, eagerly waiting for the revelation of our Lord Jesus Christ, who will also confirm you to the end, that you may be blameless in the day of our Lord Jesus Christ.

1 Corinthians 2:9-10 NKJV "Eye has not seen, nor ear heard, nor have entered into the heart of man the things which God has prepared for those who love Him." But God has revealed them to us through His Spirit. For the Spirit searches all things, yes, the deep things of God.

Galatians 1:11-12 WEB But I make known to you, brothers, concerning the Good News which was preached by me, that it is not according to man. For neither did I receive it from man, nor was I taught it, but it came to me through revelation of Jesus Christ.

Revelation 1:1 NKJV The Revelation of Jesus Christ, which God gave Him to show His servants—things which must shortly take place.

Deuteronomy 8:18 NKJV And you shall remember the LORD your God, for it is He who gives you power to get wealth.

Proverbs 3:9-10 NKJV Honor the LORD with your possessions, and with the firstfruits of all your increase; so your barns will be filled with plenty, and your vats will overflow with new wine.

Proverbs 10:22 NASB It is the blessing of the LORD that makes rich, and He adds no sorrow to it.

Proverbs 11:28 TMB He that trusteth in his riches shall fall, but the righteous shall flourish as a branch.

Proverbs 22:1-2 NKJV A good name is to be chosen rather than great riches, loving favor rather than silver and gold. The rich and the poor have this in common, the LORD is the maker of them all.

Proverbs 28:6 NLT It is better to be poor and honest than rich and crooked.

Isaiah 55:2 NKJV Why do you spend money for what is not bread, and your wages for what does not satisfy? Listen carefully to Me, and eat what is good, and let your soul delight itself in abundance.

Matthew 6:24 WEB No one can serve two masters. . . . You can't serve both God and Mammon.

2 Corinthians 8:9 NKJV For you know the grace of our Lord Jesus Christ, that though He was rich, yet for your sakes He became poor, that you through His poverty might become rich.

2 Corinthians 9:6-8 NIV Remember this: Whoever sows sparingly will also reap sparingly, and whoever sows generously will also reap generously. Each man should give what he has decided in his heart to give, not reluctantly or under compulsion, for God loves a cheerful giver. And God is able to make all grace abound to you, so that in all things at all times, having all that you need, you will abound in every good work.

1 Timothy 6:17-19 NKJV Command those who are rich in this present age not to be haughty, nor to trust in uncertain riches but in the living God, who gives us richly all things to enjoy. Let them do good, that they be rich in good works, ready to give, willing to share, storing up for themselves a good foundation for the time to come, that they may lay hold on eternal life.

Hebrews 11:24-26 NKJV By faith Moses, when he became of age, refused to be called the son of Pharaoh's daughter, choosing rather to suffer affliction with the people of God than to enjoy the passing pleasures of sin, esteeming the reproach of Christ greater riches than the treasures in Egypt; for he looked to the reward.

James 1:9-11 NLT Christians who are poor should be glad, for God has honored them. And those who are rich should be glad, for God has humbled them. They will fade away like a flower in the field. The hot sun rises and dries up the grass; the flower withers, and its beauty fades away. So also, wealthy people will fade away with all of their achievements.

James 2:5-7 NKJV Listen, my beloved brethren: Has God not chosen the poor of this world to be rich in faith and heirs of the kingdom which He promised to those who love Him? But you have dishonored the poor man. Do not the rich oppress you and drag you into the courts? Do they not blaspheme that noble name by which you are called?

Psalm 18:21–24 NKJV For I have kept the ways of the Lord, and have not wickedly departed from my God. For all His judgments were before me, and I did not put away His statutes from me. I was also blameless before Him, and I kept myself from my iniquity. Therefore the Lord has recompensed me according to my righteousness, according to the cleanness of my hands in His sight.

Psalm 24:3–5 WEB Who may ascend to Yahweh's hill? Who may stand in his holy place? He who has clean hands and a pure heart; who has not lifted up his soul to falsehood, and has not sworn deceitfully. He shall receive a blessing from Yahweh, righteousness from the God of his salvation.

Psalm 37:29–31 NKJV The righteous shall inherit the land, and dwell in it forever. The mouth of the righteous speaks wisdom, and his tongue talks of justice. The law of his God is in his heart; none of his steps shall slide.

Proverbs 12:26–28 NKJV The righteous should choose his friends carefully, for the way of the wicked leads them astray. The lazy man does not roast what he took in hunting, but diligence is man's precious possession. In the way of righteousness is life, and in its pathway there is no death.

Proverbs 20:7 NIV The righteous man leads a blameless life; blessed are his children after him.

Isaiah 54:17 WEB "No weapon that is formed against you will prevail; and you will condemn every tongue that rises against you in judgment. This is the heritage of the servants of Yahweh, and their righteousness which is of me," says Yahweh.

Hosea 14:9 NKJV Who is wise? Let him understand these things. Who is prudent? Let him know them. For the ways of the Lord are right; the righteous walk in them, but transgressors stumble in them.

Romans 5:17-18 NKJV For if by the one man's offense death reigned through the one, much more those who receive abundance of grace and of the gift of righteousness will reign in life through the One, Jesus Christ. Therefore, as . . . through one Man's righteous act the free gift came to all men, resulting in justification of life.

Romans 6:12-13 NKJV Therefore do not let sin reign in your mortal body, that you should obey it in its lusts. And do not present your members as instruments of unrighteousness to sin, but present yourselves to God as being alive from the dead, and your members as instruments of righteousness to God.

Romans 14:17 NLT For the Kingdom of God is not a matter of what we eat or drink, but of living a life of goodness and peace and joy in the Holy Spirit.

1 Corinthians 6:20 WEB For you were bought with a price. Therefore glorify God in your body and in your spirit, which are God's.

2 Timothy 2:22 WEB Flee from youthful lusts; but pursue righteousness, faith, love, and peace with those who call on the Lord out of a pure heart.

Hebrews 12:11-13 NKJV Now no chastening seems to be joyful for the present, but painful; nevertheless, afterward it yields the peaceable fruit of righteousness to those who have been trained by it. Therefore strengthen the hands which hang down, and the feeble knees, and make straight paths for your feet, so that what is lame may not be dislocated, but rather be healed.

1 John 3:7-8 NKJV Little children, let no one deceive you. He who practices righteousness is righteous, just as He is righteous. He who sins is of the devil, for the devil has sinned from the beginning. For this purpose the Son of God was manifested, that He might destroy the works of the devil.

Psalm 50:2-6 NASB Out of Zion, the perfection of beauty, God has shone forth. May our God come and not keep silence; fire devours before Him, and it is very tempestuous around Him. He summons the heavens above, and the earth, to judge His people: "Gather My godly ones to Me, those who have made a covenant with Me by sacrifice." And the heavens declare His righteousness, for God Himself is judge.

Psalm 51:15-17 NIV O Lord, open my lips, and my mouth will declare your praise. You do not delight in sacrifice, or I would bring it; you do not take pleasure in burnt offerings. The sacrifices of God are a broken spirit; a broken and contrite heart, O God, you will not despise.

Proverbs 21:3 NIV To do what is right and just is more acceptable to the Lord than sacrifice.

Micah 6:6-8 NRSV "With what shall I come before the Lord, and bow myself before God on high? Shall I come before him with burnt offerings, with calves a year old? Will the Lord be pleased with thousands of rams, with ten thousands of rivers of oil? Shall I give my firstborn for my transgression, the fruit of my body for the sin of my soul?" He has told you, O mortal, what is good; and what does the Lord require of you but to do justice, and to love kindness, and to walk humbly with your God?

Luke 18:29-30 NIV "I tell you the truth," Jesus said to them, "no one who has left home or wife or brothers or parents or children for the sake of the kingdom of God will fail to receive many times as much in this age and, in the age to come, eternal life."

John 12:25-26 NASB He who loves his life loses it, and he who hates his life in this world will keep it to life eternal. If anyone serves Me, he must follow Me; and where I am, there My servant will be also; if anyone serves Me, the Father will honor him.

Ephesians 5:1-2 NKJV Therefore be imitators of God as dear children. And walk in love, as Christ also has loved us and given Himself for us, an offering and a sacrifice to God for a sweet-smelling aroma.

2 Timothy 4:6-7 NIV For I am already being poured out like a drink offering, and the time has come for my departure. I have fought the good fight, I have finished the race, I have kept the faith.

Hebrews 7:26-27 NKJV For such a High Priest was fitting for us, who is holy, harmless, undefiled, separate from sinners, and has become higher than the heavens; who does not need daily, as those high priests, to offer up sacrifices, first for His own sins and then for the people's, for this He did once for all when He offered up Himself.

Hebrews 9:26-28 WEB Or else he must have suffered often since the foundation of the world. But now once at the end of the ages, he has been revealed to put away sin by the sacrifice of himself. Inasmuch as it is appointed for men to die once, and after this, judgment, so Christ also, having been offered once to bear the sins of many.

Hebrew 10:26-27 NKJV For if we sin willfully after we have received the knowledge of the truth, there no longer remains a sacrifice for sins, but a certain fearful expectation of judgment, and fiery indignation which will devour the adversaries.

Hebrews 13:15-16 NASB Through Him then, let us continually offer up a sacrifice of praise to God, that is, the fruit of lips that give thanks to His name. And do not neglect doing good and sharing, for with such sacrifices God is pleased.

1 John 3:16 NLT We know what real love is because Christ gave up his life for us. And so we also ought to give up our lives for our Christian brothers and sisters.

Isaiah 43:10-11 NIV "You are my witnesses," declares the LORD, "and my servant whom I have chosen, so that you may know and believe me and understand that I am he. Before me no god was formed, nor will there be one after me. I, even I, am the LORD, and apart from me there is no savior."

John 1:10-13 WEB He was in the world, and the world was made through him, and the world didn't recognize him. He came to his own, and those who were his own didn't receive him. But as many as received him, to them he gave the right to become God's children, to those who believe in his name: who were born not of blood, nor of the will of the flesh, nor of the will of man, but of God.

John 1:29 NIV The next day John saw Jesus coming toward him and said, "Look, the Lamb of God, who takes away the sin of the world!"

John 3:5-8 WEB Jesus answered, "Most certainly I tell you, unless one is born of water and the Spirit, he can't enter into the Kingdom of God! That which is born of the flesh is flesh. That which is born of the Spirit is spirit. Don't marvel that I said to you, 'You must be born anew.' The wind blows where it wants to, and you hear its sound, but don't know where it comes from and where it is going. So is everyone who is born of the Spirit."

John 3:16-17 NCV God loved the world so much that he gave his one and only Son so that whoever believes in him may not be lost, but have eternal life. God did not send his Son into the world to judge the world guilty, but to save the world through him.

John 5:24 NCV I tell you the truth, whoever hears what I say and believes in the One who sent me has eternal life. That person will not be judged guilty but has already left death and entered life.

John 14:6 NCV Jesus answered, "I am the way, and the truth, and the life. The only way to the Father is through me."

Romans 10:8-10 WEB But what does it say? "The word is near you, in your mouth, and in your heart;" that is, the word of faith, which we preach: that if you will confess with your mouth that Jesus is Lord, and believe in your heart that God raised him from the dead, you will be saved. For with the heart, one believes unto righteousness; and with the mouth confession is made unto salvation.

2 Corinthians 6:1-2 WEB Working together, we entreat also that you not receive the grace of God in vain, for he says, "At an acceptable time I listened to you, in a day of salvation I helped you." Behold, now is the acceptable time. Behold, now is the day of salvation.

Ephesians 2:8-10 NKJV For by grace you have been saved through faith, and that not of yourselves; it is the gift of God, not of works, lest anyone should boast. For we are His workmanship, created in Christ Jesus for good works, which God prepared beforehand that we should walk in them.

2 Peter 3:9 NIV The Lord is not slow in keeping his promise, as some understand slowness. He is patient with you, not wanting anyone to perish, but everyone to come to repentance.

1 John 5:11-12 NASB And the testimony is this, that God has given us eternal life, and this life is in His Son. He who has the Son has the life; he who does not have the Son of God does not have the life.

Joshua 1:8–9 NKJV This Book of the Law shall not depart from your mouth, but you shall meditate in it day and night, that you may observe to do according to all that is written in it. For then you will make your way prosperous, and then you will have good success. Have I not commanded you? Be strong and of good courage; do not be afraid, nor be dismayed, for the LORD your God is with you wherever you go.

Psalm 119:102–108 NIV I have not departed from your laws, for you yourself have taught me. How sweet are your words to my taste, sweeter than honey to my mouth! I gain understanding from your precepts; therefore I hate every wrong path. Your word is a lamp to my feet and a light for my path. I have taken an oath and confirmed it, that I will follow your righteous laws. I have suffered much; preserve my life, O LORD, according to your word. Accept, O LORD, the willing praise of my mouth, and teach me your laws.

Isaiah 40:8 NCV The grass dies and the flowers fall, but the word of our God will live forever.

Luke 4:20–22 WEB He closed the book, gave it back to the attendant, and sat down. The eyes of all in the synagogue were fastened on him. He began to tell them, "Today, this Scripture has been fulfilled in your hearing." All testified about him, and wondered at the words of grace which proceeded out of his mouth.

Acts 17:11–12 NCV These Jews were more willing to listen than the Jews in Thessalonica. The Bereans were eager to hear what Paul and Silas said and studied the Scriptures every day to find out if these things were true. So, many of them believed.

Romans 15:4 NASB For whatever was written in earlier times was written for our instruction, so that through perseverance and the encouragement of the Scriptures we might have hope.

Ephesians 6:17-18 NIV Take the helmet of salvation and the sword of the Spirit, which is the word of God. And pray in the Spirit on all occasions with all kinds of prayers and requests. With this in mind, be alert and always keep on praying for all the saints.

Colossians 3:16 NIV Let the word of Christ dwell in you richly as you teach and admonish one another with all wisdom, and as you sing psalms, hymns and spiritual songs with gratitude in your hearts to God.

2 Timothy 3:13-15 WEB But evil men and impostors will grow worse and worse, deceiving and being deceived. But you remain in the things which you have learned and have been assured of, knowing from whom you have learned them. From infancy, you have known the holy Scriptures which are able to make you wise for salvation through faith, which is in Christ Jesus.

2 Timothy 3:16-17 NASB All Scripture is inspired by God and profitable for teaching, for reproof, for correction, for training in righteousness; so that the man of God may be adequate, equipped for every good work.

Hebrews 4:12 WEB For the word of God is living, and active, and sharper than any two-edged sword, and piercing even to the dividing of soul and spirit, of both joints and marrow, and quick to discern the thoughts and intents of the heart.

2 Peter 1:19-21 NKJV And so we have the prophetic word confirmed, which you do well to heed as a light that shines in a dark place, until the day dawns and the morning star rises in your hearts; knowing this first, that no prophecy of Scripture is of any private interpretation, for prophecy never came by the will of man, but holy men of God spoke as they were moved by the Holy Spirit.

1 Chronicles 16:10-11 NLT Exult in his holy name; O worshipers of the Lord, rejoice! Search for the Lᴏʀᴅ and for his strength, and keep on searching.

1 Chronicles 28:9-10 NRSV And you, my son Solomon, know the God of your father, and serve him with single mind and willing heart; for the Lᴏʀᴅ searches every mind, and understands every plan and thought. If you seek him, he will be found by you; but if you forsake him, he will abandon you forever. Take heed now, for the Lᴏʀᴅ has chosen you to build a house as the sanctuary; be strong, and act.

2 Chronicles 7:14-15 NASB [If] My people who are called by My name humble themselves and pray and seek My face and turn from their wicked ways, then I will hear from heaven, will forgive their sin and will heal their land. Now My eyes will be open and My ears attentive to the prayer offered in this place.

Psalm 9:9-10 NIV The Lᴏʀᴅ is a refuge for the oppressed, a stronghold in times of trouble. Those who know your name will trust in you, for You, Lᴏʀᴅ, have never forsaken those who seek you.

Psalm 14:2 WEB Yahweh looked down from heaven on the children of men, to see if there were any who did understand, who did seek after God.

Psalm 16:11 WEB You will show me the path of life. In Your presence is fullness of joy. In Your right hand there are pleasures forevermore.

Psalm 27:8-10 NKJV When You said, "Seek My face," my heart said to You, "Your face, Lᴏʀᴅ, I will seek." Do not hide Your face from me; do not turn Your servant away in anger; You have been my help; do not leave me nor forsake me, O God of my salvation. When my father and my mother forsake me, then the Lᴏʀᴅ will take care of me.

Psalm 42:1-3 NRSV As a deer longs for flowing streams, so my soul longs for you, O God. My soul thirsts for God, for the living God. When shall I come and behold the face of God? My tears have been my food day and night, while people say to me continually, "Where is your God?"

Psalm 63:1-2 NKJV God, You are my God; early will I seek You; my soul thirsts for You; my flesh longs for You in a dry and thirsty land where there is no water. So I have looked for You in the sanctuary, to see Your power and Your glory.

Psalm 70:4 WEB Let all those who seek you rejoice and be glad in you. Let those who love your salvation continually say, "Let God be exalted!"

Psalm 91:14 TMB Because he hath set his love upon Me, therefore will I deliver him; I will set him on high, because he hath known My name.

Isaiah 55:6-7 NCV So you should look for the Lord before it is too late; you should call to him while he is near. The wicked should stop doing wrong, and they should stop their evil thoughts. They should return to the Lord so he may have mercy on them. They should come to our God, because he will freely forgive them.

Matthew 6:33 NIV But seek first his kingdom and his righteousness, and all these things will be given to you as well.

Matthew 7:7-8 NASB Ask, and it will be given to you; seek, and you will find; knock, and it will be opened to you. For everyone who asks receives, and he who seeks finds, and to him who knocks it will be opened.

Proverbs 11:24 NASB There is one who scatters, and yet increases all the more, and there is one who withholds what is justly due, and yet it results only in want.

Luke 9:23-24 NKJV If anyone desires to come after Me, let him deny himself, and take up his cross daily, and follow Me. For whoever desires to save his life will lose it, but whoever loses his life for My sake will save it.

Romans 8:13 NIV For if you live according to the sinful nature, you will die; but if by the Spirit you put to death the misdeeds of the body, you will live.

2 Corinthians 5:14-15 WEB For the love of Christ constrains us; because we judge thus, that one died for all, therefore all died. He died for all, that those who live should no longer live to themselves, but to him who for their sakes died and rose again.

Philippians 2:3-4 NCV When you do things, do not let selfishness or pride be your guide. Instead, be humble and give more honor to others than to yourselves. Do not be interested only in your own life, but be interested in the lives of others.

Philippians 2:21 NCV Other people are interested only in their own lives, not in the work of Jesus Christ.

2 Timothy 3:1-5 WEB In the last days, grievous times will come. For men will be lovers of self, lovers of money, boastful, arrogant, blasphemers, disobedient to parents, unthankful, unholy, without natural affection, unforgiving, slanderers, without self-control, fierce, no lovers of good, traitors, headstrong, conceited, lovers of pleasure rather than lovers of God; holding a form of godliness, but having denied its power. Turn away from these.

Proverbs 13:3 NCV Those who are careful about what they say protect their lives, but whoever speaks without thinking will be ruined.

Proverbs 16:32 NIV Better a patient man than a warrior, a man who controls his temper than one who takes a city.

1 Corinthians 9:24–25 WEB Don't you know that those who run in a race all run, but one receives the prize? Run like that, that you may win. Every man who strives in the games exercises self-control in all things.

1 Corinthians 15:58 NASB My beloved brethren, be steadfast, immovable, always abounding in the work of the Lord, knowing that your toil is not in vain in the Lord.

Galatians 5:22–25 NKJV The fruit of the Spirit is love, joy, peace, longsuffering, kindness, goodness, faithfulness, gentleness, self-control. . . . And those who are Christ's have crucified the flesh with its passions and desires. If we live in the Spirit, let us also walk in the Spirit.

Colossians 2:6-7 NIV So then, just as you received Christ Jesus as Lord, continue to live in him, rooted and built up in him, strengthened in the faith as you were taught, and overflowing with thankfulness.

Titus 2:1–5 NRSV But as for you, teach what is consistent with sound doctrine. Tell the older men to be temperate, serious, prudent, and sound in faith, in love, and in endurance. Likewise, tell the older women to be reverent in behavior, not to be slanderers or slaves to drink; they are to teach what is good, so that they may encourage the young women to love their husbands, to love their children, to be self-controlled, chaste, good managers of the household, kind, being submissive to their husbands, so that the word of God may not be discredited.

Titus 2:11-14 NASB For the grace of God has appeared, bringing salvation to all men, instructing us to deny ungodliness and worldly desires and to live sensibly, righteously and godly in the present age, looking for the blessed hope and the appearing of the glory of our great God and Savior, Christ Jesus, who gave Himself for us to redeem us from every lawless deed, and to purify for Himself a people for His own possession, zealous for good deeds.

Titus 3:8-9 NIV This is a trustworthy saying. And I want you to stress these things, so that those who have trusted in God may be careful to devote themselves to doing what is good. These things are excellent and profitable for everyone. But avoid foolish controversies and genealogies and arguments and quarrels about the law, because these are unprofitable and useless.

James 4:1-4 WEB Where do wars and fightings among you come from? Don't they come from your pleasures that war in your members? You lust, and don't have. You kill, covet, and can't obtain. You fight and make war. You don't have, because you don't ask. You ask, and don't receive, because you ask with wrong motives, so that you may spend it for your pleasures. You adulterers and adulteresses, don't you know that friendship with the world is enmity with God? Whoever therefore wants to be a friend of the world makes himself an enemy of God.

2 Peter 1:5-9 NKJV But also for this very reason, giving all diligence, add to your faith virtue, to virtue knowledge, to knowledge self-control, to self-control perseverance, to perseverance godliness, to godliness brotherly kindness, and to brotherly kindness love. For if these things are yours and abound, you will be neither barren nor unfruitful in the knowledge of our Lord Jesus Christ. For he who lacks these things is shortsighted, even to blindness, and has forgotten that he was cleansed from his old sins.

Psalm 19:9-11 NIV The fear of the LORD is pure, enduring forever. The ordinances of the Lord are sure and altogether righteous. They are more precious than gold, than much pure gold; they are sweeter than honey, than honey from the comb. By them is your servant warned; in keeping them there is great reward.

Psalm 65:4 WEB Blessed is one whom you choose, and cause to come near, that he may live in your courts. We will be filled with the goodness of your house, your holy temple.

Psalm 100:1-3 NRSV Make a joyful noise to the LORD, all the earth. Worship the LORD with gladness; come into his presence with singing. Know that the LORD is God. It is he that made us, and we are his; we are his people, and the sheep of his pasture.

Isaiah 41:9-10 NCV I took you from places far away on the earth and called you from a faraway country. I said, "You are my servants." I have chosen you and have not turned against you. So don't worry, because I am with you. Don't be afraid, because I am your God. I will make you strong and will help you; I will support you with my right hand that saves you.

Isaiah 42:1-3 NCV Here is my servant, the one I support. He is the one I chose, and I am pleased with him. I have put My Spirit upon him, and he will bring justice to all nations. He will not cry out or yell or speak loudly in the streets. He will not break a crushed blade of grass or put out even a weak flame. He will truly bring justice.

Jeremiah 1:9-10 NKJV The LORD put forth His hand and touched my mouth; and the LORD said to me: "Behold, I have put My words in your mouth. See, I have appointed you this day over the nations and over the kingdoms, to pluck up and to break down, to destroy and to overthrow, to build and to plant."

Matthew 25:21 NIV His master replied, "Well done, good and faithful servant! You have been faithful with a few things; I will put you in charge of many things."

Mark 10:43–45 NKJV Whoever desires to become great among you shall be your servant. And whoever of you desires to be first shall be slave of all. For even the Son of Man did not come to be served, but to serve, and to give His life a ransom for many.

John 15:14–16 NKJV You are My friends if you do whatever I command you. No longer do I call you servants, for a servant does not know what his master is doing; but I have called you friends, for all things that I heard from My Father I have made known to you. You did not choose Me, but I chose you and appointed you that you should go and bear fruit, and that your fruit should remain, that whatever you ask the Father in My name He may give you.

2 Corinthians 8:3–5 NASB For I testify that according to their ability, and beyond their ability, they gave of their own accord, begging us with much urging for the favor of participation in the support of the saints, and this, not as we had expected, but they first gave themselves to the Lord and to us by the will of God.

2 Corinthians 8:7 TMB Therefore as ye abound in everything—in faith, and utterance, and knowledge, in all diligence, and in your love for us—see that ye abound in this grace also.

2 Timothy 2:24–25 WEB The Lord's servant must not quarrel, but be gentle towards all, able to teach, patient, in gentleness correcting those who oppose him; perhaps God may give them repentance leading to a full knowledge of the truth, in gentleness correcting those who oppose him; if perhaps God may give them repentance to the knowledge of the truth.

Romans 13:14 NIV Rather, clothe yourselves with the Lord Jesus Christ, and do not think about how to gratify the desires of the sinful nature.

1 Corinthians 6:19-20 NKJV Or do you not know that your body is the temple of the Holy Spirit who is in you, whom you have from God, and you are not your own? For you were bought at a price; therefore glorify God in your body and in your spirit, which are God's.

Galatians 5:19-21 NIV The acts of the sinful nature are obvious: sexual immorality, impurity and debauchery; idolatry and witchcraft; hatred, discord, jealousy, fits of rage, selfish ambition, dissensions, factions and envy; drunkenness, orgies, and the like.

Ephesians 5:3-5 NLT Let there be no sexual immorality, impurity, or greed among you. Such sins have no place among God's people. Obscene stories, foolish talk, and coarse jokes—these are not for you. Instead, let there be thankfulness to God. You can be sure that no immoral, impure, or greedy person will inherit the Kingdom of Christ and of God. For a greedy person is really an idolater who worships the things of this world.

1 Thessalonians 4:3-8 NKJV This is the will of God, your sanctification: that you should abstain from sexual immorality; that each of you should know how to possess his own vessel in sanctification and honor, not in passion of lust, like the Gentiles who do not know God; that no one should take advantage of and defraud his brother in this matter, because the Lord is the avenger of all such, as we also forewarned you and testified. For God did not call us to uncleanness, but in holiness. Therefore, he who rejects this does not reject man, but God, who has also given us His Holy Spirit.

James 1:21 WEB Putting away all filthiness and overflowing of wickedness, receive with humility the implanted word, which is able to save your souls.

Psalm 31:16-17 WEB Make your face to shine on your servant. Save me in your loving kindness. Let me not be disappointed, Yahweh, for I have called on you.

Psalm 34:5-6 NKJV They looked to Him and were radiant, and their faces were not ashamed. This poor man cried out, and the LORD heard him, and saved him out of all his troubles.

2 Corinthians 5:17 NASB Therefore if anyone is in Christ, he is a new creature; the old things passed away; behold, new things have come.

Philippians 3:20-21 NKJV For our citizenship is in heaven, from which we also eagerly wait for the Savior, the Lord Jesus Christ, who will transform our lowly body that it may be conformed to His glorious body, according to the working by which He is able even to subdue all things to Himself.

2 Timothy 1:12 NIV That is why I am suffering as I am. Yet I am not ashamed, because I know whom I have believed, and am convinced that he is able to guard what I have entrusted to him for that day.

2 Timothy 2:15 NASB Be diligent to present yourself approved to God as a workman who does not need to be ashamed, accurately handling the word of truth.

Hebrews 11:16 NIV Instead, they were longing for a better country—a heavenly one. Therefore God is not ashamed to be called their God, for he has prepared a city for them.

1 John 3:20-21 TMB For if our heart condemns us, God is greater than our heart and knoweth all things. Beloved, if our heart condemn us not, then we have confidence toward God.

Jeremiah 3:15 NASB Then I will give you shepherds after My own heart, who will feed you on knowledge and understanding.

Jeremiah 10:21 NLT The shepherds of my people have lost their senses. They no longer follow the LORD or ask what he wants of them. Therefore, they fail completely, and their flocks are scattered.

John 21:15-17 NKJV "Simon, son of Jonah, do you love Me more than these?" He said to Him, "Yes Lord; You know that I love You." He said to him, "Feed My lambs." He said to him again a second time, "Simon, son of Jonah, do you love Me?" He said to Him, "Yes Lord; You know that I love You." He said to him, "Tend My sheep." He said to Him the third time, "Simon, son of Jonah, do you love Me?" Peter was grieved because He said to him the third time, "Do you love me?" And he said to Him, "Lord, You know all things; You know that I love You."

Acts 20:28-29 NKJV Therefore take heed to yourselves and to all the flock, among which the Holy Spirit has made you overseers, to shepherd the church of God which He purchased with His own blood. For I know this, that after my departure savage wolves will come in among you, not sparing the flock.

Hebrews 13:17 NIV Obey your leaders and submit to their authority. They keep watch over you as men who must give an account. Obey them so that their work will be a joy, not a burden, for that would be of no advantage to you.

1 Peter 5:2-4 NASB Shepherd the flock of God among you, exercising oversight not under compulsion, but voluntarily, according to the will of God; and not for sordid gain, but with eagerness; nor yet as lording it over those allotted to your charge, but proving to be examples to the flock. And when the Chief Shepherd appears, you will receive the unfading crown of glory.

Exodus 20:13-17 NKJV You shall not murder. You shall not commit adultery. You shall not steal. You shall not bear false witness against your neighbor. You shall not covet your neighbor's house; you shall not covet your neighbor's wife, nor his male servant, nor his female servant, nor his ox, nor his donkey, nor anything that is your neighbor's.

1 Samuel 12:20-22 NIV "Do not be afraid," Samuel replied. "You have done all this evil; yet do not turn away from the LORD, but serve the LORD with all your heart. Do not turn away after useless idols. They can do you no good, nor can they rescue you, because they are useless. For the sake of his great name the LORD will not reject his people, because the LORD was pleased to make you his own."

Psalm 103:8-10 WEB Yahweh is merciful and gracious, slow to anger, and abundant in loving kindness. He will not always accuse; neither will he stay angry forever. He has not dealt with us according to our sins, nor repaid us for our iniquities.

Isaiah 38:17 NASB Lo, for my own welfare I had great bitterness; it is You who has kept my soul from the pit of nothingness, for You have cast all my sins behind Your back.

Romans 6:22-23 NKJV But now having been set free from sin, and having become slaves of God, you have your fruit to holiness, and the end, everlasting life. For the wages of sin is death, but the gift of God is eternal life in Christ Jesus our Lord.

Galatians 6:1 NIV Brothers, if someone is caught in a sin, you who are spiritual should restore him gently. But watch yourself, or you also may be tempted.

Hebrews 4:13 NCV Nothing in all the world can be hidden from God. Everything is clear and lies open before him, and to him we must explain the way we have lived.

Hebrews 4:15-16 WEB For we don't have a high priest who can't be touched with the feeling of our infirmities, but one who has been in all points tempted like we are, yet without sin. Let us therefore draw near with boldness to the throne of grace, that we may receive mercy, and may find grace for help in time of need.

Hebrews 10:26-27 NIV If we deliberately keep on sinning after we have received the knowledge of the truth, no sacrifice for sins is left, but only a fearful expectation of judgment and of raging fire that will consume the enemies of God.

Hebrews 12:1-2 NKJV Therefore we also, since we are surrounded by so great a cloud of witnesses, let us lay aside every weight, and the sin which so easily ensnares us, and let us run with endurance the race that is set before us, looking unto Jesus, the author and finisher of our faith, for the joy that was set before Him endured the cross.

James 1:14-15 NCV But people are tempted when their own evil desire leads them away and traps them. This desire leads to sin, and then the sin grows and brings death.

James 4:7-8 WEB Be subject therefore to God. But resist the devil, and he will flee from you. Draw near to God, and he will draw near to you. Cleanse your hands, you sinners; and purify your hearts, you double-minded.

James 5:19-20 NASB My brethren, if any among you strays from the truth and one turns him back, let him know that he who turns a sinner from the error of his way will save his soul from death and will cover a multitude of sins.

1 John 1:8-9 NKJV If we say that we have no sin, we deceive ourselves, and the truth is not in us. If we confess our sins, He is faithful and just to forgive us our sins and to cleanse us from all unrighteousness.

Leviticus 26:6 NIV I will grant peace in the land, and you will lie down and no one will make you afraid. I will remove savage beasts from the land.

Psalm 3:5 NASB I lay down and slept; I awoke, for the LORD sustains me.

Psalm 4:8 NASB In peace I will both lie down and sleep, for You alone, O LORD, make me to dwell in safety.

Psalm 127:1-2 NCV If the LORD doesn't build the house, the builders are working for nothing. If the LORD doesn't guard the city, the guards are watching for nothing. It is no use for you to get up early and stay up late, working for a living. The LORD gives sleep to those he loves.

Proverbs 3:21-24 NKJV Keep sound wisdom and discretion; so they will be life to your soul and grace to your neck. Then you will walk safely in your way, and your foot will not stumble. When you lie down, you will not be afraid; yes you will lie down and your sleep will be sweet.

Isaiah 32:18 NCV My people will live in peaceful places and in safe homes and in calm places of rest.

Jeremiah 6:16 NIV This is what the LORD says: "Stand at the crossroads and look; ask for the ancient paths, ask where the good way is, and walk in it, and you will find rest for your souls."

Matthew 11:28-30 NKJV Come to Me, all you who labor and are heavy laden, and I will give you rest. Take My yoke upon you and learn from Me, for I am gentle and lowly in heart, and you will find rest for your souls. For My yoke is easy and My burden is light.

Isaiah 61:3 NKJV To console those who mourn in Zion, to give them beauty for ashes, the oil of joy for mourning, the garment of praise for the spirit of heaviness; that they may be called trees of righteousness, the planting of the LORD, that He may be glorified.

John 16:22 WEB Therefore you now have sorrow, but I will see you again, and your heart will rejoice, and no one will take your joy away from you.

Romans 12:15 WEB Rejoice with those who rejoice. Weep with those who weep.

Romans 15:4 TMB For whatsoever things were written in times past, were written for our learning, that we through patience and comfort of the Scriptures might have hope.

Romans 15:13 NIV May the God of hope fill you with all joy and peace as you trust in him, so that you may overflow with hope by the power of the Holy Spirit.

2 Corinthians 2:7-8 NASB So that on the contrary you should rather forgive and comfort him, otherwise such a one might be overwhelmed by excessive sorrow. Wherefore I urge you to reaffirm your love for him.

1 Thessalonians 4:13 NIV Brothers, we do not want you to be ignorant about those who fall asleep, or to grieve like the rest of men, who have no hope.

1 Thessalonians 5:11 TMB Therefore comfort yourselves together and edify one another, even as also ye do.

Revelation 21:4 NKJV And God will wipe away every tear from their eyes; there shall be no more death, nor sorrow, nor crying. There shall be no more pain, for the former things have passed away.

Psalm 23:3 NIV He restores my soul. He guides me in paths of righteousness for his name's sake.

Psalm 42:1-4 NKJV As the deer pants for the water brooks, so pants my soul for You, O God. My soul thirsts for God, for the living God. When shall I come and appear before God? My tears have been my food day and night, while they continually say to me, "Where is your God?" When I remember these things, I pour out my soul within me.

Psalm 63:1 NIV O God, you are my God, earnestly I seek you; my soul thirsts for you, my body longs for you, in a dry and weary land where there is no water.

Psalm 63:7-8 WEB For you have been my help. I will rejoice in the shadow of your wings. My soul stays close to you. Your right hand holds me up.

Psalm 66:16 WEB Come, and hear, all you who fear God. I will declare what he has done for my soul.

Psalm 72:12-14 TMB For he shall deliver the needy when he crieth; the poor also and him that hath no helper. He shall spare the poor and needy, and shall save the souls of the needy. He shall redeem their soul from deceit and violence, and precious shall their blood be in his sight.

Psalm 116:8-9 NKJV You have delivered my soul from death, my eyes from tears, and my feet from falling. I will walk before the LORD in the land of the living.

Psalm 143:8 NASB Let me hear Your lovingkindness in the morning; for I trust in You; teach me the way in which I should walk; for to You I lift up my soul.

Proverbs 11:30 NASB The fruit of the righteous is a tree of life, and he who is wise wins souls.

Isaiah 26:8-9 NKJV Yes, in the way of Your judgments, O Lord, we have waited for You; the desire of our soul is for Your name and for the remembrance of You. With my soul I have desired You in the night, yes, by my spirit within me I will seek You early; for when Your judgments are in the earth, the inhabitants of the world will learn righteousness.

Ezekiel 18:4-5, 9 NKJV Behold, all souls are Mine; the soul of the father as well as the soul of the son is Mine; the soul who sins shall die. But if a man is just and does what is lawful and right, . . . He shall surely live!

Matthew 11:28-29 NIV Come to me, all you who are weary and burdened, and I will give you rest. Take my yoke upon you and learn from me, for I am gentle and humble in heart, and you will find rest for your souls.

Matthew 16:26-27 NLT And how do you benefit if you gain the whole world but lose your own soul in the process? Is anything worth more than your soul? For I, the Son of Man, will come in the glory of my Father with his angels and will judge all people according to their deeds.

1 Thessalonians 5:23-24 NIV May God himself, the God of peace, sanctify you through and through. May your whole spirit, soul and body be kept blameless at the coming of our Lord Jesus Christ. The one who calls you is faithful and he will do it.

Hebrews 12:3 WEB For consider him who has endured such contradiction of sinners against himself, that you don't grow weary, fainting in your souls.

Proverbs 3:9-10 WEB Honor Yahweh with your substance, with the first fruits of all your increase: so your barns will be filled with plenty, and your vats will overflow with new wine.

Luke 8:14-15 NKJV Now the ones that fell among thorns are those who, when they have heard, go out and are choked with cares, riches, and pleasures of life, and bring no fruit to maturity. But the ones that fell on the good ground are those who, having heard the word with a noble and good heart, keep it and bear fruit with patience.

1 Corinthians 4:1-2 NASB Let a man regard us in this manner, as servants of Christ and stewards of the mysteries of God. In this case, moreover, it is required of stewards that one be found trustworthy.

1 Corinthians 9:16-18 WEB For if I preach the Good News, I have nothing to boast about; for necessity is laid on me; but woe is to me, if I don't preach the Good News. For if I do this of my own will, I have a reward. But if not of my own will, I have a stewardship entrusted to me. What then is my reward? That, when I preach the Good News, I may present the Good News of Christ without charge, so as not to abuse my authority in the Good News.

2 Corinthians 9:7-10 NKJV So let each one give as he purposes in his heart, not grudgingly or of necessity; for God loves a cheerful giver. And God is able to make all grace abound toward you, that you, always having all sufficiency in all things, may have an abundance for every good work. As it is written: "He has dispersed abroad, He has given to the poor; His righteousness endures forever." Now may He who supplies seed to the sower, and bread for food, supply and multiply the seed you have sown and increase the fruits of your righteousness.

Psalm 4:3-5 NASB But know that the LORD has set apart the godly man for Himself; the LORD hears when I call to Him. Tremble, and do not sin. Meditate in your heart upon your bed, and be still. Offer the sacrifices of righteousness, and trust in the LORD.

Psalm 46:9-11 NKJV He makes wars cease to the end of the earth; He breaks the bow and cuts the spear in two; He burns the chariot in the fire. Be still, and know that I am God; I will be exalted among the nations, I will be exalted in the earth! The LORD of hosts is with us; the God of Jacob is our refuge.

Psalm 62:5-6 WEB My soul, wait in silence for God alone, for my expectation is from him. He alone is my rock and my salvation, my fortress. I will not be shaken.

Isaiah 32:17-18 NIV The fruit of righteousness will be peace; the effect of righteousness will be quietness and confidence forever. My people will live in peaceful dwelling places, in secure homes, in undisturbed places of rest.

Zephaniah 1:7 WEB Be silent at the presence of the Lord Yahweh, for the day of Yahweh is at hand. For Yahweh has prepared a sacrifice. He has consecrated his guests.

Zechariah 2:10-13 NKJV Sing and rejoice, O daughter of Zion! For behold, I am coming and I will dwell in your midst," says the LORD. Many nations shall be joined to the LORD in that day, and they shall become My people. And I will dwell in your midst. Then you will know that the LORD of hosts has sent Me to you. And the LORD will take possession of Judah as His inheritance in the Holy Land, and will again choose Jerusalem. Be silent, all flesh, before the LORD, for He is aroused from His holy habitation!

Exodus 15:1–2 NKJV Then Moses and the children of Israel sang this song to the Lord, and spoke, saying: "I will sing to the Lord, for He has triumphed gloriously! The horse and its rider He has thrown into the sea! The Lord is my strength and song, and He has become my salvation; He is my God, and I will praise Him; my father's God, and I will exalt Him."

Exodus 15:13 WEB You, in your loving kindness, have led the people that you have redeemed. You have guided them in your strength to your holy habitation.

2 Samuel 22:29–35 NLT O Lord, you are my light; yes, Lord, you light up my darkness. In your strength I can crush an army; with my God I can scale any wall. As for God, his way is perfect. All the Lord's promises prove true. He is a shield for all who look to him for protection. For who is God except the Lord? Who but our God is a solid rock? God is my strong fortress; he has made my way safe. He makes me as surefooted as a deer, leading me safely along the mountain heights. He prepares me for battle; he strengthens me to draw a bow of bronze.

1 Chronicles 16:10–11 NCV Be glad that you are his; let those who seek the Lord be happy. Depend on the Lord and his strength; always go to him for help.

1 Chronicles 16:27–29 WEB Honor and majesty are before him. Strength and gladness are in his place. Ascribe to Yahweh, you relatives of the peoples, ascribe to Yahweh glory and strength; ascribe to Yahweh the glory due to his name. Bring an offering, and come before him. Worship Yahweh in holy array.

Psalm 18:31–34 NIV For who is God besides the Lord? And who is the Rock except our God? It is God who arms me with strength and makes my way perfect. He makes my feet like the feet of a deer; he enables me to stand on the heights. He trains my hands for battle; my arms can bend a bow of bronze.

Psalm 27:1 NIV The LORD is my light and my salvation—whom shall I fear? The LORD is the stronghold of my life—of whom shall I be afraid?

Psalm 46:1-5 WEB God is our refuge and strength, a very present help in trouble. Therefore we won't be afraid, though the earth changes, though the mountains are shaken into the heart of the seas; though its waters roar and are troubled, though the mountains tremble with their swelling. There is a river, the streams of which make the city of God glad, the holy place of the tents of the Most High. God is in her midst. She shall not be moved. God will help her at dawn.

Psalm 62:5-7 NKJV My soul, wait silently for God alone, for my expectation is from Him. He only is my rock and my salvation; He is my defense; I shall not be moved. In God is my salvation and my glory; the rock of my strength, and my refuge, is in God.

Psalm 84:4-8 NKJV Blessed are those who dwell in Your house; they will still be praising You. Blessed is the man whose strength is in You, whose heart is set on pilgrimage. As they pass through the Valley of Baca, they make it a spring; the rain also covers it with pools. They go from strength to strength; each one appears before God in Zion. Oh LORD God of hosts, hear my prayer; give ear, O God of Jacob!

Habakkuk 3:17-19 NIV Though the fig tree does not bud and there are no grapes on the vines, though the olive crop fails and the fields produce no food, though there are no sheep in the pen and no cattle in the stalls, yet I will rejoice in the LORD, I will be joyful in God my Savior. The Sovereign LORD is my strength; he makes my feet like the feet of a deer, he enables me to go on the heights.

2 Corinthians 12:9 NKJV And He said to me, "My grace is sufficient for you, for My strength is made perfect in weakness." Therefore most gladly I will rather boast in my infirmities, that the power of Christ may rest upon me.

Psalm 18:1-3 NKJV I will love You, O Lord, my strength. The Lord is my rock and my fortress and my deliverer; My God, my strength, in whom I will trust; my shield and the horn of my salvation, my stronghold. I will call upon the Lord, who is worthy to be praised.

Psalm 32:7 NIV You are my hiding place; you will protect me from trouble and surround me with songs of deliverance.

Psalm 55:22 NASB Cast your burden upon the Lord and He will sustain you; He will never allow the righteous to be shaken.

Psalm 61:2 NASB From the end of the earth I call to You when my heart is faint; Lead me to the rock that is higher than I.

Psalm 138:8 TMB The Lord will perfect that which concerneth me; Thy mercy, O Lord, endureth forever; forsake not the works of Thine own hands.

Isaiah 40:10-11 NKJV Behold, His reward is with Him, and His work before Him. He will feed His flock like a shepherd; He will gather the lambs with His arm, and carry them in His bosom, and gently lead those who are with young.

Hosea 11:4 NCV I led them with cords of human kindness, with ropes of love. I lifted the yoke from their neck and bent down and fed them.

Mark 4:19 NIV But the worries of this life, the deceitfulness of wealth and the desires for other things come in and choke the word, making it unfruitful.

1 John 4:4 NASB You are from God, little children, and have overcome them; because greater is He who is in you than he who is in the world.

1 Corinthians 11:3 NIV Now I want you to realize that the head of every man is Christ, and the head of the woman is man, and the head of Christ is God.

Ephesians 5:17-21 NKJV Therefore do not be unwise, but understand what the will of the Lord is. And do not be drunk with wine, in which is dissipation; but be filled with the Spirit, speaking to one another in psalms and hymns and spiritual songs, singing and making melody in your heart to the Lord, giving thanks always for all things to God the Father in the name of our Lord Jesus Christ, submitting to one another in the fear of God.

Ephesians 6:5-8 NIV Slaves, obey your earthly masters with respect and fear, and with sincerity of heart, just as you would obey Christ. Obey them not only to win their favor when their eye is on you, but like slaves of Christ, doing the will of God from your heart. Serve wholeheartedly, as if you were serving the Lord, not men, because you know that the Lord will reward everyone for whatever good he does, whether he is slave or free.

Philippians 2:9-11 NKJV Therefore God also has highly exalted Him and given Him the name which is above every name, that at the name of Jesus every knee should bow, of those in heaven, and of those on earth, and of those under the earth, and that every tongue should confess that Jesus Christ is Lord.

Hebrews 13:17 NASB Obey your leaders and submit to them, for they keep watch over your souls as those who will give an account. Let them do this with joy and not with grief, for this would be unprofitable for you.

James 4:7-10 NIV Submit yourselves, then, to God. Resist the devil, and he will flee from you. Come near to God and he will come near to you. . . . Humble yourselves before the Lord, and he will lift you up.

1 Peter 2:13–17 NKJV Therefore submit yourselves to every ordinance of man for the Lord's sake, whether to the king as supreme, or to governors, as to those who are sent by him for the punishment of evildoers and for the praise of those who do good. For this is the will of God, that by doing good you may put to silence the ignorance of foolish men—as free, yet not using liberty as a cloak for vice, but as bondservants of God. Honor all people. Love the brotherhood. Fear God. Honor the king.

1 Peter 2:18–21 NKJV Servants, be submissive to your masters with all fear, not only to the good and gentle, but also to the harsh. For this is commendable, if because of conscience toward God one endures grief, suffering wrongfully. For what credit is it if, when you are beaten for your faults, you take it patiently? But when you do good and suffer, if you take it patiently, this is commendable before God. For to this you were called, because Christ also suffered for us, leaving us an example, that you should follow His steps.

1 Peter 3:1 NCV In the same way, you wives should yield to your husbands. Then, if some husbands do not obey God's teaching, they will be persuaded to believe without anyone's saying a word to them. They will be persuaded by the way their wives live.

1 Peter 3:5–6 WEB For this is how the holy women before, who hoped in God, also adorned themselves, being in subjection to their own husbands: as Sarah obeyed Abraham, calling him lord, whose children you now are, if you do well.

1 Peter 5:5–7 NASB You younger men, likewise, be subject to your elders; and all of you, clothe yourselves with humility toward one another, for GOD IS OPPOSED TO THE PROUD, BUT GIVES GRACE TO THE HUMBLE. Therefore humble yourselves under the mighty hand of God, that He may exalt you at the proper time, casting all your anxiety on Him, because He cares for you.

2 Kings 20:5 NASB Thus says the LORD, the God of your father David, "I have heard your prayer, I have seen your tears; behold, I will heal you."

Psalm 66:10-12 NKJV For You, O God, have tested us; You have refined us as silver is refined. You brought us into the net; You laid affliction on our backs. You have caused men to ride over our heads; we went through fire and through water; but You brought us out to rich fulfillment.

Romans 5:3-4 NIV Not only so, but we also rejoice in our sufferings, because we know that suffering produces perseverance; perseverance, character; and character, hope.

Romans 8:17-18 NCV If we are God's children, we will receive blessings from God together with Christ. . . . The sufferings we have now are nothing compared to the great glory that will be shown to us.

Philippians 3:7-10 NKJV But what things were gain to me, these I have counted loss for Christ. Yet indeed I also count all things loss for the excellence of the knowledge of Christ Jesus my Lord, for whom I have suffered the loss of all things, and count them as rubbish, that I may gain Christ and be found in Him, not having my own righteousness, which is from the law, but that which is through faith in Christ, the righteousness which is from God by faith; that I may know Him and the power of His resurrection, and the fellowship of His sufferings, being conformed to His death.

2 Timothy 2:1-3 WEB You therefore, my child, be strengthened in the grace that is in Christ Jesus. The things which you have heard from me among many witnesses, commit the same to faithful men, who will be able to teach others also. You therefore must endure hardship, as a good soldier of Christ Jesus.

James 5:13-15 NKJV Is anyone among you suffering? Let him pray. Is anyone cheerful? Let him sing psalms. Is anyone among you sick? Let him call for the elders of the church, and let them pray over him, anointing him with oil in the name of the Lord. And the prayer of faith will save the sick, and the Lord will raise him up. And if he has committed sins, he will be forgiven.

1 Peter 4:1-2 NCV Since Christ suffered while He was in His body, strengthen yourselves with the same way of thinking Christ had. The person who has suffered in the body is finished with sin. Strengthen yourselves so that you will live here on earth doing what God wants, not the evil things people want.

1 Peter 4:12-13 NASB Beloved, do not be surprised at the fiery ordeal among you, which comes upon you for your testing, as though some strange thing were happening to you; but to the degree that you share the sufferings of Christ, keep on rejoicing, so that also at the revelation of His glory you may rejoice with exultation.

1 Peter 4:13-16 NIV But rejoice that you participate in the sufferings of Christ, so that you may be overjoyed when his glory is revealed. If you are insulted because of the name of Christ, you are blessed, for the Spirit of glory and of God rests on you. If you suffer, it should not be as a murderer or thief or any other kind of criminal, or even as a meddler. However, if you suffer as a Christian, do not be ashamed, but praise God that you bear that name.

1 Peter 5:8-11 NKJV Be sober, be vigilant; because your adversary the devil walks about like a roaring lion, seeking whom he may devour. Resist him, steadfast in the faith, knowing that the same sufferings are experienced by your brotherhood in the world. But may the God of all grace, who called us to His eternal glory by Christ Jesus, after you have suffered a while, perfect, establish, strengthen, and settle you. To Him be the glory and the dominion forever and ever. Amen.

Psalm 23:4 NIV Even though I walk through the valley of the shadow of death, I will fear no evil, for you are with me; your rod and your staff, they comfort me.

Psalm 32:8 NASB I will instruct you and teach you in the way which you should go; I will counsel you with My eye upon you.

Matthew 6:32-34 NKJV For your heavenly Father knows that you need all these things. But seek first the kingdom of God and His righteousness, and all these things shall be added to you. Therefore do not worry about tomorrow, for tomorrow will worry about its own things. Sufficient for the day is its own trouble.

2 Corinthians 3:4-6 NKJV And we have such trust through Christ toward God. Not that we are sufficient of ourselves to think of anything as being from ourselves, but our sufficiency is from God, who also made us sufficient as ministers of the new covenant, not of the letter but of the Spirit; for the letter kills, but the Spirit gives life.

2 Corinthians 9:8 NASB And God is able to make all grace abound to you, so that always having all sufficiency in everything, you may have an abundance for every good deed.

Ephesians 2:8-10 WEB For by grace you have been saved through faith, and that not of yourselves; it is the gift of God, not of works, that no one would boast. For we are his workmanship, created in Christ Jesus for good works, which God prepared before that we would walk in them.

2 Thessalonians 2:16-17 NCV May our Lord Jesus Christ himself and God our Father encourage you and strengthen you in every good thing you do and say. God loved us, and through his grace he gave us a good hope and encouragement that continues forever.

Proverbs 3:5-6 NIV Trust in the LORD with all your heart and lean not on your own understanding; in all your ways acknowledge him, and he will make your paths straight.

Isaiah 64:8 NASB But now, O LORD, You are our Father, we are the clay, and You our potter; and all of us are the work of Your hand.

Mark 14:35-36 NIV Going a little farther, he fell to the ground and prayed that if possible the hour might pass from him. "Abba, Father," he said, "everything is possible for you. Take this cup from me. Yet not what I will, but what you will."

Luke 9:23-24 WEB He said to all, "If anyone desires to come after me, let him deny himself, take up his cross, and follow me. For whoever desires to save his life will lose it, but whoever will lose his life for my sake, the same will save it."

Luke 23:46 NCV Jesus cried out in a loud voice, "Father, I give you my life." After Jesus said this, he died.

Romans 9:19-21 NKJV "For who has resisted His will?" But indeed, O man, who are you to reply against God? Will the thing formed say to him who formed it, "Why have you made me like this?" Does not the potter have power over the clay, from the same lump to make one vessel for honor and another for dishonor?

Romans 12:1-2 NKJV I beseech you therefore, brethren, by the mercies of God, that you present your bodies a living sacrifice, holy, acceptable to God, which is your reasonable service. And do not be conformed to this world, but be transformed by the renewing of your mind, that you may prove what is that good and acceptable and perfect will of God.

Psalm 119:33-38 NKJV Teach me, O LORD, the way of Your statutes, and I shall keep it to the end. Give me understanding, and I shall keep Your law; indeed, I shall observe it with my whole heart. Make me walk in the path of Your commandments, for I delight in it. Incline my heart to Your testimonies, and not to covetousness. Turn away my eyes from looking at worthless things, and revive me in Your way. Establish Your word to Your servant, who is devoted to fearing You.

Proverbs 9:9-10 NIV Instruct a wise man and he will be wiser still; teach a righteous man and he will add to his learning. The fear of the LORD is the beginning of wisdom, and knowledge of the Holy One is understanding.

Isaiah 48:17-18 NKJV I am the LORD your God, who teaches you to profit, who leads you by the way you should go. Oh, that you had heeded My commandments! Then your peace would have been like a river, and your righteousness like the waves of the sea.

Matthew 28:18-20 NKJV And Jesus came and spoke to them, saying, "All authority has been given to Me in heaven and on earth. Go therefore and make disciples of all the nations, baptizing them in the name of the Father and of the Son and of the Holy Spirit, teaching them to observe all things that I have commanded you; and lo, I am with you always, even to the end of the age."

John 3:2-3 NASB This man came to Jesus by night and said to Him, "Rabbi, we know that You have come from God as a teacher; for no one can do these signs that You do unless God is with him." Jesus answered and said to him, "Truly, truly, I say to you, unless one is born again he cannot see the kingdom of God."

Galatians 6:6 NIV Anyone who receives instruction in the word must share all good things with his instructor.

Proverbs 27:17 NIV As iron sharpens iron, so one man sharpens another.

Luke 10:1-2 NKJV After these things the Lord appointed seventy others also, and sent them two by two before His face into every city and place where He Himself was about to go. Then He said to them, "The harvest truly is great, but the laborers are few; therefore pray the Lord of the harvest to send out laborers into His harvest."

1 Corinthians 3:6-8 NIV I planted the seed, Apollos watered it, but God made it grow. So neither he who plants nor he who waters is anything, but only God, who makes things grow. The man who plants and the man who waters have one purpose, and each will be rewarded according to his own labor.

1 Corinthians 3:9-10 NCV We are God's workers, working together; you are like God's farm, God's house. Using the gift God gave me, I laid the foundation of that house like an expert builder. Others are building on that foundation, but all people should be careful how they build on it.

1 Corinthians 12:12-13 NCV A person's body is only one thing, but it has many parts. Though there are many parts to a body, all those parts make only one body. Christ is like that also. Some of us are Jews, and some are Greeks. Some of us are slaves, and some are free. But we were all baptized into one body through one Spirit.

Philippians 1:3-7 NKJV I thank my God upon every remembrance of you, always in every prayer of mine making request for you all with joy, for your fellowship in the gospel from the first day until now, being confident of this very thing, that He who has begun a good work in you will complete it until the day of Jesus Christ; just as it is right for me to think this of you all, because I have you in my heart, inasmuch as both in my chains and in the defense and confirmation of the gospel, you are all partakers with me of grace.

Proverbs 1:10–11, 15–16 NASB My son, if sinners entice you, do not consent. If they say, "Come with us, let us lie in wait for blood, let us ambush the innocent without cause.". . . My son, do not walk in the way with them. Keep your feet from their path, for their feet run to evil and they hasten to shed blood.

Matthew 6:13 NASB And do not lead us into temptation, but deliver us from evil. For Yours is the kingdom and the power and the glory forever. Amen.

Matthew 26:41 WEB Watch and pray, that you don't enter into temptation. The spirit indeed is willing, but the flesh is weak.

1 Corinthians 10:12–13 NKJV Therefore let him who thinks he stands take heed lest he fall. No temptation has overtaken you except such as is common to man; but God is faithful, who will not allow you to be tempted beyond what you are able, but with the temptation will also make the way of escape, that you may be able to bear it.

1 Corinthians 15:58 WEB Therefore, my beloved brothers, be steadfast, immovable, always abounding in the Lord's work, because you know that your labor is not in vain in the Lord.

2 Corinthians 9:8 NIV And God is able to make all grace abound to you, so that in all things at all times, having all that you need, you will abound in every good work.

Ephesians 6:10–13 NKJV Finally, my brethren, be strong in the Lord and in the power of His might. Put on the whole armor of God, that you may be able to stand against the wiles of the devil. For we do not wrestle against flesh and blood, but against principalities, against powers, against the rulers of the darkness. . . . Therefore take up the whole armor of God, that you may be able to withstand in the evil day, and having done all, to stand.

Hebrews 4:15-16 NIV For we do not have a high priest who is unable to sympathize with our weaknesses, but we have one who has been tempted in every way, just as we are—yet was without sin. Let us then approach the throne of grace with confidence, so that we may receive mercy and find grace to help us in our time of need.

James 1:12-15 NKJV Blessed is the man who endures temptation; for when he has been approved, he will receive the crown of life which the Lord has promised to those who love Him. Let no one say when he is tempted, "I am tempted by God"; for God cannot be tempted by evil, nor does He Himself tempt anyone. But each one is tempted when he is drawn away by his own desires and enticed. Then, when desire has conceived, it gives birth to sin; and sin, when it is full-grown, brings forth death.

James 4:17 NIV Anyone, then, who knows the good he ought to do and doesn't do it, sins.

1 Peter 5:8-9 WEB Be sober and self-controlled. Be watchful. Your adversary the devil, walks around like a roaring lion, seeking whom he may devour. Withstand him steadfast in your faith, knowing that your brothers who are in the world are undergoing the same sufferings.

2 Peter 2:9-10 NKJV The Lord knows how to deliver the godly out of temptations and to reserve the unjust under punishment for the day of judgment, and especially those who walk according to the flesh in the lust of uncleanness and despise authority.

1 John 3:5-6 NLT And you know that Jesus came to take away our sins, for there is no sin in him. So if we continue to live in him, we won't sin either. But those who keep on sinning have never known him or understood who he is.

Psalm 9:1-2 NASB I will give thanks to the LORD with all my heart; I will tell of all Your wonders. I will be glad and exult in You; I will sing praise to Your name, O Most High.

Psalm 19:7 NKJV The law of the LORD is perfect, converting the soul; the testimony of the LORD is sure, making wise the simple.

Psalm 105:1-5 NKJV Oh, give thanks to the LORD! Call upon His name; make known His deeds among the peoples! Sing to Him, sing psalms to Him; talk of all His wondrous works! Glory in His holy name; let the hearts of those rejoice who seek the LORD! Seek the LORD and His strength; seek His face evermore! Remember His marvelous works which He has done, His wonders, and the judgments of His mouth.

Psalm 106:8-12 NKJV Nevertheless He saved them for His name's sake, that He might make His mighty power known. He rebuked the Red Sea also, and it dried up; so He led them through the depths, as through the wilderness. He saved them from the hand of him who hated them, and redeemed them from the hand of the enemy. The waters covered their enemies; there was not one of them left. Then they believed His words; they sang His praise.

Psalm 119:2-3 NASB How blessed are those who observe His testimonies, who seek Him with all their heart. They also do no unrighteousness; they walk in His ways.

Psalm 119:111-112 WEB I have taken your testimonies as a heritage forever, for they are the joy of my heart. I have set my heart to perform your statutes forever, even to the end.

Psalm 119:125-127 NKJV I am Your servant; give me understanding, that I may know Your testimonies. It is time for You to act, O LORD, for they have regarded Your law as void. Therefore I love Your commandments more than gold, yes, than fine gold!

Joel 1:2-3 NIV Hear this, you elders; listen, all who live in the land. Has anything like this ever happened in your days or in the days of your forefathers? Tell it to your children, and let your children tell it to their children, and their children to the next generation.

Mark 5:19-20 NIV Jesus did not let him, but said, "Go home to your family and tell them how much the Lord has done for you, and how he has had mercy on you." So the man went away and began to tell in the Decapolis how much Jesus had done for him. And all the people were amazed.

Acts 22:14-16 NIV Then he said: "The God of our fathers has chosen you to know his will and to see the Righteous One and to hear words from his mouth. You will be his witness to all men of what you have seen and heard. And now what are you waiting for? Get up, be baptized and wash your sins away, calling on his name."

1 Timothy 1:15-16 NKJV This is a faithful saying and worthy of all acceptance, that Christ Jesus came into the world to save sinners, of whom I am chief. However, for this reason I obtained mercy, that in me first Jesus Christ might show all longsuffering, as a pattern to those who are going to believe on Him for everlasting life.

2 Timothy 1:8-9 NKJV Therefore do not be ashamed of the testimony of our Lord, nor of me His prisoner, but share with me in the sufferings for the gospel according to the power of God, who has saved us and called us with a holy calling.

1 Peter 3:15-16 NASB But sanctify Christ as Lord in your hearts, always being ready to make a defense to everyone who asks you to give an account for the hope that is in you, yet with gentleness and reverence; and keep a good conscience so that in the thing in which you are slandered, those who revile your good behavior in Christ will be put to shame.

Psalm 40:5 NIV Many, O Lord my God, are the wonders you have done. The things you planned for us no one can recount to you; were I to speak and tell of them, they would be too many to declare.

Psalm 100:4-5 NIV Enter his gates with thanksgiving and his courts with praise; give thanks to him and praise his name. For the Lord is good and his love endures forever; his faithfulness continues through all generations.

Psalm 107:1-3 NASB Oh give thanks to the Lord, for He is good, for His lovingkindness is everlasting. Let the redeemed of the Lord say so, whom He has redeemed from the hand of the adversary and gathered from the lands.

Psalm 107:8-9 WEB Let them praise Yahweh for his loving kindness, for his wonderful works to the children of men! For he satisfies the longing soul. He fills the hungry soul with good.

John 6:11 NCV Then Jesus took the loaves of bread, thanked God for them, and gave them to the people who were sitting there. He did the same with the fish, giving as much as the people wanted.

1 Corinthians 15:57-58 NKJV But thanks be to God, who gives us the victory through our Lord Jesus Christ. Therefore, my beloved brethren, be steadfast, immovable, always abounding in the work of the Lord, knowing that your labor is not in vain in the Lord.

2 Corinthians 9:10-11 NKJV Now may He who supplies seed to the sower, and bread for food, supply and multiply the seed you have sown and increase the fruits of your righteousness, while you are enriched in everything for all liberality, which causes thanksgiving through us to God.

Philippians 4:4-7 NKJV Rejoice in the Lord always. Again I will say, rejoice! Let your gentleness be known to all men. The Lord is at hand. Be anxious for nothing, but in everything by prayer and supplication, with thanksgiving, let your requests be made known to God; and the peace of God, which surpasses all understanding, will guard your hearts and minds through Christ Jesus.

Colossians 2:6-7 NKJV As you therefore have received Christ Jesus the Lord, so walk in Him, rooted and built up in Him and established in the faith, as you have been taught, abounding in it with thanksgiving.

Colossians 3:15, 17 NIV Let the peace of Christ rule in your hearts, since as members of one body you were called to peace. And be thankful. . . . And whatever you do, whether in word or deed, do it all in the name of the Lord Jesus, giving thanks to God the Father through him.

Colossians 4:2-3 NASB Devote yourselves to prayer, keeping alert in it with an attitude of thanksgiving; praying at the same time for us as well, that God will open up to us a door for the word, so that we may speak forth the mystery of Christ.

1 Thessalonians 5:16-18 NCV Always be joyful. Pray continually, and give thanks whatever happens. That is what God wants for you in Christ Jesus.

1 Timothy 1:12-13 NCV I thank Christ Jesus our Lord, who gave me strength, because he trusted me and gave me this work of serving him. In the past I spoke against Christ and persecuted him. . . . But God showed me mercy, because I did not know what I was doing. I did not believe.

Hebrews 13:15 NIV Through Jesus, therefore, let us continually offer to God a sacrifice of praise—the fruit of lips that confess his name.

Psalm 42:1-2 NIV As the deer pants for streams of water, so my soul pants for you, O God. My soul thirsts for God, for the living God. When can I go and meet with God?

Matthew 5:6 TMB Blessed are they that hunger and thirst after righteousness, for they shall be filled.

John 4:13-14 TMB Whosoever drinketh of this water shall thirst again, but whosoever drinketh of the water that I shall give him shall never thirst; but the water that I shall give him shall be in him a well of water springing up into everlasting life.

John 6:35 NCV Then Jesus said, "I am the bread that gives life. Whoever comes to me will never be hungry, and whoever believes in me will never be thirsty."

John 7:37-39 NKJV "If anyone thirsts, let him come to Me and drink. He who believes in Me, as the Scripture has said, out of his heart will flow rivers of living water." But this He spoke concerning the Spirit, whom those believing in Him would receive; for the Holy Spirit was not yet given, because Jesus was not yet glorified.

Revelation 7:15-17 NKJV Therefore they are before the throne of God, and serve Him day and night in His temple. And He who sits on the throne will dwell among them. They shall neither hunger anymore nor thirst anymore; the sun shall not strike them, nor any heat; for the Lamb who is in the midst of the throne will shepherd them and lead them to living fountains of waters. And God will wipe away every tear from their eyes.

Revelation 21:6 NCV The One on the throne said to me, "It is finished. I am the Alpha and the Omega, the Beginning and the End. I will give free water from the spring of the water of life to anyone who is thirsty."

Romans 8:10–11 NKJV And if Christ is in you, the body is dead because of sin, but the Spirit is life because of righteousness. But if the Spirit of Him who raised Jesus from the dead dwells in you, He who raised Christ from the dead will also give life to your mortal bodies through His Spirit who dwells in you.

Romans 12:2 WEB Don't be conformed to this world, but be transformed by the renewing of your mind, so that you may prove what is the good, well-pleasing, and perfect will of God.

1 Corinthians 6:19–20 WEB Or don't you know that your body is a temple of the Holy Spirit which is in you, which you have from God? You are not your own, for you were bought with a price. Therefore glorify God in your body and in your spirit, which are God's.

1 Corinthians 15:51–52 TMB We shall all be changed in a moment, in the twinkling of an eye.

2 Corinthians 3:18 NASB But we all, with unveiled face, beholding as in a mirror the glory of the Lord, are being transformed into the same image from glory to glory, just as from the Lord, the Spirit.

Hebrews 10:19–23 NKJV Therefore, brethren, having boldness to enter the Holiest by the blood of Jesus, by a new and living way which He consecrated for us, through the veil, that is, His flesh, and having a High Priest over the house of God, let us draw near with a true heart in full assurance of faith, having our hearts sprinkled from an evil conscience and our bodies washed with pure water. Let us hold fast the confession of our hope without wavering, for He who promised is faithful.

Revelation 21:5 NCV The One who was sitting on the throne said, "Look! I am making everything new!"

2 Samuel 22:2-4 NKJV The LORD is my rock and my fortress and my deliverer; the God of my strength, in whom I will trust; my shield and the horn of my salvation, my stronghold and my refuge; my Savior, You save me from violence. I will call upon the LORD, who is worthy to be praised; so shall I be saved from my enemies.

2 Samuel 22:17-20 NKJV He sent from above, He took me, He drew me out of many waters. He delivered me from my strong enemy, from those who hated me; for they were too strong for me. They confronted me in the day of my calamity, but the LORD was my support. He also brought me out into a broad place; He delivered me because He delighted in me.

Psalm 18:6 NIV In my distress I called to the LORD; I cried to my God for help. From his temple he heard my voice; my cry came before him, into his ears.

Psalm 20:1-3 NIV May the LORD answer you when you are in distress; may the name of the God of Jacob protect you. May he send you help from the sanctuary and grant you support from Zion. May he remember all your sacrifices and accept your burnt offerings.

Psalm 89:8-9 WEB Yahweh, God of Armies, who is a mighty one, like you? Yah, your faithfulness is around you. You rule the pride of the sea. When its waves rise up, you calm them.

Psalm 119:17-18 NASB Deal bountifully with Your servant, that I may live and keep Your word. Open my eyes, that I may behold wonderful things from Your law.

Romans 8:35 NASB Who will separate us from the love of Christ? Will tribulation, or distress, or persecution, or famine, or nakedness, or peril, or sword?

2 Corinthians 1:3-4 NIV Praise be to the God and Father of our Lord Jesus Christ, the Father of compassion and the God of all comfort, who comforts us in all our troubles, so that we can comfort those in any trouble with the comfort we ourselves have received from God.

James 1:2-4 NASB Consider it all joy, my brethren, when you encounter various trials, knowing that the testing of your faith produces endurance. And let endurance have its perfect result, so that you may be perfect and complete, lacking in nothing.

1 Peter 1:6-8 NIV In this you greatly rejoice, though now for a little while you may have had to suffer grief in all kinds of trials. These have come so that your faith—of greater worth than gold, which perishes even though refined by fire—may be proved genuine and may result in praise, glory and honor when Jesus Christ is revealed. Though you have not seen him, you love him.

1 Peter 4:12-14 NKJV Beloved, do not think it strange concerning the fiery trial which is to try you, as though some strange thing happened to you; but rejoice to the extent that you partake of Christ's sufferings, that when His glory is revealed, you may also be glad with exceeding joy. If you are reproached for the name of Christ, blessed are you, for the Spirit of glory and of God rests upon you. On their part He is blasphemed, but on your part He is glorified.

Revelation 3:10-12 NKJV Because you have kept My command to persevere, I also will keep you from the hour of trial which shall come upon the whole world, to test those who dwell on the earth. Behold, I am coming quickly! Hold fast what you have, that no one may take your crown. He who overcomes, I will make him a pillar in the temple of My God, and he shall go out no more. I will write on him the name of My God and the name of the city of My God, the New Jerusalem, which comes down out of heaven from My God. And I will write on him My new name.

2 Kings 18:5-7 NKJV [Hezekiah] trusted in the LORD God of Israel, so that after him was none like him among all the kings of Judah....For he held fast to the LORD; he did not depart from following Him, but kept His commandments.... The LORD was with him; he prospered wherever he went.

Psalm 9:9-10 WEB Yahweh will also be a high tower for the oppressed; a high tower in times of trouble. Those who know your name will put their trust in you, for you, Yahweh, have not forsaken those who seek you.

Psalm 18:30 WEB As for God, his way is perfect. The word of Yahweh is tried. He is a shield to all those who take refuge in him.

Psalm 20:6-8 NCV Now I know the LORD helps his appointed king. He answers him from his holy heaven and saves him with his strong right hand. Some trust in chariots, others in horses, but we trust the LORD our God. They are overwhelmed and defeated, but we march forward and win.

Psalm 28:6-9 NKJV He has heard the voice of my supplications! The LORD is my strength and my shield; my heart trusted in Him, and I am helped; therefore my heart greatly rejoices, and with my song I will praise Him. The LORD is their strength, and He is the saving refuge of His anointed. Save Your people, and bless Your inheritance; shepherd them also; and bear them up forever.

Psalm 37:3-5 NIV Trust in the LORD and do good; dwell in the land and enjoy safe pasture. Delight yourself in the LORD and he will give you the desires of your heart. Commit your way to the LORD; trust in him and he will do this; he will make your righteousness shine like the dawn.

Psalm 56:10-11 NCV I praise God for his word to me; I praise the LORD for his word. I trust in God. I will not be afraid. What can people do to me?

Psalm 62:7-8 WEB With God is my salvation and my honor. The rock of my strength, and my refuge, is in God. Trust in him at all times, you people. Pour out your heart before him. God is a refuge for us.

Psalm 84:11-12 NIV For the LORD God is a sun and shield; the LORD bestows favor and honor; no good thing does he withhold from those whose walk is blameless. O LORD Almighty, blessed is the man who trusts in you.

Psalm 91:1-2 NIV He who dwells in the shelter of the Most High will rest in the shadow of the Almighty. I will say of the LORD, "He is my refuge and my fortress, my God, in whom I trust."

Proverbs 3:5-6 NKJV Trust in the LORD with all your heart, and lean not on your own understanding; in all your ways acknowledge Him, and He shall direct your paths.

Isaiah 26:3-4 NLT You will keep in perfect peace all who trust in you, whose thoughts are fixed on you! Trust in the LORD always, for the LORD GOD is the eternal Rock.

Habakkuk 3:17-19 NKJV Though the fig tree may not blossom, nor fruit be on the vines; though the labor of the olive may fail, and the fields yield no food; though the flock may be cut off from the fold, and there be no herd in the stalls—yet I will rejoice in the LORD, I will joy in the God of my salvation. The LORD God is my strength; He will make my feet like deer's feet, and He will make me walk on my high hills.

Ephesians 1:11-12 TMB Being predestined according to the purpose of Him who worketh all things after the counsel of His own will, that we, who first trusted in Christ, should be to the praise of His glory.

Deuteronomy 32:4 TMB He is the Rock, His work is perfect; for all His ways are judgment, a God of truth and without iniquity; just and right is He.

Psalm 51:6 NIV Surely you desire truth in the inner parts; you teach me wisdom in the inmost place.

Psalm 73:23-25 NIV Yet I am always with you; you hold me by my right hand. You guide me with your counsel, and afterward you will take me into glory. Whom have I in heaven but you? And earth has nothing I desire besides you.

Psalm 86:11-12 NASB Teach me Your way, O LORD; I will walk in Your truth; unite my heart to fear Your name. I will give thanks to You, O LORD my God, with all my heart, and will glorify Your name forever.

Psalm 91:3-4 NKJV Surely He shall deliver you from the snare of the fowler and from the perilous pestilence. He shall cover you with His feathers, and under His wings you shall take refuge; His truth shall be your shield and buckler.

Proverbs 16:6 NASB By lovingkindness and truth iniquity is atoned for, and by the fear of the LORD one keeps away from evil.

John 1:14 NIV The Word became flesh and made his dwelling among us. We have seen his glory, the glory of the One and Only, who came from the Father, full of grace and truth.

John 3:20-21 NKJV For everyone practicing evil hates the light and does not come to the light, lest his deeds should be exposed. But he who does the truth comes to the light, that his deeds may be clearly seen, that they have been done in God.

John 8:31-32 NIV To the Jews who had believed him, Jesus said, "If you hold to my teaching, you are really my disciples. Then you will know the truth, and the truth will set you free."

John 16:13-14 NKJV However, when He, the Spirit of truth, has come, He will guide you into all truth; for He will not speak on His own authority, but whatever He hears He will speak; and He will tell you things to come. He will glorify me, for He will take of what is Mine and declare it to you.

John 17:17-19 NASB Sanctify them in the truth; Your word is truth. As You sent Me into the world, I also have sent them into the world. For their sakes I sanctify Myself, that they themselves also may be sanctified in truth.

2 Corinthians 2:14-16 NKJV Now thanks be to God who always leads us in triumph in Christ, and through us diffuses the fragrance of His knowledge in every place. For we are to God the fragrance of Christ among those who are being saved and among those who are perishing. To the one we are the aroma of death leading to death, and to the other the aroma of life leading to life.

1 Timothy 3:15 NCV Then, even if I am delayed, you will know how to live in the family of God. That family is the church of the living God, the support and foundation of the truth.

2 Timothy 2:15-17 NCV Make every effort to give yourself to God as the kind of person he will accept. Be a worker who is not ashamed and who uses the true teaching in the right way. Stay away from foolish, useless talk, because that will lead people further away from God. Their evil teaching will spread like a sickness inside the body.

Psalm 78:19-22, 32-33 WEB Yes, they spoke against God. They said, "Can God prepare a table in the wilderness? Behold, he struck the rock, so that waters gushed out, and streams overflowed. Can he give bread also? Will he provide flesh for his people?" Therefore Yahweh heard, and was angry. A fire was kindled against Jacob, anger also went up against Israel, because they didn't believe in God, and didn't trust in his salvation. . . . For all this they still sinned, and didn't believe in his wondrous works. Therefore he consumed their days in vanity, and their years in terror.

Matthew 13:58 WEB He didn't do many mighty works there because of their unbelief.

Matthew 17:16-18 NKJV Your disciples . . . could not cure him. Then Jesus answered and said, "O faithless and perverse generation, how long shall I be with you? How long shall I bear with you? Bring him here to Me." And Jesus rebuked the demon, and it came out of him; and the child was cured from that very hour.

Matthew 17:20 NIV He replied, "Because you have so little faith. I tell you the truth, if you have faith as small as a mustard seed, you can say to this mountain, 'Move from here to there' and it will move. Nothing will be impossible for you."

Mark 9:23-24 NIV " 'If you can?' " said Jesus. "Everything is possible for him who believes." Immediately the boy's father exclaimed, "I do believe; help me overcome my unbelief!"

Luke 8:11-13 NKJV The seed is the word of God. Those by the wayside are the ones who hear; then the devil comes and takes away the word out of their hearts, lest they should believe and be saved. But the ones on the rock are those who, when they hear, receive the word with joy; and these have no root, who believe for a while and in time of temptation fall away.

Deuteronomy 20:3-4 NIV He shall say: "Hear, O Israel, today you are going into battle against your enemies. Do not be fainthearted or afraid; do not be terrified or give way to panic before them. For the LORD your God is the one who goes with you to fight for you against your enemies to give you victory."

2 Chronicles 20:17 WEB You will not need to fight in this battle. Set yourselves, stand still, and see the salvation of Yahweh with you, O Judah and Jerusalem. Don't be afraid, nor be dismayed. Go out against them tomorrow, for Yahweh is with you.

Psalm 18:35-37 NASB You have also given me the shield of Your salvation, and Your right hand upholds me; and Your gentleness makes me great. You enlarge my steps under me, and my feet have not slipped. I pursued my enemies and overtook them, and I did not turn back until they were consumed.

Psalm 20:6-9 NKJV Now I know that the LORD saves His anointed; He will answer him from His holy heaven with the saving strength of His right hand. Some trust in chariots, and some in horses; but we will remember the name of the LORD our God. They have bowed down and fallen; but we have risen and stand upright. Save, LORD!

1 Corinthians 15:57-58 NIV But thanks be to God! He gives us the victory through our Lord Jesus Christ. Therefore, my dear brothers, stand firm. Let nothing move you. Always give yourselves fully to the work of the Lord, because you know that your labor in the Lord is not in vain.

2 Corinthians 2:14-15 NKJV Now thanks be to God who always leads us in triumph in Christ, and through us diffuses the fragrance of His knowledge in every place. For we are to God the fragrance of Christ among those who are being saved and among those who are perishing.

Genesis 22:17-18 NKJV Blessing I will bless you, and multiplying I will multiply your descendants as the stars of the heaven and as the sand which is on the seashore; and your descendants shall possess the gate of their enemies. In your seed all the nations of the earth shall be blessed because you have obeyed My voice.

Deuteronomy 28:1-2 WEB It shall happen, if you shall listen diligently to the voice of Yahweh your God, to observe to do all his commandments which I command you this day, that Yahweh your God will set you on high above all the nations of the earth: and all these blessings shall come on you, and overtake you, if you shall listen to the voice of Yahweh your God.

Psalm 12:6-7 NASB The words of the Lord are pure words; as silver tried in a furnace on the earth, refined seven times. You, O Lord, will keep them; You will preserve him from this generation forever.

Psalm 29:4, 8-9 NKJV The voice of the Lord is powerful; the voice of the Lord is full of majesty.... The voice of the Lord shakes the wilderness.... The voice of the Lord makes the deer give birth, and strips the forests bare; and in His temple everyone says, "Glory!"

Psalm 106:24-27 NASB Then they despised the pleasant land; they did not believe in His word, but grumbled in their tents; they did not listen to the voice of the Lord. Therefore He swore to them that He would cast them down in the wilderness, and that He would cast their seed among the nations and scatter them in the lands.

Psalm 119:127-130 NIV Because I love your commands more than gold, more than pure gold, and because I consider all your precepts right, I hate every wrong path. Your statutes are wonderful; therefore I obey them. The unfolding of your words gives light; it gives understanding to the simple.

Exodus 15:3-7 NKJV The L ORD is a man of war; the L ORD is His name. Pharaoh's chariots and his army He has cast into the sea . . . Your right hand, O L ORD, has become glorious in power; Your right hand, O L ORD, has dashed the enemy in pieces. And in the greatness of Your excellence You have overthrown those who rose against You.

Deuteronomy 20:1 NIV When you go to war against your enemies and see horses and chariots and an army greater than yours, do not be afraid of them, because the L ORD your God, who brought you up out of Egypt, will be with you.

2 Chronicles 20:12 NIV O our God, will you not judge them? For we have no power to face this vast army that is attacking us. We do not know what to do, but our eyes are upon you.

Psalm 27:3-4 NASB Though a host encamp against me, my heart will not fear; though war arise against me, in spite of this I shall be confident. One thing I have asked from the L ORD, that I shall seek: That I may dwell in the house of the L ORD all the days of my life, to behold the beauty of the L ORD and to meditate in His temple.

Psalm 46:4-6 NKJV There is a river whose streams shall make glad the city of God, the holy place of the tabernacle of the Most High. God is in the midst of her, she shall not be moved; God shall help her, just at the break of dawn. The nations raged, the kingdoms were moved; He uttered His voice, the earth melted.

Psalm 46:9-10 WEB He makes wars cease to the end of the earth. He breaks the bow, and shatters the spear. He burns the chariots in the fire. "Be still, and know that I am God. I will be exalted among the nations. I will be exalted in the earth."

Matthew 24:6 WEB You will hear of wars and rumors of wars. See that you aren't troubled, for all this must happen, but the end is not yet.

Zechariah 4:6 WEB "Not by might, nor by power, but by my Spirit," says Yahweh of Armies.

Luke 10:17-19 NKJV "Lord, even the demons are subject to us in Your name." And He said to them, "I saw Satan fall like lightning from heaven. Behold, I give you the authority to trample on serpents and scorpions, and over all the power of the enemy, and nothing shall by any means hurt you."

2 Corinthians 10:3-5 NASB For though we walk in the flesh, we do not war according to the flesh, for the weapons of our warfare are not of the flesh, but divinely powerful for the destruction of fortresses. We are destroying speculations and every lofty thing raised up against the knowledge of God, and we are taking every thought captive to the obedience of Christ.

Ephesians 6:12-13 NIV For our struggle is not against flesh and blood, but against the rulers, against the authorities, against the powers of this dark world and against the spiritual forces of evil in the heavenly realms. Therefore put on the full armor of God, so that when the day of evil comes, you may be able to stand your ground, and after you have done everything, to stand.

Ephesians 6:16-18 NKJV Above all, taking the shield of faith with which you will be able to quench all the fiery darts of the wicked one. And take the helmet of salvation, and the sword of the Spirit, which is the word of God; praying always with all prayer and supplication in the Spirit, being watchful to this end with all perseverance and supplication for all the saints.

Colossians 2:15 NCV God stripped the spiritual rulers and powers of their authority. With the cross, he won the victory and showed the world that they were powerless.

Deuteronomy 10:17-18 NIV For the LORD your God is God of gods and LORD of lords, the great God, mighty and awesome, who shows no partiality and accepts no bribes. He defends the cause of the fatherless and the widow, and loves the alien, giving him food and clothing.

Psalm 68:4-5 NIV Sing to God, sing praise to his name, extol him who rides on the clouds—his name is the LORD—and rejoice before him. A father to the fatherless, a defender of widows, is God in his holy dwelling.

Psalm 146:7-9 NCV He does what is fair for those who have been wronged. He gives food to the hungry. The LORD sets the prisoners free. The LORD gives sight to the blind. The LORD lifts up people who are in trouble. The LORD loves those who do right. The LORD protects the foreigners. He defends the orphans and widows, but he blocks the way of the wicked.

Isaiah 46:4 NCV Even when you are old, I will be the same. Even when your hair has turned gray, I will take care of you. I made you and will take care of you. I will carry you and save you.

Jeremiah 29:11-14 NKJV For I know the thoughts that I think toward you, says the LORD, thoughts of peace and not of evil, to give you a future and a hope. Then you will call upon Me and go and pray to Me, and I will listen to you. And you will seek Me and find Me, when you search for Me with all your heart. I will be found by you, says the LORD, and I will bring you back from your captivity.

James 1:27 NKJV Pure and undefiled religion before God and the Father is this: to visit orphans and widows in their trouble, and to keep oneself unspotted from the world.

Genesis 2:18 NASB Then the Lord God said, "It is not good for the man to be alone; I will make him a helper suitable for him."

Proverbs 12:4 NCV A good wife is like a crown for her husband, but a disgraceful wife is like a disease in his bones.

Proverbs 18:22 NLT The man who finds a wife finds a treasure and receives favor from the Lord.

Proverbs 19:14 NIV Houses and wealth are inherited from parents, but a prudent wife is from the Lord.

Proverbs 21:9, 19 WEB It is better to dwell in the corner of the housetop, than to share a house with a contentious woman. . . . It is better to dwell in a desert land, than with a contentious and fretful woman.

Proverbs 31:10–12 NKJV Who can find a virtuous wife? For her worth is far above rubies. The heart of her husband safely trusts her; so he will have no lack of gain. She does him good and not evil all the days of her life.

Song of Solomon 4:9–11 NKJV You have ravished my heart . . . my spouse; you have ravished my heart with one look of your eyes, with one link of your necklace. How fair is your love . . . my spouse! How much better than wine is your love, and the scent of your perfumes than all spices! Your lips, O my spouse, drip as the honeycomb; honey and milk are under your tongue; and the fragrance of your garments is like the fragrance of Lebanon.

1 Corinthians 7:39 NASB A wife is bound as long as her husband lives; but if her husband is dead, she is free to be married to whom she wishes, only in the Lord.

Ephesians 5:22-24 NIV Wives, submit to your husbands as to the Lord. For the husband is the head of the wife as Christ is the head of the church, his body, of which he is the Savior. Now as the church submits to Christ, so also wives should submit to their husbands in everything.

Titus 2:3-5 WNT In the same way exhort aged women to let their conduct be such as becomes consecrated persons. They must not be slanderers nor enslaved to wine-drinking. They must be teachers of what is right. They should school the young women to be affectionate to their husbands and to their children, to be sober-minded, pure in their lives, industrious in their homes, kind, submissive to their husbands, so that the Christian teaching may not be exposed to reproach.

Hebrews 13:20-21 NIV May the God of peace, who through the blood of the eternal covenant brought back from the dead our Lord Jesus, that great Shepherd of the sheep, equip you with everything good for doing his will.

1 Peter 3:1-6 WEB In the same way, wives, be in subjection to your own husbands; so that, even if any don't obey the Word, they may be won by the behavior of their wives without a word; seeing your pure behavior in fear. Let your beauty be not just the outward adorning of braiding the hair, and of wearing jewels of gold, or of putting on fine clothing; but in the hidden person of the heart, in the incorruptible adornment of a gentle and quiet spirit, which is in the sight of God very precious. For this is how the holy women before, who hoped in God, also adorned themselves, being in subjection to their own husbands: as Sarah obeyed Abraham, calling him lord, whose children you now are, if you do well, and are not put in fear by any terror.

1 John 4:18-19 TMB There is no fear in love; but perfect love casteth out fear, because fear hath torment. He that feareth is not made perfect in love. We love Him, because He first loved us.

Deuteronomy 2:7 WEB For Yahweh your God has blessed you in all the work of your hand; he has known your walking through this great wilderness: these forty years Yahweh your God has been with you; you have lacked nothing.

Deuteronomy 8:2–7 NKJV And you shall remember that the LORD your God led you all the way these forty years in the wilderness, to humble you and test you, to know what was in your heart, whether you would keep His commandments or not. So He humbled you, allowed you to hunger, and fed you with manna which you did not know nor did your fathers know, that He might make you know that man shall not live by bread alone; but man lives by every word that proceeds from the mouth of the LORD. Your garments did not wear out on you, nor did your foot swell these forty years. You should know in your heart that as a man chastens his son, so the LORD your God chastens you. Therefore you shall keep the commandments of the LORD your God, to walk in His ways and to fear Him. For the LORD your God is bringing you into a good land, a land of brooks of water, of fountains and springs.

Deuteronomy 32:10–12 WEB He found him in a desert land, in the waste howling wilderness. He surrounded him. He cared for him. He kept him as the apple of his eye. As an eagle that stirs up her nest, that flutters over her young, he spread abroad his wings, he took them, he bore them on his feathers. Yahweh alone led him. There was no foreign god with him.

Isaiah 43:18–19 NKJV Do not remember the former things, nor consider the things of old. Behold, I will do a new thing, now it shall spring forth; shall you not know it? I will even make a road in the wilderness and rivers in the desert.

Mark 1:12–13 WNT At once the Spirit impelled Him to go out into the Desert, where He remained for forty days, tempted by Satan; and He was among the wild beasts, but the angels waited upon Him.

Joshua 24:14–15 NKJV Now therefore, fear the Lord, serve Him in sincerity and in truth, and put away the gods which your fathers served on the other side of the River and in Egypt. Serve the Lord! . . . Choose for yourselves this day whom you will serve. . . . But as for me and my house, we will serve the Lord.

Proverbs 3:5-10 NASB Trust in the Lord with all your heart and do not lean on your own understanding. In all your ways acknowledge Him, and He will make your paths straight. Do not be wise in your own eyes; fear the Lord and turn away from evil. It will be healing to your body and refreshment to your bones. Honor the Lord from your wealth and from the first of all your produce; so your barns will be filled with plenty and your vats will overflow with new wine.

Proverbs 16:9 NIV In his heart a man plans his course, but the Lord determines his steps.

Proverbs 16:25 NIV There is a way that seems right to a man, but in the end it leads to death.

Mark 14:35-36 NASB And He went a little beyond them, and fell to the ground and began to pray that if it were possible, the hour might pass Him by. And He was saying, "Abba! Father! All things are possible for You; remove this cup from Me; yet not what I will, but what You will."

John 7:16-18 WNT Jesus answered their question by saying, "My teaching does not belong to me, but comes from Him who sent me. If any one is willing to do His will, he shall know about the teaching, whether it is from God or originates with me. The man whose teaching originates with himself aims at his own glory. He who aims at the glory of Him who sent him teaches the truth, and there is no deception in him."

Romans 12:1-2 WEB Present your bodies a living sacrifice, holy, acceptable to God, which is your spiritual service. Don't be conformed to this world, but be transformed by the renewing of your mind, so that you may prove what is the good, well-pleasing, and perfect will of God.

Ephesians 5:14-19 WNT For this reason it is said, "Rise, sleeper; rise from among the dead, and Christ will shed light upon you." Therefore be very careful how you live and act. Let it not be as unwise men, but as wise. Buy up your opportunities, for these are evil times. On this account do not prove yourselves wanting in sense, but try to understand what the Lord's will is. Do not over-indulge in wine—a thing in which excess is so easy—but drink deeply of God's Spirit.

Colossians 1:9-10 WEB For this cause, we also, since the day we heard this, don't cease praying and making requests for you, that you may be filled with the knowledge of his will in all spiritual wisdom and understanding, that you may walk worthily of the Lord, to please him in all respects, bearing fruit in every good work, and increasing in the knowledge of God.

1 Thessalonians 4:3-4 WEB For this is the will of God: your sanctification, that you abstain from sexual immorality, that each one of you know how to possess himself of his own vessel in sanctification and honor.

Hebrews 10:36 NLT Patient endurance is what you need now, so you will continue to do God's will. Then you will receive all that he has promised.

Hebrews 13:20-21 TMB Now the God of peace, who brought back from the dead our Lord Jesus, that great Shepherd of the sheep, through the blood of the everlasting covenant, make you perfect in every good work to do His will, working in you that which is well pleasing in His sight, through Jesus Christ, to whom be glory for ever and ever. Amen.

Proverbs 3:13-19 NRSV Happy are those who find wisdom, and those who get understanding, for her income is better than silver, and her revenue better than gold. She is more precious than jewels, and nothing you desire can compare with her. Long life is in her right hand; in her left hand are riches and honor. Her ways are ways of pleasantness, and all her paths are peace. She is a tree of life to those who lay hold of her; those who hold her fast are called happy. The LORD by wisdom founded the earth.

Isaiah 11:2 WEB The Spirit of Yahweh shall rest on him, the spirit of wisdom and understanding, the spirit of counsel and might, the spirit of knowledge.

Isaiah 33:6 NCV He will be your safety. He is full of salvation, wisdom, and knowledge. Respect for the LORD is the greatest treasure.

1 Corinthians 2:4-8 NKJV My speech and my preaching were not with persuasive words of human wisdom, but in demonstration of the Spirit and of power, that your faith should not be in the wisdom of men but in the power of God. . . . We speak wisdom among those who are mature, yet not the wisdom of this age, nor of the rulers of this age, who are coming to nothing. But we speak the wisdom of God in a mystery, the hidden wisdom which God ordained before the ages for our glory, which none of the rulers of this age knew; for had they known, they would not have crucified the Lord of glory.

1 Corinthians 2:13-14 NIV This is what we speak, not in words taught us by human wisdom but in words taught by the Spirit, expressing spiritual truths in spiritual words. The man without the Spirit does not accept the things that come from the Spirit of God, for they are foolishness to him.

James 1:5 NASB But if any of you lacks wisdom, let him ask of God, who gives to all generously and without reproach, and it will be given to him.

Psalm 96:2-3 NIV Sing to the LORD, praise his name; proclaim his salvation day after day. Declare his glory among the nations, his marvelous deeds among all peoples.

Proverbs 11:30 NIV The fruit of the righteous is a tree of life, and he who wins souls is wise.

Isaiah 43:10-12 NRSV You are my witnesses, says the LORD, and my servant whom I have chosen, so that you may know and believe me and understand that I am he. Before me no god was formed, nor shall there be any after me. I, I am the LORD, and besides me there is no savior. I declared and saved and proclaimed, when there was no strange god among you; and you are my witnesses, says the LORD.

Matthew 5:16 WEB Even so, let your light shine before men; that they may see your good works, and glorify your Father who is in heaven.

Matthew 9:37-38 NCV Jesus said to his followers, "There are many people to harvest but only a few workers to help harvest them. Pray to the Lord, who owns the harvest, that he will send more workers to gather his harvest."

Matthew 24:14 NASB This gospel of the kingdom shall be preached in the whole world as a testimony to all the nations, and then the end will come.

Matthew 28:18-20 WNT Jesus however came near and said to them, "All power in Heaven and over the earth has been given to me. Go therefore and make disciples of all the nations; baptize them into the name of the Father, and of the Son, and of the Holy Spirit; and teach them to obey every command which I have given you. And remember, I am with you always, day by day, until the Close of the Age."

Mark 8:35 NASB For whoever wishes to save his life will lose it, but whoever loses his life for My sake and the gospel's will save it.

Luke 2:17-18 WEB When they saw it, they publicized widely the saying which was spoken to them about this child. All who heard it wondered at the things which were spoken to them by the shepherds.

John 4:35-38 NCV You have a saying, "Four more months till harvest." But I tell you, open your eyes and look at the fields ready for harvest now. Already, the one who harvests is being paid and is gathering crops for eternal life. So the one who plants and the one who harvests celebrate at the same time. Here the saying is true, "One person plants, and another harvests." I sent you to harvest a crop that you did not work on. Others did the work, and you get to finish up their work.

Acts 1:8 NCV But when the Holy Spirit comes to you, you will receive power. You will be my witnesses—in Jerusalem, in all of Judea, in Samaria, and in every part of the world.

Acts 26:22 TMB Having therefore obtained the help of God, I continue unto this day, witnessing both to small and great, saying nothing other than what the prophets and Moses said should come.

Galatians 6:9 WEB Let us not be weary in doing good, for we will reap in due season, if we don't give up.

James 5:19-20 WEB Brothers, if any among you wanders from the truth, and someone turns him back, let him know, that he who converts a sinner from the error of his way will save a soul from death, and will cover a multitude of sins.

1 John 2:6 NIV Whoever claims to live in him must walk as Jesus did.

Revelation 12:11 NIV They overcame him by the blood of the Lamb and by the word of their testimony; they did not love their lives so much as to shrink from death.

Exodus 35:30-33 WEB Moses said to the children of Israel, "Behold, Yahweh has called by name Bezalel the son of Uri, the son of Hur, of the tribe of Judah. He has filled him with the Spirit of God, in wisdom, in understanding, in knowledge, and in all kinds of workmanship; and to make skillful works, to work in gold, in silver, in brass, in cutting of stones for setting, and in carving of wood, to work in all kinds of skillful workmanship."

Exodus 36:2 NASB Then Moses called Bezalel and Oholiab and every skillful person in whom the LORD had put skill, everyone whose heart stirred him, to come to the work to perform it.

Deuteronomy 28:12 NASB The LORD will open for you His good storehouse, the heavens, to give rain to your land in its season and to bless all the work of your hand; and you shall lend to many nations, but you shall not borrow.

2 Chronicles 15:7 NIV But as for you, be strong and do not give up, for your work will be rewarded.

Psalm 90:17 NIV May the favor of the Lord our God rest upon us; establish the work of our hands for us—yes, establish the work of our hands.

Proverbs 22:29 NASB Do you see a man skilled in his work? He will stand before kings; He will not stand before obscure men.

1 Corinthians 3:8-10 WNT Now in aim and purpose the planter and the waterer are one; and yet each will receive his own special reward, answering to his own special work. Apollos and I are simply fellow workers for and with God, and you are God's field—God's building. In discharge of the task which God graciously entrusted to me, I—like a competent master-builder—have laid a foundation, and others are building upon it. But let every one be careful how and what he builds.

1 Corinthians 15:58 NIV Therefore, my dear brothers, stand firm. Let nothing move you. Always give yourselves fully to the work of the Lord, because you know that your labor in the Lord is not in vain.

Galatians 6:3-4 WEB For if a man thinks himself to be something when he is nothing, he deceives himself. But let each man test his own work, and then he will take pride in himself and not in his neighbor.

Colossians 3:23-24 NCV In all the work you are doing, work the best you can. Work as if you were doing it for the Lord, not for people. Remember that you will receive your reward from the Lord, which he promised to his people. You are serving the Lord Christ.

1 Thessalonians 4:10-12 NCV And truly you do love the Christians in all of Macedonia. Brothers and sisters, now we encourage you to love them even more. Do all you can to live a peaceful life. Take care of your own business, and do your own work as we have already told you. If you do, then people who are not believers will respect you, and you will not have to depend on others for what you need.

Titus 2:6-10 NRSV Likewise, urge the younger men to be self-controlled. Show yourself in all respects a model of good works, and in your teaching show integrity, gravity, and sound speech that cannot be censured; then any opponent will be put to shame, having nothing evil to say of us. Tell slaves to be submissive to their masters and to give satisfaction in every respect; they are not to talk back, not to pilfer, but to show complete and perfect fidelity, so that in everything they may be an ornament to the doctrine of God our Savior.

Revelation 22:12 NCV Listen! I am coming soon! I will bring my reward with me, and I will repay each one of you for what you have done.

Psalm 37:1-3 NIV Do not fret because of evil men or be envious of those who do wrong; for like the grass they will soon wither, like green plants they will soon die away. Trust in the Lord and do good; dwell in the land and enjoy safe pasture.

Psalm 37:7-9 NRSV Be still before the Lord, and wait patiently for him; do not fret over those who prosper in their way, over those who carry out evil devices. Refrain from anger, and forsake wrath. Do not fret—it leads only to evil. For the wicked shall be cut off, but those who wait for the Lord shall inherit the land.

Matthew 6:25-30 NRSV Therefore I tell you, do not worry about your life, what you will eat or what you will drink, or about your body, what you will wear. Is not life more than food, and the body more than clothing? Look at the birds of the air; they neither sow nor reap nor gather into barns, and yet your heavenly Father feeds them. Are you not of more value than they? And can any of you by worrying add a single hour to your span of life? And why do you worry about clothing? Consider the lilies of the field, how they grow; they neither toil nor spin, yet I tell you, even Solomon in all his glory was not clothed like one of these. But if God so clothes the grass of the field, which is alive today and tomorrow is thrown into the oven, will he not much more clothe you—you of little faith?

Philippians 4:6-7 NASB Be anxious for nothing, but in everything by prayer and supplication with thanksgiving let your requests be made known to God. And the peace of God, which surpasses all comprehension, will guard your hearts and your minds in Christ Jesus.

Philippians 4:19 NIV And my God will meet all your needs according to his glorious riches in Christ Jesus.

Exodus 34:14 NIV Do not worship any other god, for the LORD, whose name is Jealous, is a jealous God.

Deuteronomy 8:10 WEB You shall eat and be full, and you shall bless Yahweh your God for the good land which he has given you.

Deuteronomy 10:20-22 NCV Respect the LORD your God and serve him. Be loyal to him and make your promises in his name. He is the one you should praise; he is your God, who has done great and wonderful things for you, which you have seen with your own eyes. There were only seventy of your ancestors when they went down to Egypt, and now the LORD your God has made you as many as the stars in the sky.

Deuteronomy 11:1-7 NRSV You shall love the LORD your God, therefore, and keep his charge, his decrees, his ordinances, and his commandments always. Remember today that it was not your children (who have not known or seen the discipline of the LORD your God), but it is you who must acknowledge his greatness, his mighty hand and his outstretched arm, his signs and his deeds that he did in Egypt to Pharaoh, the king of Egypt, and to all his land; what he did to the Egyptian army, to their horses and chariots, how he made the water of the Red Sea flow over them as they pursued you, so that the LORD has destroyed them to this day; what he did to you in the wilderness . . . how in the midst of all Israel the earth opened . . . along with their households, their tents, and every living being in their company; for it is your own eyes that have seen every great deed that the LORD did.

Deuteronomy 11:13-16 WEB It shall happen, if you shall listen diligently to my commandments which I command you this day, to love Yahweh your God, and to serve him with all your heart and with all your soul, that I will give the rain of your land in its season, the former rain and the latter rain, that you may gather in your grain, and your new wine, and your oil. I will give grass in your fields for your livestock, and you shall eat and be full. Take heed to yourselves, lest your heart be deceived, and you turn aside, and serve other gods, and worship them.

Psalm 29:2 WEB Ascribe to Yahweh the glory due to his name. Worship Yahweh in holy array.

Psalm 66:4-5 NCV All the earth worships you and sings praises to you. They sing praises to your name. Come and see what God has done, the amazing things he has done for people.

Psalm 66:8-9 NCV You people, praise our God; loudly sing his praise. He protects our lives and does not let us be defeated.

Psalm 81:9-10 NIV You shall have no foreign god among you; you shall not bow down to an alien god. I am the LORD your God, who brought you up out of Egypt. Open wide your mouth and I will fill it.

Psalm 145:10-12 NCV LORD, everything you have made will praise you; those who belong to you will bless you. They will tell about the glory of your kingdom and will speak about your power. Then everyone will know the mighty things you do and the glory and majesty of your kingdom.

John 4:23-24 NKJV But the hour is coming, and now is, when the true worshipers will worship the Father in spirit and truth; for the Father is seeking such to worship Him. God is Spirit, and those who worship Him must worship in spirit and truth.

John 9:31 WEB We know that God doesn't listen to sinners, but if anyone is a worshipper of God, and does his will, he listens to him.

Hebrews 12:28-29 NASB Therefore, since we receive a kingdom which cannot be shaken, let us show gratitude, by which we may offer to God an acceptable service with reverence and awe; for our God is a consuming fire.

Psalm 14:2 TMB The Lord looked down from heaven upon the children of men, to see if there were any that did understand and seek God.

Psalm 119:9-10 NIV How can a young man keep his way pure? By living according to your word. I seek you with all my heart; do not let me stray from your commands.

Psalm 144:12 NIV Then our sons in their youth will be like well-nurtured plants, and our daughters will be like pillars carved to adorn a palace.

Proverbs 6:20-22 NCV My son, keep your father's commands, and don't forget your mother's teaching. Keep their words in mind forever as though you had them tied around your neck. They will guide you when you walk. They will guard you when you sleep. They will speak to you when you are awake.

Proverbs 8:34-35 NCV Happy are those who listen to me, watching at my door every day, waiting at my open doorway. Those who find me find life, and the Lord will be pleased with them.

Proverbs 13:20 NCV Spend time with the wise and you will become wise, but the friends of fools will suffer.

Proverbs 23:15-16 NASB My son, if your heart is wise, my own heart also will be glad; and my inmost being will rejoice when your lips speak what is right.

Isaiah 40:30-31 NRSV Even youths will faint and be weary, and the young shall fall exhausted; but they who wait for the Lord shall renew their strength, they shall mount up with wings like eagles, they shall run and not be weary, they shall walk and not faint.

Jeremiah 1:7-8 WEB But Yahweh said to me, "Don't say, 'I am a child;' for to whoever I shall send you, you shall go, and whatever I shall command you, you shall speak. Don't be afraid because of them; for I am with you to deliver you," says Yahweh.

Jeremiah 31:17 NIV "So there is hope for your future," declares the LORD. "Your children will return to their own land."

1 Timothy 4:12 NIV Don't let anyone look down on you because you are young, but set an example for the believers in speech, in life, in love, in faith and in purity.

2 Timothy 2:22 NCV But run away from the evil young people like to do. Try hard to live right and to have faith, love, and peace, together with those who trust in the Lord from pure hearts.

2 Timothy 3:12-15 WNT And indeed every one who is determined to live a godly life as a follower of Christ Jesus will be persecuted. But bad men and impostors will go on from bad to worse, misleading and being misled. But you must cling to the things which you have learnt and have been taught to believe, knowing who your teachers were, and that from infancy you have known the sacred writings which are able to make you wise to obtain salvation through faith in Christ Jesus.

Titus 2:6-8 NCV In the same way, encourage young men to be wise. In every way be an example of doing good deeds. When you teach, do it with honesty and seriousness. Speak the truth so that you cannot be criticized. Then those who are against you will be ashamed because there is nothing bad to say about us.

1 Peter 5:5 WEB Likewise, you younger ones, be subject to the elder. Yes, all of you clothe yourselves with humility, to subject yourselves to one another; for "God resists the proud, but gives grace to the humble."

Psalm 84:10 WEB For a day in your courts is better than a thousand. I would rather be a doorkeeper in the house of my God, than to dwell in the tents of wickedness.

Psalm 119:136 NIV Streams of tears flow from my eyes, for your law is not obeyed.

Psalm 119:137-140 NASB Righteous are You, O LORD, and upright are Your judgments. You have commanded Your testimonies in righteousness and exceeding faithfulness. My zeal has consumed me, because my adversaries have forgotten Your words. Your word is very pure, therefore Your servant loves it.

Romans 10:1-4 WNT Brethren, the longing of my heart, and my prayer to God, on behalf of my countrymen is for their salvation. For I bear witness that they possess an enthusiasm for God, but it is an unenlightened enthusiasm. Ignorant of the righteousness which God provides and building their hopes upon a righteousness of their own, they have refused submission to God's righteousness. For as a means of righteousness Christ is the termination of Law to every believer.

Titus 2:14 TMB [He] gave Himself for us, that He might redeem us from all iniquity and purify unto Himself a peculiar people, zealous for good works.

Hebrews 6:11-12 WEB We desire that each one of you may show the same diligence to the fullness of hope even to the end, that you won't be sluggish, but imitators of those who through faith and patience inherited the promises.

In Appreciation:

To the team at Howard Books—with special thanks to Philis, Denny, and Mary.

Rick Graham for his willingness to help in all areas.

Kim Beck for leading Merry to Jesus.

Tiffany, Timothy, Shiloh, and David for blessing their Momma Merry.

Kaflin for letting mum (Rachel) visit the USA—often!

Priscilla Ussery for showing us how to climb over fences.

Debbie Forstall and Heather Phillips for always believing in us.

To those who keep us in their prayers!

And once again, to our Lord Jesus!